HISTORIC TRACKS

Exploring Britain's Heritage

HISTORIC TRACKS

Exploring Britain's Heritage

◆

DES HANNIGAN

PAVILION

For Pauline

ACKNOWLEDGEMENTS
My thanks to Lesley Billingham and Barry Hitchcox
for their generous help and guidance.
Special thanks to Doris Rasdall for her unstinting moral support.
Thanks to T and D for giving me hell…

First published in Great Britain in 1997
by Pavilion Books Limited
26 Upper Ground, London SE1 9PD

Text and photographs © Des Hannigan 1997
Maps © Don Sargeant 1997

Designed by Andrew Barron and Collis Clements Associates

A CIP catalogue record for this book is available from the British Library

ISBN 1 85793 913 1

Typeset by Textype, Cambridge, in Adobe Garamond & Gill Sans
Printed and bound in Great Britain by WBC

1 2 3 4 5 6 7 8 9 10

This book may be ordered by post direct from the publisher.
Please contact the Marketing Department.
But try your bookshop first.

The routes of the walks described in this book are believed to follow public footpaths,
rights of way or permitted paths that existed at the time of the book going to press.
No responsibility can be taken by the author or publisher for any accidents that may befall
walkers, or for any action that may be taken against users of the book.

Front jacket photograph: Chun Quoit, The Tinners' Way, Cornwall
Back jacket photograph: Avebury, The Circle Road, Wiltshire

Contents

THE ROAD TO THE ISLES

Skye Cannich
KINTAIL Inverness *STRATHSPEY* Craigellachie
THE WHISKY ROAD
Tomintoul Aberdeen

Fort William

Lochearnhead Perth Dundee
A ROUGH, ROMANTIC ROAD
Callander

Glasgow Edinburgh

Kelso
Kirk Yetholm
THE REIVERS' ROAD
Alwinton Newcastle

A LEAD-MINERS' TRACK

SWALEDALE Richmond

THE WEAVERS TROD
Todmorden Hebden Bridge
Manchester

Chester
Wrexham
Llangollen Chirk
THE WATER WAY

Birmingham

THE CELTIC FRINGE Hereford

Fishguard
St David's *PEMBROKE* THE CASTLE ROAD A PAINTER'S WAY
Abergavenny Monmouth Bures
Colchester Manningtree
Cardiff Bristol
London
Marlborough
THE CIRCLE ROAD
THE SAXON SHORE Deal
THE GIANT'S ROAD Dover
THE STONE ROAD Cerne Abbas
Princetown Exeter Dorchester
St Just St Ives Ivybridge
Abbotsbury
THE TINNERS' WAY

Introduction

Travelling on foot along the old paths and tracks of rural landscapes is one of the most rewarding ways of interpreting the past. History may have been 'bunk' to Henry Ford, but engaging with the past through travel and through observation of historic and prehistoric artefacts helps us to judge the present and gives us some perspective of the future. Ford revolutionized transport and made a triumph of destination over journey. With the machine, we shrank the world and cheated time, but we also reduced the experience of slow, reflective movement through landscapes and of the close – quarter engagement with Nature that such experience brings.

In Britain today there are still hundreds of miles of very old paths and tracks, whose often tortuous courses mark out the line of least resistance, rather than the line of the bulldozer. Many of them were first created, and then maintained, by early hunters, herdspeople and settlers, merchants, monks, soldiers, brigands, refugees from war and pestilence, weavers and miners with their pack-horse trains, farmers, carters and those early 'tourists', the religious pilgrims. It would be naïve of us to think that any of these travellers would not have welcomed the machine age as a literal leap forward. Their way of life is not one to which many of us would wish to return. But by retracing their steps through the landscapes that shaped them, and which were shaped by them, we may still experience something of the colour and the intensity of their lives and times.

Preparation

Many of the lowland routes and most of the circular routes described can be undertaken by walkers who are generally fit. The long-distance routes through hill and mountain country should be undertaken only by very fit parties of at least two people. In winter they should be undertaken only by experienced and well-equipped parties. Leave details of the planned route including date and estimated time of completion – allowing for reasonable delays – with a responsible person. Walking speed in mountain areas is approximately 2 miles/ 3 kms per hour. This is steady progress. Allow a longer estimate in bad weather and for very steep terrain. Confirm your safe return *as soon as possible* to avoid a potentially wasteful call-out of the emergency services. Obtain local weather forecasts before setting out. These are available at Tourist Information Centres (TICs) and National Park Centres.

Equipment

Carry weatherproof clothing and footwear, even in fine weather. Specialist winter clothing and equipment are essential for winter walking in hill and mountain country. Carry emergency bivouac equipment in mountain areas and in remote hills. Always take an Ordnance Survey map, a compass, a whistle and a head-torch. Skilled use of map and compass is vital for walking on mountains, hills and moorland, where poor visibility is common. Carry a first-aid kit. At least one member of the party should have first-aid experience.

Maps

The sketch maps that accompany each route direction give an excellent and useful reference to the line of the route (shown by a broken line and numbered points within squares) and its main features, as well as to the circular walks (shown by a dotted line and numbered points within circles). For precise route-finding, walkers are advised to use the relevant Ordnance Survey maps.

Travel

Many of the areas covered by these walks have summer bus services only. Winter bus services in rural areas are generally limited. Timetables may vary from year to year. Local TICs have up-to-date information about seasonal services, and it is strongly, advised that current services are verified.

Accommodation

On lowland routes there is usually a good choice of hotels, guest houses, bed and breakfast (B&B) establishments, hostels and camp sites along the way. In mountain areas a more limited choice of accommodation is available at either end of the route. Local TICs have up-to-date information on availability.

Health and welfare

Take plenty of food and liquid on long-distance walks. Hot, dry weather may cause dehydration. Do not drink from lowland rivers and streams. Do not drink from mountain streams, unless you are certain of the purity of the water. Guard against potential sunburn or sunstroke.

The infamous 'biting midge' is a major pest in the Scottish Highlands, especially during the period from June to October, and particularly during late afternoon and evening. Midges are present in other upland areas of England and Wales, too. There are numerous 'anti-midge' products on the market. The basic antidote is thick skin and gritted teeth. Do not swim at dusk.

The tick, which sucks blood from animals and humans, is on the increase in upland areas and there is evidence that it may cause potentially serious illnesses, such as Lyme disease. Currently there are 200 reported cases annually of Lyme disease in humans, caused by ticks. Bare limbs are an inevitable target, especially in areas of long grass and heather. Examine the skin closely after a day's walking. Remove ticks carefully by using tweezers. *Never squeeze a tick while it is still attached to you*; it may re-inject infected blood into the host.

Access

All the routes described in this book follow rights of way, sections of official regional or long-distance trails, or permissive paths. *In areas where shooting may be in progress, it is wise to check details beforehand.*

TICs in such areas usually have current details of shooting schedules. Rights of way remain open to walkers during shooting seasons.

A huge amount of good work is done by various local authorities, conservation bodies and voluntary groups in maintaining access to the countryside. There are also many private landowners who have a positive attitude to public access. Acknowledgement of the good work carried out in areas covered by this book is made to the National Trust, National Trust for Scotland, Glenlivet Estate, Yorkshire Dales National Park Authority, Calderdale District Council, British Waterways Board, Pembrokeshire National Park Authority, Dartmoor National Park Authority; the County Councils of Scottish Borders, Northumberland, Clwyd, Monmouthshire, Suffolk, Essex, Kent, Wiltshire, Dorset, and Cornwall; English Heritage, English Nature, The Countryside Commission, The Ramblers' Association, The Scottish Rights of Way Association and many individual landowners.

Historic Tracks has been written with attention to the *Guidelines for the Writers of Path Guides*, issued by the Outdoor Writers' Guild.

Conservation

Today, the impact of walkers' feet, horses' hooves and the wheels of mountain bikes and all-terrain vehicles causes unsightly and cumulative erosion on many paths and tracks. The dilemma is obvious for all outdoor users, and especially for the writer of a book such as this one. But to travel on foot along established ways that lead through beautiful landscapes is an enriching experience. To follow such ways with the minimum of physical intrusion, and with an active and vigilant concern for the environment, is the best way forward. Please respect the work of countryside managers, rangers and wardens and comply with any requests for restraint on environmental grounds.

Follow the country code

Enjoy the countryside and respect its life and work.
Guard against all risk of fire.
Fasten all gates.
Keep your dogs under close control.
Keep to public paths across farmland.
Use gates and stiles to cross fences, hedges and walls.
Leave livestock, crops and machinery alone.
Take your litter home.
Help to keep all water clean.
Protect wildlife, plants and trees.
Take special care on country roads.
Make no unnecessary noise.

The Road to the Isles
West Highlands

Cannich to Sheil Bridge 29 miles/46.7 kms

The modern road bridge between Kyle of Lochalsh and Skye may
have wrecked the romance of the 'Skye Boat Song', but for most
people, the bridge is simply the end of a famous 'Road to the Isles' that
symbolizes the romantic heritage of the Highlands. This walk eschews
the modern road, and instead follows the Highlanders' ancient way to
the Isles through the remote mountains of Glen Affric and Kintail.

The modern road to the Isles runs north-east from Fort William
through the Great Glen. At Invergarry it turns west to Loch Garry,
from where it uncoils like a river through Strath Cluanie and Glen
Shiel. It is always longer than you remember from previous journeys.
It tantalizes with its promise of the western sea, of Skye and the
Hebrides and of the way north to Torridon and Assynt where the deep
Highlands envelop the traveller inescapably.

It is an inspiring road to drive along, an antidote to the fast,
impersonal world of motorways. Spectacular views and free-ranging
sheep impose a speed limit of their own. To the south of the road lies
a tumult of ridges and valleys that runs for miles into the heart of
Lochaber. To the north lies the long ridge of Beinn Mhor, the 'Big
Mountain', with its succession of peaks that are known enticingly as
the Five Sisters; Sgurr na Moraich, Sgurr nan Saighead, Sgurr
Fhuaran, Sgurr na Carnach, and Sgurr na Ciste Duibhe. Sgurr
translates as 'peak'. The Sisters' Gaelic names translate as the Sea Plain,
Arrows, Cold Place, Stony Place, and Black Chest (The Coffin), hard
names in an alien tongue for such elegant maidens, but they suit the
local legend that portrays the Sisters as the spirits of princesses,
forlornly waiting for the promised hands of five royal Irishmen, who
never came to claim them.

To the casual motorist, the deep trench of Glen Shiel must seem the
only possible way through these mountains. Yet the line of today's A87
main road was not the only road to the Isles in the days when the
world moved on its own two feet, and when Inverness was of greater
significance to the people of the North West Highlands than Fort
William ever was. The Glen Shiel route became the 'official' way to
the west only when the English Commander-in-Chief in Scotland,
General George Wade, engineered a military road through the glen in
the 1720s as part of the 'pacification' of the Highlands after the failed
Jacobite rebellion of 1715. Until then, most travellers had used a long-
established east–west route that ran through the remote mountains of
Affric and Kintail to the north of Glen Shiel. This ancient route was
the first Road to the Isles.

This other Road to the Isles led from Inverness, by Beauly, Strath
Glass, and Glen Affric, and then on to Loch Duich through the lonely
mountain pass of Bealach an Sgairne, the 'pass of the rumbling stones'.
It was a route associated with the Dark Age Irish missionary St

Duthac, whose followers were said to travel along it, to and from the saint's religious house at Tain on the Dornoch Firth. Loch Duich was named after the saint and an alternative name for the Bealach an Sgairne is said to be Cadha Dhuich, 'St Duthac's Pass'; somewhere, amidst the tumbled rocks of the Bealach there is a spring that was known as Duthac's Well.

The Belloch
The old route is the only one that is marked on maps of 1725 and 1755. It was described in the *Statistical Account of Scotland* of 1792 as being the main route from the west to Inverness. Records state that it was 'daily frequented by people from Skye and other places, to Inverness and Dingwall, with heavy loads'. It was known as the 'Belloch', and the highest point of the pass was described in the *Statistical Account* as being 'a high ridge of hills which environs this district on the east, and would render it inaccessible from that quarter, if nature had not left a small gap in the mountain, as if it had been sawn down the middle, which leaves room for three passengers to go abreast'. The Belloch was used by all types of traveller and it continued to be the preferred route of native Highlanders for some time, even after the military road was built through Glen Shiel. By the late eighteenth century, the military road was virtually impassable and was reported as having only 'some remains'. Such roads, at the extremes of the Highlands, depended on local goodwill for their upkeep. Until the nineteenth century, Wade's Glen Shiel road – today's tourist road to the Isles – continued to be purposely neglected by those who had not wanted it in the first place and who held to the high passes of the old way.

The preference of native Highlanders for the high, mountain route as opposed to the military road was understandable. For most of the eighteenth century they were at odds with English and Lowland interests. The Kintail area was particularly troublesome. In 1719 a minor battle was fought in Glen Shiel between Hanoverian Crown forces under General Wightman and a Jacobite mix of clansmen and Spanish soldiers. The latter had been provided by the King of Spain, who was no friend of George I at the time. The Jacobite force was commanded by the Mackenzie Earl of Seaforth and the Marquis of Tullibardine. When the smoke cleared, the Castle of Eilean Donan on Loch Duich had been blown up by Wightman, and the Jacobites had been defeated. The brave, but forlorn Spaniards were imprisoned, but their weapons disappeared into the hills, to reappear in the rebellion of 1745. The hill on which the main action took place was called thereafter Sgurr nan Spainteach, 'The Peak of the Spaniards'.

In the wake of such turbulence, General Wade's initial burst of roadbuilding was seen by disaffected Highlanders as strengthening the hand of the Crown. Anxious local people also believed that a military road increased the threat of raids by rival clans. 'The more inaccessible, the more secure' was a canny mountain maxim of the time. Keeping to the high road has always been a Scottish preference.

The route of the old road to the Isles leads west from the Beauly Firth through Strath Glass to Cannich, then on to Alltbeithe at the head of Glen Affric. From Alltbeithe, alternative routes run through the mountain passes of the Bealach an Sgairne and the Fionngleann, to the north and south of the vast bulk of Ben Fhada, 'the long mountain'. They link again at Strath Croe and the head of Loch Duich, from where the line of the A87 follows the last miles of the old route, to Kyle of Lochalsh. In its roadless section, from Loch Affric to Strath Croe, this old road to the Isles is remote and beautiful, and is one of the finest walking routes in the north-west Highlands.

Frontier Settlement

Modern roads now traverse both sides of Strath Glass from Beauly, and, for the walker, the old road is best started from Cannich at the head of Strath Glass. Cannich has a hint of frontier settlement about it, like most communities at a modern road end, where fast travel fetches you up against a wall of wilderness. There is always a whiff of cut wood in the air round Cannich. Forestry has dominated the area for centuries. During the latter part of the eighteenth century larch and spruce were introduced to Strath Glass, and there were later plantings of alien conifers. There was much felling during the early part of the twentieth century and especially during the two world wars. In the lower reaches of Strath Glass, the industry was wholesale. Overhead cableways, precursors of today's ski-lifts, sent cut logs hissing through the air to Beauly. Newfoundlanders and Canadians, even German prisoners of war, worked in the forest. It was international logging country. During the 1950s the Forestry Commission purchased the lower part of Glen Affric and introduced an admirable policy of using only Scots pine for replanting within the ancient forest to either side of Loch Beinn a' Mheadhoin. The result today is the magnificent woodland of birch and Caledonian pine that fills the heart of lower Glen Affric.

Sheep rearing came to these great mountains in the eighteenth century, and the people of Affric and Strath Glass suffered from the evil of forced evictions during the notorious Highland Clearances. This is a hideous period of Scottish history that should never be glossed over. It arose, perhaps inevitably, from the new culture of enterprise that emerged in Europe during the eighteenth century. The Highlands were seen as assets rather than as homelands, and, in the wake of failed Jacobite rebellions, there were enough Scots landowners and clan chiefs – many of whom were either bankrupt or avaricious – who were ready to exploit the green hills and glens. The old kinship that had fostered the extended family of the clan was fatally undermined after the last Jacobite rebellion of 1745. The simple economies of isolated Highland communities were not in tune with the new economies of land ownership; the people were surplus to requirements. They had few legal rights, and the will to resist had bled into the dreary moss of Culloden. It is this betrayal of a people's true inheritance that has given Scotland its sentimental 'heritage' of vacant straths and hills that we so admire today.

Strath Glass and Affric were Chisolm country and though the last of the hereditary Chisolm lairds, Alexander Chisolm, known as An Siosal Ban, the 'Fair Haired One', resisted the lure of higher rents from sheep farming, his death in 1793 prompted a reversal of human rights in the glens. The main perpetrator was the detested Marsailidh Bhinneach, 'Light-headed Marjorie', widow of Duncan Macdonell of Glengarry and mother of Elizabeth Chisolm, the wife of Alexander's sickly half-brother who had inherited the clan lands. Between them the two women forced the depopulation of Glen Affric and Strath Glass and by 1830 only two named Chisolms remained in the district. Today, the Chisolms own no hereditary lands in their old glens.

Loch Affric

The public road west from Cannich is long and relentless; its accessibility has robbed this great way to the mountains of some of its exclusiveness. The road runs as far as the mouth of Loch Affric. There is no public transport from Cannich to the road-end and if a lift is not arranged, then the road has to be walked. From the halfway point at Dog Falls a forestry track can be followed along the south side of Loch Beinn a' Mheadhoin as an alternative to foot-bashing tarmac. The road is best walked in the early morning when deer are drinking from the River Affric, or foraging amidst the roadside birches. Disturbed, they start away, leaving a swirl of pungent musk in the air. On still, clear mornings, the silken water of Loch Beinn a' Mheadhoin reflects pine-clad islands on its mirrored surface.

From the road-end car park, near the mouth of Loch Affric, a track winds above small lochans, where pale reeds speckle the calm waters. It passes outside the environs of Affric Lodge, then climbs high above the main loch across the steep slopes of Sgurr na Lapaich. Ahead, the summits of Mullach Fraoch Choire and A' Chralaig crowd the western horizon above Athnamulloch. In early summer this is a relentlessly green country, hazy with sunlight, or blurred by drenching mist and rain. The greenness is the legacy of sheep grazing, and of the 100 inches of rain that pour onto these mountains each year. On the slopes of An Tudair Beag near the western end of Loch Affric, the great waterfall of Sputan Ban sends down a dazzling stream of white water between rock walls.

Athnamulloch was the scene of a strange sequel to the Battle of Glen Shiel. After the battle, the Hanoverian government attempted to punish the Jacobite Earl of Seaforth and other local lairds by forfeiting their rents in Kintail and elsewhere. Two east-coast officials, William and Robert Ross were appointed as Estate Commissioners and rent-collectors. They set off from Inverness along the old road to Kintail, escorted by a company of North British Fusiliers. Word of their coming raced ahead, and they were met, first at Knockfin, near Cannich, and later at Athnamulloch, by a force of 300 Kintail men who had crossed the mountains by the Bealach an Sgairne. Shots were exchanged. One of the Commissioners was wounded, as was his son, who later died. The Commissioners retreated. The Highlanders faded back into the great hills. 'Pacification' was a slow process in Kintail.

Weather

Beyond Loch Affric, the glen runs clear into the mountains; the green flanks of the enclosing hills sweep up and over towards unseen spiny ridges. Ahead, at the mouth of the deeper glens, the great eastern shoulder of Ben Fhada looms above Alltbeithe and above the morass of the river plain. Here, the tumbling streams of Cam-ban, Chomlain, and the Allt Beithe Gharbh spill into the headwaters of the River Affric where the draining waters of the moss brim underfoot.

Midsummer heat can be oppressive here. The dusty white ribbon of the track winds languidly through the green trench of the glen. The Affric river seems diminished within its stony course. It shadows the road, first through broad river flats where the mossy ruins of old settlements stand isolated on low mounds, then is more defined, where the valley floor becomes irregular and the slopes of the flanking hills crowd in. Pace falters at times in the heat; the Kintail mountains and Ben Fhada fade amidst the blue haze on the edge of the great bowl of the hills; the air is parched. Such heat is enervating, but it is more welcome than the bleak weather that so often drenches these mountains with mist and rain. The desert heat of clear, settled weather is a bonus amidst the uncertainties.

Highland weather has always been extreme and, in our time, predictable only in its unpredictability, its coldness and dampness. Yet records suggest remarkable climatic differences in the past. The *Statistical Account of Scotland* gives this description of weather in Strath Glass and Glen Affric during the mid-eighteenth century: 'About twenty years ago, the farmers, without a coat upon them, were obliged to yoke their labouring cattle, even in the month of March, about three or four o' clock in the morning, as neither the ploughman nor cattle could stand the heat of the day after six or seven. But how great the reverse. No sight more common now, in the latter end of April, and beginning of May, than a ploughman, his body wrapt up in a great coat, and his hands muffled in worsted mitts, to preserve him from the frosty air. Showers of snow and hail are not unusual in June.'

Fellow Travellers

Hot or cold, the climate has always been hard on travellers in these great mountains, where determination is an essential part of the baggage. On the road west, you follow a ghostly train of those who have used this rough way, when it was the chosen route to and from the Isles, and later, when it became the high road, the way of the proscribed and the hunted. They are all good company, these ghostly fellow travellers; the pilgrims of the Dark Ages; the fugitives from Culloden; the hard-faced drovers and herdsmen on their journeys to and from the cattle trysts of Muir of Ord; the driven crofters, who travelled west to the emigrant ships of the eighteenth and nineteenth centuries; the shepherds who supplanted them, and the stalkers and gillies of the Victorian period, who had the hills to themselves, until a more democratic age sent people from all quarters to find gratuitous recreation in the 'great outdoors'.

Through Glen Affric in 1911 came an Edwardian outdoorsman, Arthur L. Bagley, who set off, according to his journal, armed with 'alarming tales of the treatment that a common or garden tourist might expect in this region . . . The Tibet of the Highlands . . .' Faced with such anxieties cometh the man, however. Armed also with dauntless conceits and certainties, Bagley knew the price of patronage. At Loch Beinn a' Mheadhion, he met a man who was heading for Affric Lodge and who offered to carry his rucksack. To the manner born, Arthur offered the man a tip, in spite of mild reservations on the grounds that his benefactor might be a 'gentleman'. 'I felt a little anxious as to whether I had committed a solecism in offering him a tip,' mused Arthur. 'But he was (only) a keeper, for I inquired later.' The shilling that was pressed on the keeper was rejected by him as 'being too much'. Bagley's genuine bewilderment at this diffidence leaps from the page.

At Alltbeithe, Bagley enjoyed a 'copious tea', courtesy of a deerwatcher's family. He was served by a young girl. Out popped the purse: 'I proffered the handmaiden a shilling, whereupon she exclaimed that it was too much, and only took it after some considerable pressure, figurative and moral be it strictly understood, not literal or corporeal.' Perish the thought. Thus fortified Arthur pressed on through the Fionngleann to Gleann Lichd, where the Bagley shilling was deposited also at the 'poor little shanty' of Gleann Lichd cottage in exchange for 'excellent tea and eggs'. In some ways, Arthur L. Bagley, with his naive sense of superiority, is a startling symbol of a culture that within two centuries had put paid to the Highland way of life, first by military attrition and then by patronage and exploitation.

Today, there are no deerwatchers or shepherds, or 'handmaidens', who actually live in the remote corners of these great hills. But at Alltbeithe, the Scottish Youth Hostels Association has one of its most famous hostels that has served walkers and mountaineers for many years and is now equipped with its own wind generator. Beyond Alltbeithe there lies a compelling wilderness, much of which is in the care of the National Trust for Scotland whose wise policies of protection and sustainment are aimed at enriching this already outstanding landscape. Respect and active care for that landscape is a small price to pay by those of us who pass through for pleasure.

The Bealach an Sgairne

Beyond Alltbeithe comes a choice of routes; one is by the ancient track to the north of Beinn Fhada through the Bealach an Sgairne, the other, to the south, through the Fionngleann to Gleann Lichd. Both are marvellous journeys into the heart of the mountains. The people who used these hill passes through necessity rather than for pleasure chose the Bealach an Sgairne, probably from custom, but also because it is shorter than the southern route by about 2 miles/3.2 kms. Today, the National Trust has carried out excellent path stabilization on many of the more difficult sections of both routes.

The way through the Bealach an Sgairne has antiquity to commend it. From Alltbeithe the path leads north-west through the green trough of Gleann Gniomhaidh, a landscape of blanket bog and sheep-grazed heath. It skirts the southern edge of Loch a' Bhealaich at the mouth of the lonely Gleann Gaorsaic, the 'glen of the loud bird calls', then climbs steeply to the mouth of the Bealach an Sgairne. The path runs a twisting course through the rock-littered chaos of the Bealach. There is a sparse, ragged beauty here, although an eighteenth-century commentator warned: 'The traveller finds himself in passing through this gut, inclosed with hills of rueful aspects, inspiring awe, and often quickening his pace.' We linger nowadays in such remote places to relish that rueful aspect. The sun gleams on smooth facets of the drenched rocks, hooded crows patrol the ribbed pinnacles of the skyline, croaking their lonely disdain, and, in the west, the slate-blue hills of Inverinate slice across the hazy distance beneath often turbulent skies.

The western end of the Bealach drops suddenly from small, peaked hillocks into Gleann Choinneachain. But the path sidesteps the downfall, and takes a tumbling zigzag way across the swooping western slopes of Meall a' Bhealaich. It levels off by the little waterfalls of the streams that drain the remote northern corries of Sgurr a' Choire Ghairbh, where the white-flowered alpine saxifrage and the tiny, pink-flowered mountain azalea grow on the gloomy cliffs. Beyond here, the path runs helter-skelter down the southern side of

Gleann Choinneachain above a pinched ravine, to a junction with Strath Croe, and the path north to the Falls of Glomach and Glen Elchaig. From here, the way leads easily down to the low ground alongside the Abhainn Chonaig and on to a surfaced road at the mouth of Gleann Lichd, above Morvich.

The Fionngleann and Gleann Lichd

The route from Alltbeithe through the southern pass of the Fionngleann and the Allt Grannda seems more remote than the Bealach an Sgairne. The mountains here have a greater complexity of form, and there is greater scale; the soaring, northern faces of the Five Sisters add to the grandeur. From Alltbeithe, a sturdy track leads for 2 miles/3.2 kms up the Fionngleann to Camban Bothy where once there were croft meadows filled with corn; the outlines of the little fields are still visible. A shepherd's family lived here until early in the twentieth century.

Beyond Camban, a path winds on through the long, lonely pass amidst dark peat hags, deer grass and sedges. To the south and west, the shapely peaks of the Five Sisters fill the horizon, their northern faces a mottled purple and deep green. Here the path runs in tandem with the young stream of the Allt Grannda that seems to linger amidst the scooped hollows of the pass. Rounded stones glimmer beneath the surface. Soon the stream veers off through a chaotic wilderness of slabby rocks and grass. It enters a deep ravine that slices down from Creag Ghlas to end, abruptly, where the stream plunges in its long fall to the valley below. The path winds its careful way round the northern side of the great cirque of cliffs and swooping slopes. There is an echoing rush of wind and falling water here, the sound of high places, where a sense of exposure and of great space is overpowering. It is this enduring, fierce and at times frightening emptiness that defines the heart of the remote Highlands.

The path edges its way above the vast cauldron of the falls and then drops steeply into the wide bed of Gleann Lichd over well-pitched stone setts. A stout bridge crosses the deep gorge of the Allt Grannda, where rowan and birch trees sprout from the rocky walls. A second bridge spans the quieter stream of the Allt a' Choire Dhomdain, from where the path winds downriver to Gleann Lichd Cottage. Just beyond the cottage, a broad estate track is reached and the way down Gleann Lichd becomes a plain trudge. But the swooping slopes of the Five Sisters and of Beinn Fhada, and the sinuous river, keep close company all the way to the mouth of the glen. Here the route merges with that of the Bealach an Sgairne and leads along surfaced lanes to Morvich and Shiel Bridge and to the steel torrent of the modern 'Road to the Isles'.

The Road to the Isles
Information

Distance 29 miles/46.7 kms

Maps OS Landranger 25 (Glen Carron &
Surrounding Area); OS Landranger 26
(Inverness & Strath Glass)

Nature of walk A long, tough walk through a
remote mountain area, with no handy escape
routes. The walking distance can be reduced by
11 miles/17.7 kms if transport is available from
Cannich to the road-end at the mouth of Loch
Affric. Sections of the route through the high
passes of the Bealach an Sgairne and the
Fionngleann may be wet and peaty. Weather
conditions can change quickly for the worse at any
time of the year, especially outside summer.
A winter crossing should only be made by those
with winter mountaineering experience, full winter
clothing and emergency bivouac equipment.

*Selective culling of deer is carried out in the
privately-owned ground of Glen Affric and
Inverinate, and in the National Trust for Scotland's
properties of West Affric and Kintail. The key period
is from mid-August to mid-February. The routes
described here are rights of way, but walkers should
be aware that deer-stalking may be in progress*

*during certain times. Contact the National Trust's
Ranger Service at Morvich for details.*

Accommodation Hotel and B&Bs at Cannich
and at Shiel Bridge. Youth hostels at Cannich,
Alltbeithe and Ratagan, near Shiel Bridge. Camp
sites at Cannich, Morvich and Shiel Bridge.

Transport Bus connections from Beauly to
Cannich and from Shiel Bridge to Kyle of
Lochalsh, from where trains run to Inverness.

Further information Tourist Information
Centre, Inverness, tel. (01463) 234353; National
Trust for Scotland Ranger Service, Morvich
Farm, Shiel Bridge, Kintail.

Start Cannich

1 Follow the public road west from the hotel at
Cannich to the Hydro Electric works at Fasnakyle
and continue to the road-end at the east end of
Loch Affric. (11 miles/17.7 kms)
Alternative: Follow the road from Cannich for
5 miles/8 kms to reach a car park close to the Dog
Falls at OS 283283. A forestry road leads from
here along the southern side of Loch Beinn a'

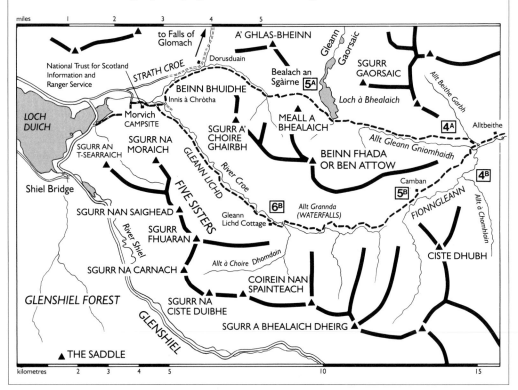

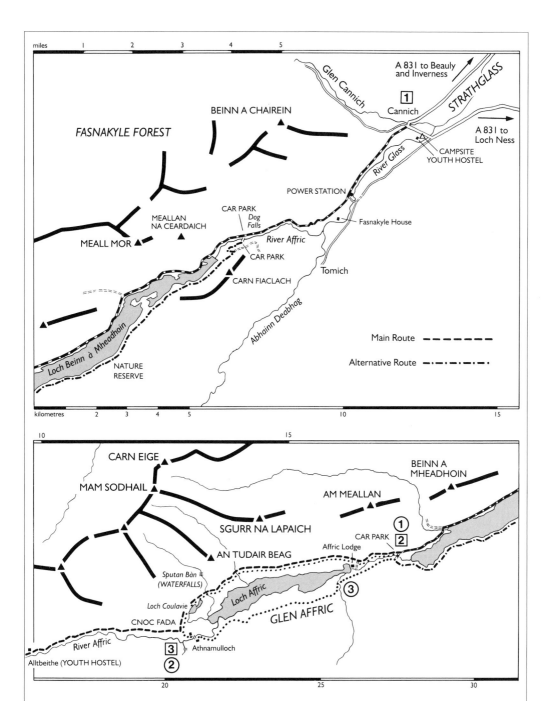

miles 1 2 3 4 5

Mheadhoin to the car park at the east end of
Loch Affric.

2 Turn west out of the Loch Affric car park and
where the track forks, take the right-hand track
for about 1 mile/1.6 kms until abreast of Glen
Affric Lodge. Keep ahead and to the right of the
lodge, then follow the good track that runs high
above the loch and along the slopes of Sgurr na
Lapaich. Pass above the tiny Loch Coulavie to
reach Cnoc Fada, at OS 129209, where the track
reaches a junction with an estate road from
Athnamulloch. (5 miles/8 kms)

3 Go right along the estate track and follow it
through Upper Glen Affric to Alltbeithe Youth
Hostel. (3¼ miles/5.2 kms)

Alternative routes to Morvich from Alltbeithe

The Bealach an Sgairne

4a From Alltbeithe cross the wooden bridge and
follow the track alongside the River Affric for just
under ½ mile/0.8 kms to where a small wooden
bridge crosses a stream. Just beyond this bridge
an indistinct grassy path veers off to the right.
Follow it, keeping by the stream for several
hundred yards, then bear due west to cross
another stream. Continue across the slope of
Beinn an t-Socaich and follow the path alongside
the stream of the Allt Gleann Gniomhaidh to the
southern end of Loch a' Bhealaich. Continue
steeply to the mouth of the Bealach an Sgairne at
OS 014214. (4¼ miles/6.8 kms)

5a Follow the path through the rocky pass and then descend steeply through a series of zigzags. Ignore a side path that leads off left towards the summit of Beinn Fhada. Continue on a good path past a small waterfall and descend Gleann Choinneachain. Pass opposite Dorusduain at the mouth of the glen, then continue alongside the Abhainn Chonaig. Keep on the path and pass below the house at Innis a' Chrotha to reach a lane end at the mouth of Gleann Lichd. Go right and follow the lane to Morvich and a T-junction. Go left to reach the A87 and Shiel Bridge. (6 miles/9.6 kms)

The Fionngleann and Gleann Lichd

This route extends the walk, making the overall distance from Cannich 31 miles/49.9 kms

4b From Alltbeithe, cross the wooden footbridge and follow the track alongside the River Affric, to where a narrow, stone-laid path veers off alongside the tributary stream of the Allt Gleann Gniomhaidh to a footbridge. Cross over, then turn left and go downstream on a made-up path to where it joins the old track close to its river crossing. Turn right along the track and climb steadily up the Fionngleann to Camban Bothy. (2¼ miles/3.6 kms)

5b Continue along the track to where it becomes a path. Follow the path to where it descends steeply, at OS 023173, past the spectacular waterfalls of the Allt Grannda. Continue steeply downhill into Gleann Lichd, cross two bridges and reach Gleann Lichd Cottage (Hadden-Woodburn Memorial Hut). (3½ miles/5.6 kms)

6b Continue along the path, then follow a broad track down Gleann Lichd to reach a junction with a surfaced lane at the mouth of the glen. Go left and follow the lane to Morvich and a T-junction. Go left to reach the A87 and Shiel Bridge. (6 miles/9.6 kms)

CIRCULAR WALK
Loch Affric Circuit 10 miles/16 kms

This is a pleasant, though mildly strenuous, circuit of Loch Affric on good paths and forestry tracks, and with few inclines.

Start Loch Affric car park, OS 200234

1 Follow direction **2** on the main walk to reach Cnoc Fada, at OS 129209, where the track reaches a junction with an estate road from Athnamulloch. (5 miles/8 kms)

2 Go left along the estate road to reach Athnamulloch, then cross the River Affric by the bridge. Turn left and join a broad track. Continue above Loch Affric to reach a forestry gate by a signpost to Cougie at OS 181224. (3½ miles/5.6 kms)

3 Continue along the main track, through conifers, to the mouth of Loch Affric, keeping left where the track forks. Cross a bridge over the river and ascend a short track to reach the car park. (1½ miles/2.4 kms)

The Whisky Road
Grampian

Tomintoul to Craigellachie 27 miles/43.4 kms

Whisky is an essential part of Scotland's heritage; its name is synonymous with that of the nation; its secrets are in the very air of the hills through which this walk passes, and its substance is in the famous distilleries that signpost the way.

A long walk that passes several whisky distilleries could well remain unfinished; from amble to shamble might be the result, if the product of every distillery is sampled along the way. G. K. Chesterton claimed that the rolling English drunkard made the rolling English road. Nothing so coarse would do for Scotland. But the famous Highland fiddler, Scott Skinner, is credited with a similar epigram. Skinner told the Duke of Atholl that it was not the *length* of the road home from the whisky den that delayed him, but the distance from side to side.

The whisky heritage clings like peat smoke to the sentimental image of traditional distilling. It is immortalized in Landseer's painting *The Highland Whisky Still*, a piece of whimsy that portrays eighteenth-century distilling in all its illicit glory, amidst heather, homestead and high hills. Drink this, the message implies, and the air will fill with the skirl of the pipes and the smoky fragrance of the peat fire. The hidden message should be: drink too much and you may become a social liability. There are other distillations that can have the same effect; but they are not conventionally, or even legally, acceptable; this is a cultural ambivalence that should not be ignored, even while we enjoy good whisky as a civilized pleasure.

In the whisky country of north-east Scotland the famous-name distilleries still stand in famously named glens. They are mostly stark, functional buildings without architectural merit, and they can be jarringly intrusive on the green fields and mellow hills. There are other unromantic realities, too. Approach within a hundred yards of a distillery and the pungent smell of mashed barley – mildly nauseous, yet with a *frisson* of whisky fragrance – might easily turn your head. Clouds of steam gush from tall aluminium chimneys; the subdued hum of generators echoes round the blank walls; the long, low warehouses where the casks are stored squat darkly amidst lush meadows; massive articulated lorries crunch through the gears on the uphill drives to lane-locked buildings. It is all a long way from Landseer's image of a once delinquent domestic trade.

The Irish Connection

Whisky distilling began in Ireland, according to some, though no Scot would consider Irish whiskey to be in the same exalted league as Scotland's 'barley-bree'. Distilling is probably as ancient as the Stone Age, and the word 'alcohol' derives from an early Arabic term, *aqua ardens*, meaning the 'burning water'. The word 'whisky' derives from the Gaelic *uisge beatha*, meaning the 'water of life'. These ancient languages encouraged loquacity. Whisky sounds just about right – a simple word that is more easily voiced, after you've had a few.

The first Scottish record of whisky distilling dates from the late fifteenth century. Distilling was certainly common in the Scottish Highlands by the seventeenth century, when every community, even individual farms and homes, had whisky stills. It was a morning-to-evening drink and was supped by everyone, including children. When asked solicitously if whisky did not 'bite', an eighteenth-century urchin famously replied: 'Ay, but I like the bite.' Whisky was thus a casual drink of the common people, used for medicinal purposes as well as for comfort and pleasure. Its production was so widespread that in the 1640s a jealous Scots Parliament imposed a spirit tax. During the following century numerous tough laws against private distilling were enacted. What was once lawful by nature now became illicit.

Regulation was inevitable, partly because distilling was legal in the Scottish Lowlands and was attracting the attention of investors. Pressure from Lowland whisky producers, backed by the government's determination to rationalize distilling, led to an Act of 1823, by which sensible levels of duty were set and reasonable licence fees introduced.

Today, Scotch whisky exports earn nearly a billion pounds annually. Over 100 brands are sold in Britain, and many other brands are exported. Modernization has made the image of Landseer's *The Highland Whisky Still* even more whimsical, although modern distillers promote the old image with convincing style. Ask awkward questions, however, and you discover that hard-headed economics now controls the industry. Ask a distillery guide where the peat fires burn and you quickly learn that they burn nowhere near the traditional source. Few modern distilleries use their own 'malting' floors, where germinated barley, known as 'green malt' and plump with starch, is kiln-dried over peat fires. Today, most malting is done by commercial maltsers and is then sold to individual distilleries. Peat is still used in the drying process, but it is supplemented with coal or coke. In some cases, peat-flavoured air is wafted across the barley like bursts of perfume.

Home to the Hills
The distilling process is where whisky-making comes home to the hills, and to alchemy. The malted barley is cleansed of rootlets and chaff and then ground in a mill, after which it is 'mashed' in huge vats containing the distillery's cherished local water. The water is heated and the liquid that results is drawn off after three or four mashings. It is known, unromantically, as 'worts'. Mashing produces the heavy, sickly smell that wafts round the distillery buildings. The worts is quickly cooled to preserve maltose and is then piped into large

wooden vats known as wash-backs. Yeast is added, and the yeast enzymes convert dextrose in the worts into alcohol. The process is a lively one. The liquid in the vats heaves and bubbles like a tidal pool as the released carbon dioxide escapes. The resulting mixture is called 'wash' and is a beer-like liquid, with an alcohol content of about 6 per cent.

Next comes the misty mystery of distillation, in which the wash is heated in copper pot-stills. These are large bulbous vessels, with tall slender necks. The swirling vapour from the wash rises through the pot-still and is condensed in a coiled copper pipe. There are always two pot-stills – the initial wash-still, which produces a fairly impure spirit, called 'low wines'; and the smaller spirit-still, which re-distills the low wines into something approaching whisky. The resulting liquid is then run out into a 'spirit safe'.

The spirit safe is the focus of the distillery. It is a glass-sided brass tank, only a few square feet in size, like a tabernacle, into which spills a narrow stream of distillate. There is more than a hint of religiosity about the apparatus. Stillmen hover before it like priestly acolytes awaiting a sign. The initial run of impure liquor from the stills is called 'foreshot' and is drained from the safe and recycled through the stills. So too is the impure 'feints', the last of the run. It is the 'middle cut' that the distiller wants, and this is diverted into a hydrometer vessel called the spirit receiver, which measures its specific gravity. The spirit safe is kept securely locked and the stillman makes a visual judgement of when to accept the middle cut. His decision determines the final quality of a malt whisky several years away.

Individuality

The uniqueness of a malt may be determined by subtle differences in the workings of each distillery, but much still rests on maturation. The new, colourless and very strong whisky is piped to the spirit store, where it is diluted, using local spring water, and is then run into casks for storage. Oak casks that once held sherry are used to add good colour and lustre to the maturing liquor. Three years is the minimum storage period before whisky becomes legally recognized as Scotch. Eight years is considered a good age for a mature malt, but maturation may continue beyond fifteen years.

Warehouse storage of whisky has its own mystique. The casks are porous, to allow the maturing whisky to 'breathe', and the percentage of whisky lost through evaporation is known as 'ullage', or more appealingly as the 'Angel's Share'. The outside walls of whisky warehouses look soot-black and grimy, but this effect is caused by a lichen that thrives on the slow, misty passage of whisky vapour through the stonework; permanent inebriation for the lichen. It is during the lengthy maturation period that magic things are supposed to happen to whisky. It seems a reasonable hypothesis, given the volatility of the mix and the potency of the Highland climate. In the distilleries on the island of Islay, the sea air is said to contribute its own indefinable quality. Island mist or mountain dew – who cares when the glass is primed?

Beyond the simple basics of whisky production there lies a complex and colourful culture. There is much room in the glass for all of whisky's attendant myths and genuine mysteries, and although we cannot hope to understand the romance and the heritage of *uisge beatha* at one sip, to walk through the great distilling country of north-east Scotland is one way of releasing the spirit from the bottle.

The Speyside Way

The long-distance footpath known as the Speyside Way leads from the sea at Spey Bay on the Moray Firth to Ballindalloch, 15 miles/24 kms from Tomintoul. It was opened in 1981 by the Countryside Commission for Scotland and is looked after by Moray District Council's Ranger Service. For much of its length the Way follows the disused track of the old Speyside Railway. Plans to extend the Speyside Way from Ballindalloch to Glenmore, near Aviemore, remain unrealized at present, but in 1988 a 15-mile/24-km extension was introduced from Ballindalloch across the Avonside hills to Tomintoul. Official descriptions of the Speyside Way favour a north–south walk, but the route from Tomintoul north to Craigellachie is the objective here, signposted as it is by a succession of distilleries.

Tomintoul was a product of the 'improving' ethic of the late eighteenth century. It was a planned settlement, like nearby Grantown-on-Spey, and like Oban and Ullapool on Scotland's west coast. Such model communities were a form of social engineering imposed on Scotland at the close of a century that had destroyed the Jacobite dream of a Stewart king and that had seen the Highland people robbed of purpose and cohesion. It was aimed at converting Highlanders from their alleged 'idle and wicked practices' to gainful employment. In 1775 the Duke of Gordon set out plans for a village on the bleak height of land where Tomintoul now stands. The village was to be a base for linen manufacture, but growing of flax proved uneconomic in the bitter ground of the hills. Tomintoul survived, but with a struggle, its people dependent on farming and cattle-rearing and on a stubborn momentum. Today, the village's position between the glorious mountains of the Cairngorms and the whisky country of Glenlivet and Speyside has made it a popular tourist centre.

Crown Property

The whisky road from Tomintoul follows the A939 towards Grantown, swinging west beyond the last houses of the village. A woodland track leads north-east from here. The route ahead runs through the Glenlivet Estate, a Crown property, where diversification into leisure use has resulted in an impressive network of waymarked walks and cycle trails. The waymarking is of a quality rarely seen outside national parks, an achievement that says much for the skills and commitment of the estate's management team.

In half a mile/o.8 kms the route crosses Conglass Water, then climbs a steep field to reach a minor road that curls edgily round the wooded slopes of the valley. A short distance along this road, a narrow path leads onto the hill of Carn Sleibhe and the boggy ground of the Feith Musach. In the nineteenth century local women worked long hours here, cutting peat for use at the Glenlivet Distillery.

In bright sunlight, the moorland is as tawny as whisky. In mist it is Macbeth country, menacing and featureless, yet always invigorating. The peat ground runs up to the high point of Carn Daimh, but beyond the open moor, the path leads first through a conifer plantation where, in hot weather, the pines smell of sweet, dusty resin, as they do in the Mediterranean. In driving rain, there is a rich odour of peat and damp decay, the elusive whisky air. Beyond the trees, a rough, stony track leads to the summit of Carn Daimh, the Hill of the Stags. This is just under 2,000 feet/609 metres, and the views are genuinely panoramic beneath huge skies.

To the south, the snow-patched corries of Ben A'an rise above the Cairngorm foothills, which themselves crowd skyward in rounded tiers above the flat shelf of Tomintoul. You should raise a glass to those true mountains, where water from the ice can taste as exquisite as good malt whisky. To the west of Carn Daimh, dense conifers lie combed out on the Strath Avon Hills. Beyond is the smooth ridge of Cromdale, with its highest point of Creagan a Chaise. To the north-east lies the handsome Ben Rinnes, crowned by a granite tor and dominating the true whisky country through which the River Spey glides effortlessly towards the sea.

The Glenlivet

From Carn Daimh, paths and tracks lead north across the shoulder of Carn Liath to emerge close to the Glenlivet Distillery. On the bleak, ragged moorland above the distillery there is a plain memorial stone. It stands alongside a small reservoir and marks the site of the original distillery, which was set up by a local farmer, George Smith, in 1824. In the early decades of the nineteenth century there were 200 illicit stills in the Glenlivet area alone, and Smith operated one of these. He was a trained architect as well as a farmer, and was well connected to such powerful figures as the Duke of Gordon, the major landowner in the whisky country of north-east Scotland. Gordon had persuaded the government that if it introduced legislation that was not punitive, he and his fellow landowners would encourage their tenants to apply for licences. Smith was so persuaded. He had the advantage of living in a district where illicit whisky was already famous as being the finest in Scotland.

Smith faced violent opposition from other local stillmen and from smugglers, who recognized the threat of a legalized monopoly. He employed armed workers, and himself carried 'hair-trigger' pistols for several years until his position was assured. By 1880 Smith's product was given added lustre by being named 'The Glenlivet' to distinguish it from a number of local competitors. Today it is synonymous with all that defines the greatest of Highland malts.

The modern distillery is now owned by the Canadian firm, Seagram. It is a complex of mainly functional buildings. On one side of the road there is a processing plant that uses the draff and other residue of distilling to produce cattle food. The distillery is open to the public and there are guided tours of the complex. They start from the splendidly refurbished Visitor Centre, which was once the Victorian maltings building. The tour ends with a complimentary glass of pale, amber whisky, the inimitable 'The Glenlivet', mellow and smooth, and with a defining malty taste; it sends you on your way with warmth.

To Ballindalloch

A short distance from the distillery, a side lane leads down to the River Livet, which is crossed by a sturdy bridge. The sudden contrast with the sometimes sterile moorland is exquisite. In season, there are masses of white, starry stitchwort amidst the tall grasses and mellow trees of the river bank. In hot summer weather, the undergrowth seethes with insect life.

A riverside path leads to the main road and a junction with a lane, which passes in front of the Glenlivet Village Hall and climbs past Deskie Farm, to join a track that leads steeply onto the Hill of Deskie. The Glenlivet Distillery dominates the swooping slopes opposite; a scarf of white steam billows from its tall chimney and fades into the mottled landscape. The Hill of Deskie has its own scarf of saffron-coloured broom below a bare summit. Beyond lies another stretch of darkly peated moorland. Ahead lies Ben Rinnes. The route across the moor ends at a track that runs down to the main road, which, in turn, leads to a junction with a great broad crescent of the busy A95.

The modern road has swept all before it here. A brutal span of concrete strides across the River Avon by the gatehouse to Ballindalloch Castle. The gatehouse is baronial Gothic in style, more impressive now because of its isolation. It was built in 1850 and is inscribed with the motto of Clan Chattan, 'Touch not the cat but a glove'. One arm of the old approach road has been abruptly cut off by the blank wall of the new bridge. But the gatehouse, with its witch's hat of a turret, retains its appealing style. Modern brutalism is dismissed by Victorian confection; the rumble of heavy traffic barely intrudes. Deep within the wooded countryside, beyond the gatehouse, lies Ballindalloch Castle, originally a sixteenth-century tower house.

A short distance along the main road, and just before the turn-off to Ballindalloch Station, are the remains of two chambered cairns, burial sites dating from the Neolithic, Late Stone Age period. All that survives of the original mounds of earth and stone are the broken outer rings; scant relics, but still impressive symbols of a society that owned this landscape, long before it was overtaken by concrete.

The Speyside Railway

A side road leads down to the old Ballindalloch Station and to the southern terminus of the Speyside Way. A few hundred yards further on is Cragganmore Distillery. Cragganmore was opened in 1870 and had its own railway siding linked to the main line at Ballindalloch. The Speyside Railway was opened in 1863. It was single-track and carried whisky, timber and grain; rich pickings from a rich land. The line was in use for over 100 years. It was closed in 1971 and left derelict, until the opening of the Speyside Way ten years later.

Today, the old line offers a delightful walking and cycling route through the Speyside countryside. There are stretches of the route that are so deeply embedded in the landscape that they have a remoteness to match that of the Glenlivet Hills to the south. The track follows closely the course of the River Spey. In places, the river steals up on you without warning, then veers off in yet another gentle meander between its densely wooded banks. About 1 mile/1.6 kms from Ballindalloch it runs close to the track. It is broad and restless, though its surface is unbroken. Thick coils and smooth shields of water slide past the banks, fretted with oily ripples; the river is like a seething tideway, where the water does not know its own mind.

The track leads arrow-straight past the preserved station house at Blacksboat. A ferryman operated on the river here for nearly fifty years prior to the building of a bridge in 1908. He never lost anyone in that broad, swift flood, although he 'made Baptists of a good few'. From Blacksboat, the track runs on for 2 miles/3.2 kms between dense walls of trees – hawthorn, elder, sycamore, beech and conifer; the stillness and silence are exquisite. Even when there is raw weather on the hills, there is shelter here amidst the trees. Soon Tamdhu Distillery is reached. Tamdhu produces another of those characteristic Glenlivet malts. The old station buildings have been carefully preserved as a Visitor Centre for the summer months and there are conducted tours of the distillery, with a sampling of its product: rounded, mellow and with subtle sweetness.

Aberlour

The next distillery alongside the track is Knockando, a name that might make Americans pause. Whisky country has some wonderful names, some of them strange hybrids between mountain Gaelic and Lowland, 'Lalland' dialect. One of the most endearing is Maggieknockater, the name of a village near Craigellachie. It somehow goes with good whisky in a low-life shebeen, and one explanation of the name indeed refers to a woman called Maggie who kept a lively drinking house during the eighteenth century. Unlike Maggie's shebeen, the Knockando distillery is not open to the public, and neither is the Imperial Distillery at Carron, a short distance further on. Both produce single malts that are also used in blending.

From Carron, the Speyside Way leads through its green channel to Charlestown of Aberlour, another of those planned settlements of the early nineteenth century. The village was laid out by local laird, Charles Grant, whose name was appended for posterity, although the village is better known as Aberlour. It has a fine, broad main street and the area round the old station is now a charming park and amenity area. The Aberlour Distillery is open to the public. It produces a single malt that has some of the heady fragrance of the heather moors on nearby Ben Rinnes. In the pubs and hotels of Aberlour, the range of local malt whiskies makes your head spin.

Just beyond Aberlour, the track goes through a tunnel like a dark, smoky hangover. Beyond the tunnel, only a short distance remains to Fiddich Park at Craigellachie, where, at Boat o' Fiddich, there is a Speyside Way Visitor Centre. Nearby, Thomas Telford's 1814 bridge still spans the River Spey, its elegant ironwork an enduring rebuke to the functional concrete of the modern road bridge that supplanted it. Craigellachie is a handsome village, Highland Victorian in its architecture and handsomely placed above the confluence of the Spey and the River Fiddich. The Craigellachie Distillery produces a light-bodied single malt with a smoky fragrance. A few miles south-east along the A941 lies Dufftown, proclaimed as the malt whisky 'capital', with Glenfiddich, Glendullan, Mortlach and Dufftown distilleries within its bounds.

Whisky distilleries lie in all quarters from Craigellachie. Most are within a pastoral landscape, which seems far removed from the great mountains of the Cairngorms and the Tomintoul Hills and could be anywhere in Lowland Britain. But the air of the whisky country is still the air of the hills, of clear, singing winds blended with mellow rain and breezy sunlight, the fragrance of the heather moor and, in winter, the biting sharpness of frost and snow. Like whisky itself, it defines a nation, in the best possible taste.

The Whisky Road
Information

NOTE: The route follows part of the Speyside Way, an established long-distance footpath. It is waymarked throughout, by posts bearing the Countryside Commission for Scotland's symbol, a thistle within a hexagon.

Distance 25 miles/40 kms

Maps OS Landranger 28 (Elgin, Dufftown & Surrounding Area); OS Landranger 36 (Grantown, Aviemore & Cairngorm Area)

Nature of walk Hill tracks and forestry roads dominate the first half of the route, followed by undemanding walking on a disused railway line. Several whisky distilleries stand close to this latter section. Parts of the route on the high ground may be wet and muddy. Temperatures can be low here, even in midsummer. Strong boots and reliable weatherproof clothing are essential. A winter crossing of Carn Daimh and Hill of Deskie should be made only by those with winter hill-walking experience.

Accommodation Hotels, pubs and B&B at Tomintoul, Charlestown of Aberlour and Craigellachie. Youth hostel at Tomintoul. Camp site at Charlestown of Aberlour.

Transport Bus connections to Tomintoul from main centres, and between Tomintoul and Aberlour/Craigellachie, may be subject to annual changes. Contact TICs for current details.

Further information Tourist Information Centre, The Square, Tomintoul. Open April–November, tel. (01807) 580285. Out of season, tel. (01343) 542666/543388; Speyside Way Visitor Centre & Ranger Service, Craigellachie. Open May–September, tel. (01340) 881266; Glenlivet Estate Office & Information Centre, Main Street, Tomintoul, tel. (01807) 580283.

Start The Square, Tomintoul

1 Walk north-west along Main Street, the A939, to the outskirts of the village. Where the road bends left, turn off right at a parking area, where there are signs for the Speyside Way. Follow a track, then a path, and after about ½ mile/0.8 kms cross a bridge over a stream, then go uphill to reach a narrow road. Go left along the road for about 400 yards/365 metres to reach a signpost at a path leading off right. (1½ miles/2.4 kms)

2 Follow the path uphill between fences, and pass through several metal squeeze-gates. At a conifer plantation turn left, then follow the path through the next belt of conifers. At open ground continue, with conifers on your left, cross a stream, then climb steadily uphill on a bearing of 30 degrees, for 1¼ miles/2 kms to reach another plantation. Follow the track into the plantation for about 150 yards/137 metres to reach a junction, signposted Tomnavoulin, Tomintoul and Ballindalloch. (2½ miles/4 kms)

3 Go left at the junction and follow a good track to reach the northern edge of the plantation. Go through a gate, then continue along the track, with a wire fence on your left, to reach the summit of Carn Daimh. From the summit, go north and downhill towards a belt of conifers to reach a gate near the place where the plantation ends. Go through the gate and follow a track across the west flank of Carn Liath to reach a conifer plantation. Soon, pass a ruined house, then reach a junction with a road. Keep straight ahead, pass the entrance to Blairfindy Lodge Hotel, then turn left to reach the Glenlivet Distillery. (2½ miles/4 kms)

4 Continue down the road from the distillery and, just beyond the Minmore House Hotel, turn right down a narrow lane. At a right-hand bend, turn off left and cross the River Livet by a sturdy bridge. Go left along a riverside path to reach the B9008 main road. Go left along the road for a short distance, then turn off right by Glenlivet Village Hall. Walk up a track that curves up left to Deskie Farm at OS 201300. Just past the first house, bear off left to pass behind another cottage, then go right and follow a path steadily uphill and between wire fences. Continue over the top of Hill of Deskie. Descend, then continue uphill over the shoulder of Cairnacay. Follow the track downhill to reach a junction with an unsurfaced road. Turn left and go downhill to join surfaced road. Continue past Auldich to a junction with the B9008. (5 miles/8 kms)

5 Turn right and follow the B9008, with care, to reach a junction with the A95, by a war memorial. Turn left and follow the A95, with care, then turn right down the B9137 to Cragganmore at OS 167366 to reach the old Ballindalloch Station, now a private hostel. (1½ miles/2.4 kms)

6 From the old Ballindalloch Station, the Speyside Way now follows the track of the disused Speyside Railway. The route is well signposted and is easily followed to Charlestown of Aberlour and on to Craigellachie. (12 miles/19.3 kms)

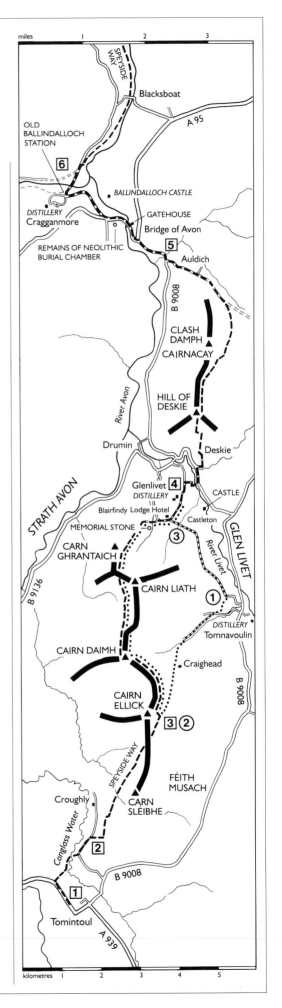

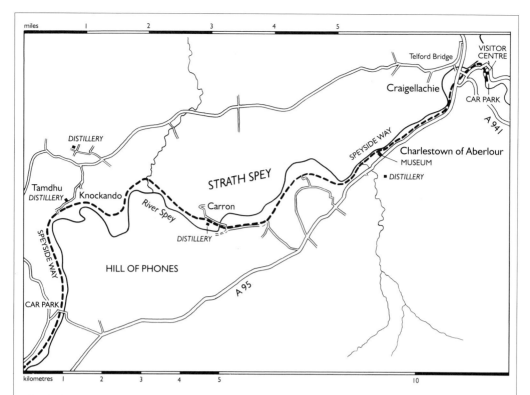

CIRCULAR WALK
6 miles/9.6 kms

Walking boots and reliable weatherproof clothing are advised. A winter crossing of Carn Daimh should be made only by those with winter hill-walking experience. The route has been very well waymarked by the Glenlivet Estate Ranger Service.

For safety reasons the off-road section of the route is closed between 6pm/1800 hours and 8am/0800 hours, during which time the culling of roe deer may take place. Duration: end April–12 August, and 1–21 October. Dogs must be kept under close control so as not to disturb livestock and wild creatures.

Start Tomnavoulin. There is limited parking at a cleared area by the Clash Wood forestry gate at OS 208265. This is about ½ mile/0.8 kms along a side road that leads off the B9008 on the north side of Tomnavoulin.

1 Cross a stile by the forestry gate. Follow the forest road for about 200 yards/183 metres, then go left along a woodland path that is waymarked as Walk 5. Continue alongside a fence, with trees on your right, then cross a stile, and go immediately left over a second stile onto a farm track. Where this track forks, take the left fork, signposted Westerton/Walk 5. Just past Westerton, follow a track round left, cross a stream, then continue uphill and round to the right and pass through a narrow belt of conifers.

Continue past the ruins of Craighead and keep uphill to enter another conifer plantation. Reach a junction with the Speyside Way, signposted Tomnavoulin, Tomintoul and Ballindalloch.

2 Follow direction **3** on the main walk to reach the Glenlivet Distillery.

3 Retrace your steps uphill from the Glenlivet Distillery, then turn left at the junction for Tomnavoulin. Follow the winding road to return to the car park.

A Rough, Romantic Road
The Trossachs

Lochearnhead to Callander 14¼ miles/22.9 kms

'Oh Caledonia!
stern and
wild. . .'
Walter Scott, *Lay of the
Last Minstrel*

The nineteenth-century novels and poems of Sir Walter Scott are often credited with introducing 'tourism' to Scotland. But, at the end of the eighteenth century, enthusiasts for the 'picturesque' were already thronging accessible areas such as The Trossachs, though few ventured very far into the more remote mountains through which this walk leads.

Walter Scott's vision of Caledonia is typically exclamatory – Scott was a great enthusiast; for him, the 'rugged strand' of the Highlands was a tangible symbol of Scottish nationhood. On the threshold of the nineteenth century, Scotland was without direction and without much identity. Scott secured for the nation a cultural heritage by transforming its eighteenth-century political confusion into romantic patriotism. His novels, especially, won international recognition, and they have great stature still. But in defining a style that leaned heavily on medievalism, they condemned Scottish literature to a century of costume drama.

A generation before Walter Scott, Robert Burns had displayed more pragmatism, and less bland patriotism. Burns was the better poet, too. 'A parcel of rogues in a nation' was how he judged his fellow Scots for their internal history of betrayal and treachery and their ultimate capitulation to English influence. Burns portrayed a Scotland with its trews down. His people, and their bad behaviour, are timeless. Scott created a rosier image through his romanticism; and though Scott created colourful characters alongside his rather stiff historical figures, they are frozen in time, brilliant characterizations that remain theatrical.

Walter Scott mixed the characteristics of the industrious Presbyterians of the Scottish Lowlands with the feckless, colourful 'mountain Irish' of the Highlands to add colour and verve to his historical storytelling. He had the advantage of being of 'mountain' stock himself. He was descended from a Border clan of notorious marauders and, in childhood, had been exposed to and had absorbed the powerful oral history of the Borders. Highland sentiment was easily absorbed, in kind. But Scott's romantic appreciation of the rough bounds of the hills and mountains was tempered by good Lowland values and by forensic discipline. He belonged, after all, to the Scottish bourgeoisie of the Age of Enlightenment; he was committed to England's Hanoverian establishment and was thus Anglicized, though he remained in thrall to what he saw as Scotland's rich heroic past. He was thus ideally equipped to give a cultural identity to late eighteenth-century Scotland, a nation that stood on the threshold of the modern world, where social and cultural traditions – those 'old, forgotten, far off things' – were being steadily eroded by politics and commerce.

Border Ballads

Scott's first literary efforts produced *The Border Minstrelsy*, a collection of old folk tales in verse, which Scott embellished and probably added to. Soon he was writing original epics such as *The Lay of the Last Minstrel* and *The Lady of the Lake*. Both were set against the background of The Trossachs, and they became the bestsellers of their day: 20,000 copies of *The Lady of the Lake* were sold within a few months of publication in 1810, and 50,000 copies had been sold by the 1830s. The tone of these epic poems was more Arthurian chivalry than Scottish romance, but Scott was following the cultural trend that had started with Rousseau and had been embraced by the Lake Poets. The mood of the times was for romantic idealism.

Walter Scott found rich ground for such idealism in The Trossachs of the early nineteenth century. Here was the 'Lake District of the Scottish Highlands', given the seal of approval by William and Dorothy Wordsworth, who had stayed at Strathyre and Callander in 1803. The Trossachs of the previous century had already been labelled 'picturesque' and as having 'such an assemblage of wildness and of rude grandeur, as beggars all description and fills the mind with the most sublime conceptions'. By the 1780s leisured visitors to the area were taking boat trips along 'Loch-Ca-therine', as Loch Katrine was then known, to visit such 'sights' as The Rock and Den of the Ghost, described by one writer as being a cave 'whose dark recesses, from their gloomy appearance, the imagination of superstition conceived to be the habitation of supernatural beings'. Wickerwork shelters were erected at strategic viewpoints, 'for the accommodation of strangers, who visit this wild and picturesque landscape', and local people were already willing to offer their services as tour guides. All this took place within a bare forty years of the murderous battle of Culloden and the brutal 'pacification' of the Highlands. The blood was barely dry on the heather.

By the beginning of the nineteenth century, The Trossachs area was purged of many of the realities of 'old, forgotten, far off things'. Sentimentality, and curiosity, filled the void. The *Statistical Account of Scotland* of 1791–9 says of the area: 'The Trosachs [*sic*] are often visited by persons of taste, who are desirous of seeing nature in her rudest and most unpolished state.' The rude, unpolished Highlanders, who had survived the eighteenth century, were probably fast withdrawing into the northern mountains in sheer terror at the thought of it. Among the persons of taste who visited The Trossachs was the Hon. Mrs Murray, of Kensington, who in 1799 published *A Companion and Useful Guide to the Beauties of Scotland*. Her Kensington terms of reference apart, the redoubtable Mrs Murray's book title alone seems a deeply ironic epitaph on the passing of the Highland way of life. In 1818 the poet John Keats complained that The Trossachs were 'vexatiously full of visitors'. Tourism has a long pedigree, as well as long queues.

Rich Theatre

Into this rich theatre of the picturesque came Sir Walter Scott, first with his medieval epic poems, and then with his great Scottish novels of the Highlands. The Trossachs became the accessible workshop of Scott's imagination, the background to such bustling, brawling novels as *Rob Roy* and *A Legend of Montrose*. The latter was based on the 1644–5 campaign of James Graham, the Marquis of Montrose, the bright star of seventeenth-century principled revolution, who epitomized the perfect merging of Noble Savage with chivalry in the Scottish heroic mould. Montrose had chosen to support Charles II in his war with Cromwell and Parliament, and for a short while he blazed a brave, but ultimately futile, trail of battle and skirmish across Scotland, with his army of formidable clansmen.

Scott used Ardvorlich House, on the south shore of Loch Earn, as the setting for the early chapters of *A Legend of Montrose*. He renamed it Darnlinvarlach Castle, and it was here that Scott had Montrose's Highlanders gather at the wooded mouth of Glen Vorlich. The novel is vintage Scott in its heroic mould; the setting is The Trossachs at their romantic best.

Loch Earn defines the northern bounds of Ardvorlich with a flourish; its cool waters are the focus of smoothly textured hills and crowded woods, and of lochside meadows where Highland cattle graze. Today, Ardvorlich House sits comfortably amidst its lawns and shrubbery. The present building is neither modest nor ostentatious, but there is a sturdy dignity about it. In the grounds, rhododendrons glow with blood-red flowers in early summer, a startling contrast to the emerald green of the surrounding fields and woods.

Bad blood in plenty stains the real history of Ardvorlich. By the bridge before the east gate there is an inscribed stone marking the re-interment of seven Macdonalds of Glen Coe, who in 1629 'were attempting to harry Ardvorlich' and were killed by the resident Stewarts. There is a more hideous tale from the sixteenth century about raiders who killed, then decapitated, the Keeper of the Royal Forest of Glen Artney in return for his having cut off the ears of MacGregor poachers. Not content with such summary revenge, the MacGregors took advantage of the hospitality of the Keeper's pregnant sister, the unwitting Mistress of Ardvorlich Castle, whose Stewart husband was absent. The MacGregors ate the food she offered, and then left her brother's severed head on the castle's dining table, his gaping and bloodied mouth stuffed with bread and cheese. The shock was too much for the lady. She fled to the cold hills and hid for weeks, but returned eventually to the castle, where she gave birth to a son, James Stewart. He was to lead, in kind, a dark, brutal life of cruelty and murder. So much for Highland 'romance'.

The Kilpont Murder

Walter Scott wove the bloody story of the MacGregor atrocity into *A Legend of Montrose* and based the volatile character of the novel's Allan McAuley on that of James Stewart of Ardvorlich. As always, Scott made a rattling good tale from such brutal raw material. But the historical record portrays Stewart of Ardvorlich as a dangerously embittered and quarrelsome man. During the civil war of the seventeenth century, he fought with the Marquis of Montrose on the Royalist side and, in 1644, was at the Battle of Tippermuir, near Perth. Soon after the battle, Stewart killed, in a quarrel, Lord Kilpont, his close friend and the eldest son of the Earl of Mentieth, whose lands lay near Callander. An early explanation for this seemingly random act was that Stewart was involved in a plot to assassinate Montrose and had asked Kilpont to assist him. Kilpont refused and Stewart then stabbed him to death and escaped from Montrose's camp to join the Parliamentarian side. He was later pardoned, by Parliament, for Kilpont's murder, giving credence to the allegation of treachery.

These were the incidents on which Scott based, very loosely, the background to *A Legend of Montrose*. But there was another explanation for the murder of Lord Kilpont, and it is one that sits more convincingly with the wasteful war of attrition between the Highlanders themselves. Scott had told the conventional story of the Kilpont murder in several publications and, in 1830, while *A Legend of Montrose* was being printed, he received a letter from Robert Stewart, the contemporary Laird of 'Ardvoirlich' (as it was then known). Robert Stewart's version of the Kilpont murder was aimed at clearing his family's honour and the name of his ancestor. His story has the stamp of authenticity, yet it reveals the dark, destructive nature of the Highland temperament.

Robert Stewart explained to Scott that his ancestor's killing of Kilpont was due to drunkenness and bad temper – less dishonourable than political treachery, it seems. The details of the incident reflect the volatility of the times. Before the Battle of Tippermuir, James Stewart had been angered by the behaviour of a band of Irish MacDonnells, brought in on Montrose's side by a western chieftain, Alasdair Macdonald – the famous MacColla Coitach, 'son of Colla Coitach, the left-handed one'. The Irish troops were savage men, as foreign and menacing to many of their fellow Gaels of Scotland as Viking raiders had been five centuries before. They were also Catholic, in name at least, a fact that did not sit easily with the non-Catholic Highlanders in Montrose's army. On their way through the Ardnamurchan Peninsula from the western shore, MacColla's men plundered

Campbell homes – something that would not have upset Montrose or his men, given that the Campbells were the traditional enemies of many of the clans. But, later in their progress east, the Irish troops caused trouble on other clan territories, including that of Ardvorlich. Gaelic bards lionized MacColla and his fierce band as 'the men with fair locks, with sharp cleaving blades, and red shield bosses'. But for many who fought uneasily alongside them, they were nothing less than rabid.

James Stewart of Ardvorlich demanded from Montrose some redress for the alleged damage to Ardvorlich land. Montrose was indifferent to the demand, not least due to being preoccupied with battle plans. But he was then forced to arrest Stewart and MacColla because of a threatened duel between them. Montrose ordered peace between the two men, and in the reluctant hand-shaking that followed, Stewart 'took such a hold of Macdonald's hand as to make the blood start from his fingers'. There was never much grace in Highland conciliation.

Montrose won a spectacular victory at Tippermuir. His men were outnumbered two to one by the Godly Lowlanders of Fife and Stirlingshire, who had been sent out by their church ministers, but were no match for a berserker charge by clansmen. In spite of the victory, Stewart of Ardvorlich continued to brood about his dispute with MacColla. He resented the attitude of his friend Lord Kilpont, who had supported Montrose's judgement in the dispute. During a drinking bout after Tippermuir, Stewart argued with Kilpont, finally stabbing him to death. He then killed a sentry and escaped. He later joined the Parliamentarians, not through treachery, argued his descendant, but on the pragmatic grounds that his life on the Royalist side was forfeit. The distinction was crucial to the maintenance of Highland honour.

The Route to the South
Today, Ardvorlich is a peaceful place, although the image of Scott's gathering of the clans can still be set against the background of hills and loch and the 'scathed branches' of pine trees. Here came the Macdonnells of Glengarry under Vich Alistair Mor, the Camerons of Lochiel under Evan Dhu, the Macdougalls of Lorn, the Macaulays, Macleans, Macdonalds – each clan eyeing the other with suspicion while their pipers strutted like fighting cocks and the air heaved with the drone of competing war tunes. From Ardvorlich, at one time or another, such wild bands probably set off south, across the hill passes, for the Lowland plains. The route to the south, through Glen Vorlich and over the hills to Callander, survives today as a right of way and offers a wilder view of The Trossachs than the 'picturesque' world of the loch shore.

The route through the hills begins from the east gate of Ardvorlich House; it passes through the grounds on a strictly defined track that winds amongst trees and shrubs. The fragrance of damp woodland fills the air. Above the house, the bulky shoulder of Ben Vorlich looms through the trees. Rowans and birches line the banks of the stream. The track divides below a steep bank; the right-hand branch climbs steadily towards the steep, rounded shoulder of Ben Vorlich, a tempting way for the peak-bagger; while the left branch first leads down by the river, then begins its long, winding rise up Glen Vorlich.

High Pastures

The track up Glen Vorlich is well defined and where it gives out amidst shaggy heather, a slight path leads alongside the stream towards the saddle of the Bealach Gliogarsnaiche. The ground is dense with heather and blaeberry. There are sketchy ruins of old buildings at various places in the glen. It was to these high pastures that the black cattle of Ardvorlich would be taken in summer, in the days of James Stewart; the herd watchers lived in the shielings.

The summit of the Bealach is soon reached at the gaunt remains of an iron fence. Beyond lies a narrow valley, down which small streams drain from the watershed. The white-breasted ring ouzel, the 'mountain blackbird', frequents this high country and its harsh, crackling call, the counterpoint of a sweet fluting song, pierces the silence. A vestigial path runs down the valley, through a boggy maze of hidden streams. This is raw ground, where snow lies long into the early spring and where, even in the driest summer, the ground remains waterlogged. It is swathed in a mixture of rough grasses, including sheep's fescue and bent, with purple moor grass on the lower ground. It is a landscape of low, crouching vegetation, where the tiny yellow flowers of tormentil and the purple specks of milkwort are woven through the tiding grass.

The route from the summit of the pass leads along sketchy paths to a junction with the main stream of the Allt an Dubh Choirein, which flows down from the great saucer of land below Ben Vorlich and Stuc a' Chroin. At the junction of the streams are the ruins of a shepherd's cottage, the tumbled stones of its walls dark with lichen and moss. There was probably a dwelling on this site for many centuries, a settlement even, now abandoned to the cold, lonely air of the hills. On the slopes to the north-west stand the remains of a small hill shelter built of corrugated iron, the 'crinkly tin' that became a ubiquitous building material in the Highlands during the twentieth century, though its rust-red walls sit uneasily on the brocaded moor.

From the ruined cottage on the river bank there are alternative routes to the low ground. For those who prefer the certainty of a clear track, a 4¼ mile/7-km route leads down the north bank of the Allt an

Dubh Choirein to a junction with the Glen Artney hill road, which then leads west to the main track to Callander. The alternative, traditional route climbs south-west through rough ground to a low saddle on the flank of Meall na h-Iolaire, the 'Hill of the Eagles'.

To the north of this path, the seamed faces of the great hills turn into each other above the hollow emptiness of Dubh Choirein, the Black Corrie. Light and shade play across the mottled slopes in bright, breezy weather, the sharp sunlight flooding the pale deer grass with golden light, the cloud shadows dark blue and purple on the scooped face of Ben Vorlich. At the saddle of Meall na h-Iolaire, there is a desolate spread of land, of broken peat hags and bleached stones. On the far side of the saddle, it falls steeply in a tumble of broken ground towards the broad headwaters of the Keltie Water. After the cramped quarters of the high hills, the view across this flowing landscape is panoramic, although it is diminished by the flat distance and by the blurred edge of the horizon. There is no clear path from the saddle, and the way to the low ground requires good route-finding in mist and rain. The objective is the sprawl of sheep folds and the old cottage of Arivurichardich – a name to take a run at.

From the cottage, a broad track leads by the Keltie Water out of the hills. Within a mile or two/1.5–3 kms, the supple, wooded countryside round Callander is reached, where birches and Scots pines, beeches, oak and larch blanket the low hills. The narrow road from Braeleny and Drumardoch farms leads directly to Callander, but partway along it a worthwhile detour can be made onto the high escarpment of Callander Craig. From the roadside a muddy path twists steeply uphill through the trees, amidst butter-yellow globe flowers and the blue-petalled meadow cranesbill. On the narrow summit ridge, cotton grass speckles the blaeberry and heather. From the summit cairn, which was raised in honour of Queen Victoria's jubilee of 1897, there are exhilarating views to Ben Ledi, Loch Venachar and Callander, and across the unfolding plains of the River Teith as far as Stirling. To the north, Ben Vorlich seems suitably distant and withdrawn.

From the top of the Craig, the way lies steeply through dappled woods. It follows stepped pathways, where Victorian excursionists once pursued, robustly, the spirit of the picturesque within shouting distance of civilization. The line of Callander Craig can be followed in a direct descent to Callander, but a pleasant alternative leads south-east on a delightful route through the woods, to regain the road from the hills near the Bracklinn Falls car park. From here Callander is soon reached, its broad, generous main street a bustling contrast to the loneliness of the hills. In the Tourist Information Centre there are splendid displays that depict The Trossachs in a way that the murderous James Stewart of Ardvorlich, and the brawling clansmen of the hills, might not recognize.

A Rough, Romantic Road
Information

Distance 14¼ miles/22.9 kms

Maps: OS Landranger 51 (Loch Tay); OS Landranger 57 (Stirling & The Trossachs Area)

Nature of walk A good, tough route through the more remote Ben Vorlich area of The Trossachs, crossing two mountain passes. The middle section of the route is pathless in places. There is some rough waymarking using wooden posts, though their continued presence should not be assumed. Skill with map and compass is necessary in bad visibility. Waterproof boots and reliable weatherproof clothing are essential, even in summer. A winter crossing should be made only by those with winter hill-walking experience and with full winter clothing and equipment. Walkers are asked to stay on defined paths during the deer-stalking season, 1 July to 15 February. Sheep graze throughout the area of the walk and there are ground-nesting birds on the higher reaches. *Dogs should be kept on leads at all time.*

Accommodation Hotels and B&B at Lochearnhead and Callander. Camp sites by the A84 south of Lochearnhead, and at Strathyre.

Transport Main bus connections to Callander from Stirling. A seasonal bus service runs between Callander and Lochearnhead via Strathyre. Walkers can leave a car at Callander and take a bus to the start of the South Loch Earn Road.

Further information Tourist Information Centre, Callander, tel. (01877) 330342.

Start Lochearnhead. Alternatively, if private transport is available, a start can be made from the east gate of Ardvorlich House. This saves several miles of road walking.

1 Walk south along the A84 for about ¾ mile/1.2 kms to the junction with the South Loch Earn Road. Follow the South Loch Earn Road as far as the east gate of Ardvorlich House at OS 633232. This lies just beyond a bridge, where there is a memorial stone to executed Macdonalds by the roadside. (3½ miles/5.6 kms)

2 Go through the east gate and follow the drive for a short distance to a junction by Home Farm. Take the right branch and cross a bridge over a stream, then bear left just before Ardvorlich House (private). Reach a kissing-gate beside a wooden bridge. Beyond the gate, keep uphill to another gate, then continue on a stonier path for about 1 mile/1.6 kms, to the place where the track forks at OS 639212, just past a wooden bridge. (The right-hand track is signposted to Ben Vorlich.) Take the left-hand, grassier track. Soon, cross a small stream, then cross a larger stream by a wooden bridge. Continue uphill on a track that fades gradually. Just before the track levels off, bear off along a narrow path that starts abreast of a large boulder. Keep straight ahead alongside a stream, and in line with poles. *The path is indistinct in places.* Reach the level summit of the rock-strewn Bealach Gliogarsnaiche, between Ben Vorlich and Meall na Fearna, at OS 638188. (2¼ miles/3.6 kms)

3 Continue to the summit of the pass, where there is a line of iron fence posts. Follow a slight path downhill on the left of a stream, then cross over where the ground levels off. Bear south along the bed of the shallow valley. The path is indistinct, but keep to the right bank of the stream. Near the mouth of the valley, by some small waterfalls, keep high along a slight path to reach the ruins of Dubh Choirein. ✎ (1½ miles/2.4 kms)

4 *The next section is pathless in places and requires good navigation in mist.* Cross the stream that comes in from the right and just below the ruins of Dubh Choirein. (This position can also be reached if you cross the stream on the left, then walk downstream for a short distance to re-cross by a good bridge. Walk upstream until opposite the ruins.) Follow a narrow path upstream, cross a subsidiary stream after about 50 yards/45 metres, then continue uphill on the right of the main stream to the spot where it becomes very narrow. When abreast of a large isolated boulder on the right, cross the stream to reach a flat boulder. (¾ miles/1.2 kms)

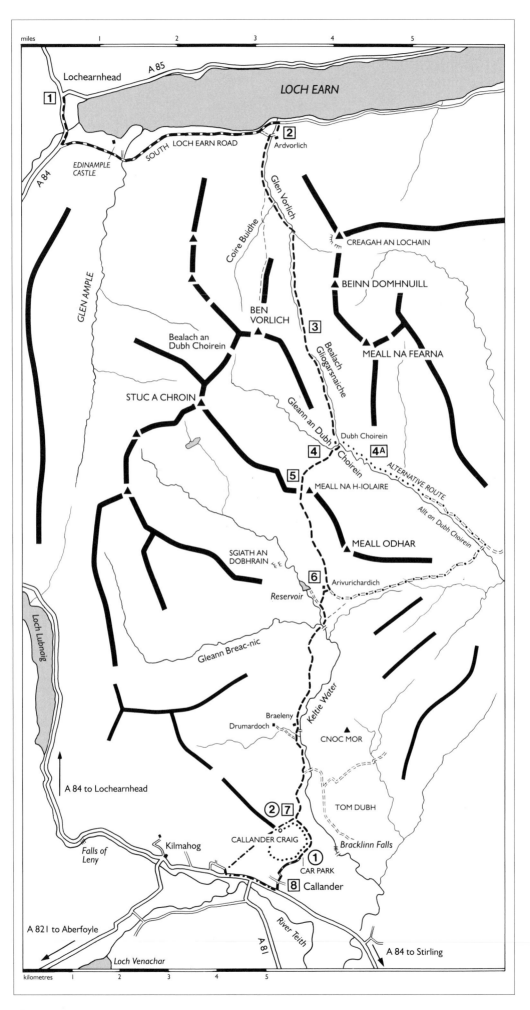

miles

Lochearnhead
A 85
LOCH EARN
1

SOUTH LOCH EARN ROAD
2
Ardvorlich

A 84
EDINAMPLE CASTLE

GLEN AMPLE

Coire Buidhe

Glen Vorlich

CREAGAH AN LOCHAIN

BEINN DOMHNUILL

BEN VORLICH

3

Bealach an Dubh Choirein

Bealach Gliogarsnaiche

MEALL NA FEARNA

STUC A CHROIN

Gleann an Dubh Choirein

Dubh Choirein
4
4A
ALTERNATIVE ROUTE

5
MEALL NA H-IOLAIRE

Allt an Dubh Choirein

SGIATH AN DOBHRAIN

MEALL ODHAR

6
Arivurichardich
Reservoir

Gleann Breac-nic

Loch Lubnaig

Keltie Water

Braeleny
Drumardoch
CNOC MOR

A 84 to Lochearnhead

TOM DUBH

②7

Falls of Leny
Kilmahog
CALLANDER CRAIG
Bracklinn Falls
①
CAR PARK
8 Callander

A 821 to Aberfoyle

A 81

River Teith

A 84 to Stirling

Loch Venachar

kilometres

4a *An alternative, though longer route, leads south-east from the ruins at Dubh Choirein. Cross the left-hand stream, then continue along the north bank of the Allt an Dubh Choirein to a junction with the track from Glen Artney. A right turn at the junction leads to Arivurichardich (4¼ miles/7 kms)*

5 Continue towards the saddle on the west side of Meall nah-Iolaire, on a bearing of 200 degrees. Reach a stony patch with prominent peat hags ahead. Bear up right from here and follow a sketchy path due south over the saddle to reach a large boulder on a prominent knoll. Go left from the boulder along a faint path that winds downhill. The path soon fades and it is best to descend steadily on a bearing of 160 degrees across the slope of Meall Odhar. Keep above the line of a fence that runs across the bottom of the slope, then descend more directly to reach the bothy and sheep pens at Arivurichardich. (1½ miles/2.4 kms)

6 From Arivurichardich, follow a track south and cross a bridge over the Keltie Water. Keep right along a good track to reach Braeleny and the start of a surfaced road. Follow the road for about 1 mile/1.6 kms to reach a corner by a black-and-white traffic pole and a faded footpath sign. (3 miles/4.8 kms)

7 Go off to the right up a steep, narrow path through some trees. Follow the path uphill to reach a cairn on top of Callander Craig. Continue on a path along the rim of the escarpment, go through a kissing-gate, then descend a rocky section. Cross a small bridge to the place where the path forks. (The path ahead leads directly to Ancaster Road, Callander.) Take the left fork and go down some steep wooden steps. Reach a rough forestry track. Turn left and after about 50 yards/45 metres go off to the left along a winding path through woodland which takes you to the surfaced lane from Braeleny. (1 mile/1.6 kms)

8 Turn right and walk downhill. Keep straight across where the road bends sharply left, then follow a surfaced path alongside two houses. At a junction with Ancaster Road, turn right and continue to where the road bears left over a

bridge to reach the car park by the Dreadnought Hotel. (¾ miles/1.2 kms)

CIRCULAR WALK
2 miles/3.2 kms

Start Car park for Bracklinn Falls, OS 637083

1 Leave the car park by its upper exit, then go right and walk up the narrow lane to reach a corner by a black-and-white traffic pole and a faded footpath sign. Turn off left on a path through the trees.

2 Follow direction 7 on the main route. At the surfaced road, turn left to reach the Bracklinn Falls car park.

The Reivers' Road
The Borders

Town Yetholm to Alwinton 17 miles/27.3 kms

'I ride on my fleet-footed grey, My sword hanging down by my knee. I never was afraid of a foe, And wha daur meddle wi' me?'

Seventeenth-century Border ballad

The Cheviot Hills were once part of a medieval 'state' of robber clans whose armed men, known as 'reivers', terrorized the whole of the Border area between Scotland and England. This walk crosses the Cheviots by an ancient track that was used by invading armies, by gypsies, smugglers, traders and cattle drovers, and by the reivers themselves, as they set about the business of 'shaking loose the Border'.

The Cheviot Hills seem unremarkable when viewed from the broad, fertile plain called The Merse, which lies south of Edinburgh. Grudgingly they rise from the horizon; they are like distant islands that seem never to grow in size no matter how closely you approach. At the Border town of Kelso there is still no hint of the dense, interlocking valleys and tangled hills that mark the East March between Scotland and England. You must travel further south-east, towards Town Yetholm, where suddenly the landscape becomes parochial; where roads grow narrow and begin to twist and turn between field boundaries, and to dip in and out of wooded hollows. Here at last the smooth, billowing hill country draws itself round you like a cloak.

Borders have always been battlegrounds. They are the fault lines of history, where the only common ground lies in the graveyards of those who died defending them. People who live to either side of national borders are less concerned with the defence of those borders than with daily survival amidst the violent tides of history. The medieval people of the Anglo-Scottish Border were innately lawless. They were typical of most people who live close to wild and ungovernable frontiers; they were suspicious of outsiders and their aggressiveness was sharpened by distrust of each other.

It was always difficult for successive generations to draw boundaries across the green running sea of hills that spans the waist of Britain. At one time a notional kingdom of Northumbria extended northward as far as Edinburgh, and ancient Scots kingdoms laid claim to parts of Cumbria. The Romans alone drew physical lines at the limits of their endurance by building first Hadrian's Wall and then the Antonine Wall. The latter was the most audacious attempt to demarcate the hostile north from the largely passive south. It ran from the River Forth to the River Clyde; had it prevailed as a political border, Scotland might have been more of a province than a proud nation today.

The Romans drew their lines with precision. Hadrian's Wall was the axis of the Empire's northern defences until the Roman army withdrew from Britain in AD407. For the next 600 years Britain was ravaged by conflicts between aggressive races, whose territories remained uncertain and random until the Norman Conquest of 1066 recast the north–south divide of the Romans.

The Conqueror

William the Conqueror at first drew a harsh line. He wrecked the northern provinces of his new land and turned Northumbria into a charred desert. He invaded Scotland with such forcefulness that the Scottish king, Malcolm Canmore, wisely submitted. It was an act that may have ensured Scotland's political subservience to England. Subsequent English monarchs believed that, by Malcolm's capitulation, Scotland had surrendered its independence for ever. It was a view that condemned the borderland between the two countries to centuries of strife.

Norman influence in Scotland grew strongly in the twelfth century during the reign of Scotland's Norman-educated King David. Amongst these 'new Scots' were a de Bailleul, and a de Brus, forebears of future Scottish kings. Throughout the Borders, Norman barons founded a hierarchy of famous names, such as Maxwell, Graham, Elliot, Armstrong, Johnstone and Hume. In Northumbria the names were no less Norman – Dacre, Ridley, Forster, Fenwick.

For the kings of Scotland and England, the Borders served as both battleground and buffer. During the thirteenth and fourteenth centuries, the kings of both countries bludgeoned their way towards the violent conclusion of the Battle of Bannockburn and the winning of Scottish 'independence'. It was an independence that left the Borders in turmoil, as successive kings of Scotland and England confronted each other politically and militarily. In 1513 Scotland's savage defeat at the Battle of Flodden ended the dynastic struggle of the monarchs, but left the Borders irretrievably lawless.

After Flodden, Henry VIII sought to 'pacify' the Border clans. It was a forlorn hope, not least because Henry had used the old device of keeping the Borders unstable by keeping the Borderers in arms. There ensued, for the following hundred or so years, the violent heyday of the reivers. The leading families were based in fortified stone towers, known as peels, from which they conducted raids and feuds in a climate of general anarchy. A readiness for violence was inured from birth, despite lip-service to the rites of religion. The right hand of a male child was often left unchristened, so that later it might kill without compunction.

The Scottish Borderers depended on a cattle economy in a hard land, and they believed that the robbing of cattle from the lush valleys of Cumbria and Northumbria was by natural law ordained. The robbing of household goods came an easy second. The murder and rape of those who got in the way was inevitable. Retribution followed, just as inevitably.

The forceful recovery of stolen goods was legally condoned by the authorities, and the close pursuit of a reiving band by a group of aggrieved farmers and others was known as following a 'hot trod'.

Pursuit of a 'cold trod', several days after a raid, was just as legal. The result was often summary justice by sword, lance or pistol amidst the raw, brimming hills of the Marches, an act that itself invited revenge from the victim's family. The novelist Walter Scott, himself of Border stock, called the trod 'the fatal privilege'. Thus was the grim cycle of violence sustained.

Rough Justice

The anarchy of the Borders had been recognized by the authorities of Scotland and England as early as the thirteenth century. At that time both sides appointed commissioners with orders to formulate special laws for the area, the *leges Marchiarum*, aimed at delivering efficient 'rough justice'. The commissioners also drew up a geographical division of the Border area into East, Middle and West 'Marches', which, in turn, were divided into Scottish and English equivalents.

By the fourteenth century the commissioners were known as 'Wardens of the Marches'. There were three Scottish and three English wardens. They were men of substance, though not necessarily of rectitude, often being involved in violence themselves, or at least in turning a blind eye to it. Both sides appointed men who would best further each nation's interest. The wardens were expected to impose the martial law of the Borders and to judge the rights or wrongs of an affray. They held occasional 'Days of Truce' at which aggrieved parties met to plead cases. In practice, the wardens lent only a veneer of order to an ungovernable wilderness.

Within this wilderness, certain robber clans were dominant. The Armstrongs of the West March could summon a raiding party of 3,000 men from their immediate clan and from related families known as 'graynes'. This was a private army by any measure. A typical reiver band numbered 100 armed and mounted men. Their tough little horses were known as hobblers and were noted for their sure-footedness and stamina. Their hard-faced riders wore steel bowl-bonnets or peaked burgonets on their heads; over their rough shirts they wore leather coats called jacks, which had metal or horn plates sewn into the quilting; their breeches were tucked into leather thigh boots, against which rested a long-barrelled handgun known as a 'dag'. At their waists hung sword and dagger, and across their backs was strung the reiver's favourite weapon, the lance.

The most notorious reivers included such colourful characters as Kinmont Willie Armstrong, Ill Will Sandy Armstrong, Nebless Clem Croser, Curst Eckie, Fingerless Will Nixon, God's Curse Scott and Archie Fire-the-Braes. The reivers were said to have cool tongues to go with such fiery names, and often talked their way out of retribution. The bleak violence of their lives was enlivened by epic adventures and rough humour, and certainly by a mad courage. But this is to romanticize a way of life that was rooted in greed and cruelty, however conditioned that life was by brutal times. It was sustained by official connivance for long enough. But the gangsterism of those such as Kinmont Willie and Ill Will Sandy could not long survive the centralizing and ordering of society that began with the Union of the Crowns in 1603.

Hostile Confrontation

Reiving's political 'cover' of a Scotland and England in hostile confrontation ended with the Union. James I, of the newly united kingdom, ordered stricter control of the Borders, a region that he renamed, rather belatedly, the 'Middle Shires'. Imprisonment, exile or hanging were now the lot of those Borderers who did not come to heel. The reiving culture became less clan-based. The leading families were absorbed into the more structured and secure way of life that new economic opportunities offered. They were absorbed also by the political and religious changes of the seventeenth century and lent their warrior skills to the struggles between Crown and commons, Church and State.

Many repentant reivers were transported to Northern Ireland, where they gave to Ulster Unionism its intractable Protestantism. In the Borders themselves, the large organized bands were succeeded by individuals, who were known as moss-troopers, after their secret hiding places in the peat bogs, or 'mosses', of the Middle and West Marches. The moss-troopers were more easily categorized, and dealt with, as common thieves by the authorities and, without the security of the clan or grayne, their numbers were steadily reduced. By the latter part of the seventeenth century the Borders had been 'pacified'. Society had moved on from the feudal independence that was the Norman inheritance of the Border clans, and commerce had become too powerful and too organized to tolerate anarchy of the reiving kind. A historic end to the old Border ways was hauntingly expressed by the lament of one exiled reiver:

This is my departing night,
For here no longer must I stay,
There's neither friend nor foe of mine
But wishes me away.

A Compelling Landscape

Today's Borderers are civilized, good-natured inheritors of the reivers' compelling landscape. Within this landscape, the Cheviot Hills seem the most remote part. Historically, they lay within the East March and offered less convenient border crossings than did the cross-border valleys of Teviotdale and Liddlesdale to the south-west. Crossings of the East March are by long climbs to high ground and equally long descents into the remote, hidden corners of Northumbria. Ancient routes do cross these hills, however, and one of the most significant is the route that leads from Yetholm in Roxburghshire to Alwinton in Northumbria, which was known throughout its southern half as Clennel Street.

Yetholm is in two parts, Town Yetholm and Kirk Yetholm. The name derives from a mix of Scots and Anglo-Saxon, *yett* being Old Scots for gate, and *holm* being Old English for river-flat or meadow. The two Yetholms lie on either side of the Bowmont Water. Kirk Yetholm is the older of the two, having been a churchtown in the thirteenth century. Its present church is Victorian, but its style is reminiscent of the medieval peel towers in which the Border reivers found a less than spiritual sanctuary. Its church tower seems equally impregnable: its dour whinstone walls are webbed with pale mortar and are as hard as iron. The church stands on high ground above the river flats and in summer its sternness is mellowed by the trees and shrubs that crowd round it. At the centre of Kirk Yetholm there is an attractive village green; it is flanked on its northern side by the Border Hotel, the symbolic terminus of the long-distance national trail, the Pennine Way, which leads along the rim of the high hills to the east.

Town Yetholm, or more properly 'Toun' Yetholm, proclaims its yeoman roots with a broad market street. The 'toun' evolved in the fourteenth century as a market for local farmers and as a staging post on the drove roads that led south across the Cheviots. The growth of sheep-rearing added to Town Yetholm's importance and today the Yetholm Border Shepherds' Show, held in early October, is said to be the area's most traditional display of sheep in prime condition. Both Yetholms sit prettily in the landscape. Their rural charms have not been compromised by too much modern intrusion, and in the languid dusk of a summer's evening there is an air of serenity amidst the mellow hills and the cool river meadows.

Gypsies

Yetholm has a curious association with gypsies, which dates from the sixteenth century and may have coincided with the arrival of definitive gypsy people in Scotland. Always self-confident, the gypsies contrived special status in the Scotland of James IV, a monarch of liberal sympathies. But soon they overreached themselves and were persecuted in later years. Yetholm may have seemed a useful refuge for medieval gypsies. But another tradition suggests that Kirk Yetholm became the 'capital' of the Scots gypsies because a gypsy soldier of the French wars of the 1690s saved the life of a British officer during the Battle of Namur. The officer owned property in Yetholm and is said to have granted land and houses to his saviour. Yetholm certainly became the base for successive gypsy 'kings and queens', most notably the 'royal' family of the Faas. The most famous gypsy king was 'canny Wull Faa o' Kirk Yetholm', an accomplished smuggler of whisky and gin across the Cheviots. His sister Esther, 'Etta' Faa Blyth, was the last gypsy queen. She died in 1883; her cottage, known as the Gypsy Palace, still stands in Town Yetholm's Muggers Row, where gypsies made mugs and pots for sale.

The last gypsy coronation took place in Yetholm in 1898. It was attended by 10,000 people, and there are surviving photographs of gypsy 'royalty' in eccentric, but quite stylish, regalia. Groups of gypsies passed through the area for many years after this event. During the early nineteenth century a Yetholm minister, the Revd John Baird, established a school for gypsy children, the first step towards integration with the settled community. Today, the Romany tradition is still upheld in Yetholm. During Yetholm Civic Week in June, a young man and woman are elected as leaders of the celebrations under the old Romany titles of Bari Gadgi, the 'good man', and Bari Manushi, the 'good woman', symbols of the travelling people's heritage.

The Bowmont Valley

From Town Yetholm the traveller's route south to Cocklawfoot and the Border runs through the valley of the Bowmont Water. In early summer the valley is thick with vivid white hawthorn blossom, which makes the coiled hedgerows look like drifts of snow. It is a long tramp along the Bowmont to Cocklawfoot, but the road through the valley is pleasant enough. At Cocklawfoot, the Cheviots rise like a green wall ahead. The track from the valley climbs round the plump little hills of White Knowe and The Bank. On White Knowe there are the remains of an Iron Age fortification, its terraced embankments still visible. Above The Bank the track levels off, then, without fanfare, reaches the great national border, at a wooden gate in a wire fence. Nothing more – gate and fence seem arbitrary and flimsy. But how else should borders be?

There are few points of reference here. South-east is Windy Gyle and the vast emptiness of the military training ground of Otterburn. To the north-west is the swelling summit of The Cheviot, from which high point the whole range takes its name. Southward lies the Kidland Forest and the lonely hills of Upper Coquetdale. In summer, the greenness of the hills is intense; the dense hues of emerald and jade bleed into each other, or meet emphatically at the dividing line between conifer plantation and open hillside. In fine weather, light and shade flicker across the chameleon slopes beneath spinnaker clouds; the air fizzes with the tangy smell of heather and peat. In autumn, the colours on the hill are old gold and purple and the skies are slate-blue. In winter, it is all black peat moss and bleached grass, the whole streaked with licks of snow, or blanketed white after a blizzard, when the air is as sharp as blades beneath gloomy skies.

The Border Gate is a gloomy enough place, summer or winter. It lies amidst peat bog and heather bank, an indeterminate, flat landscape between the high points of King's Seat and Windy Gyle. At the Border Gate, the Pennine Way crosses Clennel Street. Massive stone slabs have been bedded into the quaking peat along the line of the Way. They are a solution to the problem of footpath erosion, and they continue in the tradition of the paved trods that were laid for hundreds of miles across the moors of northern England during the medieval period of pack-horse transport. Here, on the Cheviots, the slab pavement runs for miles along the line of the border.

Day of Truce

The Border Gate was known historically as Cocklawgate, or the Hexpethgate. It was a traditional meeting place of the wardens of the East and Middle Marches and was the scene, in 1585, of a typical Border fracas during which Lord Francis Russell, son of the Earl of Bedford, was shot dead. Russell is commemorated by an eponymous cairn to the south-west of the Border Gate. The incident was symptomatic of volatile Border politics. Russell had accompanied his father-in-law, the English warden Sir John Forster, on a Day of Truce at Cocklaw. They met with the Scottish warden, Sir John Ker of Ferniehirst. Records show that the Scots came in greater force than was merited, and the tension may have been heightened at what was always a fraught occasion.

Both sides confronted each other at a distance. The rough-haired ponies wheeled and turned upon the heather and the trampled grass. Between the two sides, ragged youngsters and unmounted messengers passed to and fro. Riders broke away from the main bands, and groups from both sides may even have come together for friendly gossip and to share gulps of whisky in the clean, edgy air of the hills. But, in spite of occasional goodwill, these were battle lines drawn.

At some point in the exchanges, and inexplicably, Lord Russell was shot dead. Fighting broke out; one report states that the Scots pursued the English for several miles south of the Border Gate. Later reports were confused, alternating between claims that the fracas was started deliberately by the Scots and allegations of a 'little pickery', or thieving, which led to violence and to the killing of Russell. The truth may lie in evidence that there was bad feeling between Russell and Ferniehirst. Russell had earlier foiled a Scottish plan to invade England. Ferniehirst had been involved in the plan and, on the bleak heights of Cocklaw and Windy Gyle, Russell may have paid the price of bad blood, by a sidelong bullet.

The Road to the Isles: West Highlands
TOP Loch Beinn a` Mheadhoin
BELOW Ciste Dhubh, from Camban in the Fionnglean

The Whisky Road: Grampian
TOP Telford Bridge, Craigellachie
BELOW Old Tamdhu Station on the Speyside Way

A Rough, Romantic Road: The Trossachs
TOP Ben Vorlich from above Gleann an Dubh Choirein
BELOW Ardvorlich House, Loch Earn
OVERLEAF In the woods of Callander Craig

The Reivers' Road: The Borders
TOP South of the Border, towards the hills of Upper Coquetdale
BELOW Clennell Hill, above Alwinton
OVERLEAF Looking towards the Bowmont Valley

A Lead Miners' Track: The Yorkshire Dales
TOP Above Birbeck Wood, Gunnerside Gill
BELOW The old peat store at Blakethwaite Mill, Gunnerside Gill
OVERLEAF Lead mine adit at Bunton, Gunnerside Gill

Lonely Landscape

From the Border Gate, the way south leads through a lonely landscape of grassy hills and vast conifer plantations. There is something sweetly forlorn about such vacant land. This side of the border may be England by decree, but it is still frontier land by nature – unquantifiable, and indistinguishable from its Scottish counterpart beyond Cocklaw; the merging of the nations is seamless. It is tempting to linger in this no-man's-land, and the temptation is encouraged by a sense of unaccountability that may have been the imperative of Border lawlessness.

Across these hills rode the dark horsemen of the Marches, the truly unaccountable, the rough-cheeked, hard-bitten reivers, bristling with weaponry, their horses shrouded with steam in the cold air, their coming heralded by the creak of leather and the clank of cold steel beneath plated jacks. The riders thought no further than the hours ahead, to the immediacy of brute existence, violence, plunder and intractable revenge. You find yourself uneasily scanning the hill crests for sudden thickets of horsemen; and the cold company of those bleak riders dogs your heels on the descent into a cross-cleft of valleys dense with conifers. Ahead, the red weal of a forestry road snakes through the dark trees and draws the eye towards a horizon of low hills.

In the green sump of the main valley, a sturdy footbridge spans the Usway Burn. On the stream bank is a circular sheep stell, one of those stone corrals that punctuate the Border hills. Its geometric shape is in keeping with the severe lines of the conifer plantations and the clean curves of the hills. Beyond the burn, the path climbs the open hillside and is sucked deep into the Kidland Forest. Here, Clennel Street is rendered featureless by forestry; the splendidly named summits of Bloodybush Edge, Hog Lairs, Nettlehope, Sneer Hill and Flesh Shank are swamped by the ubiquitous pine. Forestry tracks wind gently on towards Alwinton, with little of landscape merit to break the monotony. Beyond Wholehope Knowe, the track descends to a broad, open apron of reedy turf, across which brawny sheep wander.

On the forest's edge a ruined building and a shed of gleaming aluminium squat messily amidst rubble and weeds. To the south, there is a falling away to England. The eye seeks out high places in the hazy distance, but the track leads always downhill, across springy turf and on through interlocking hills to the peaceful little village of Alwinton and the lush fields of Coquetdale. Beyond these remote quarters lies the green weight of England. Its existence, and its ambition, must always have pressed against the Border region with menacing force. In turn, England's promise – its plump meadows and corn-fed cattle, its yeoman wealth – drew down like gathering storm clouds the hard-faced reivers from their cold lairs in the hills.

The Reivers' Road
Information

Distance 17 miles/27.3 kms

Maps OS Landranger 74 (Kelso & Surrounding Area); OS Landranger 80 (Cheviot Hills & Kielder Forest)

Nature of walk Some steep inclines, but they are short-lived. Tracks and paths over the high ground are in good condition and are generally dry. The route on the English side of the border is mainly along forestry tracks. Walking boots and reliable weatherproof clothing are essential, even in summer. A winter crossing should be made only by those with winter hill-walking experience and with full winter clothing and equipment.

Accommodation Hotels, pubs and B&B at Kelso and Yetholm. Hotel and B&B at Alwinton. Youth hostel at Kirk Yetholm. Camp site at Alwinton.

Transport Main bus connections to Yetholm from Edinburgh and from other Border towns to Kelso. Regular bus service from Kelso to Yetholm. Annual travel guide for the Kelso area available from Kelso TIC. Post bus between Alwinton and Morpeth, via Rothbury, Mon–Fri and Sat morning. School bus between Alwinton and Rothbury, Mon–Fri, term time only. Main bus connections between Rothbury and Morpeth, and between Morpeth and Newcastle upon Tyne; further information from Kelso and Morpeth TICs.

Further information Tourist Information Centre, Kelso, tel. (01573) 223464; Tourist Information Centre, Morpeth, tel. (01670) 511323.

Start Town Yetholm, OS 820280

1 Take the B6401 leading south out of Town Yetholm. After about 1 mile/1.6 kms take the side road on the left and pass through Primsidemill. Continue along the valley road, past Cliftoncote, Belford and Swindon. Where the road forks for Sourhope and Cocklawfoot, take the right-hand branch and continue to Cocklawfoot. (7 miles/11.2 kms)

2 Cross a bridge to the farmyard, then go sharp right and through a gate by a large sycamore tree. Follow a good track uphill, through a belt of conifers, and then go across open ground to reach a gate. Just beyond the gate, where the track forks, take the left branch and climb steadily uphill. Continue round the hillside, then bear left and uphill to reach the Border Gate and a junction with the Pennine Way at OS 871160. (2¼ miles/3.6 kms). *The Pennine Way alternative from Kirk Yetholm joins the main route here.*

3 Go through the Border Gate into England. Continue south for ½ mile/0.8 kms to reach a signpost indicating Salters Road and Clennel Street. Keep on the track signposted Clennel Street, go through a gate and then follow the track, with walls of conifers to left and right, to reach a signpost indicating Uswayford via a side path on the left. Keep on the main track downhill to reach a broad forestry road. Cross this road, then continue to a gate and stile in a fence, where a signpost indicates that it is 6½ miles (10.5 kms) to Alwinton. Go through the gate and descend the sloping field to pass a circular sheep fold. Cross the Usway Burn by a bridge and follow the path uphill to enter a conifer plantation. Follow a forestry track to the spot where it emerges below Nettlehope Hill and rises to a junction with a track coming in from the left, just before a gate. (3½ miles/5.6 kms)

4 Beyond the gate, follow the track for about 1 mile/1.6 kms to enter another belt of conifers. Just before the trees end, the track divides. Take the right-hand branch, signposted Border County Ride, and descend to a gate. Continue along the track, and pass through another gate beside an old corrugated-iron shed and ruined building. Continue along the track, with conifers to the left, then descend to cross open ground on a sketchy track. Pass some sheep folds, then climb steadily to a gate. Continue along a good track that leads to a surfaced lane into Alwinton. (4¼ miles/6.8 kms)

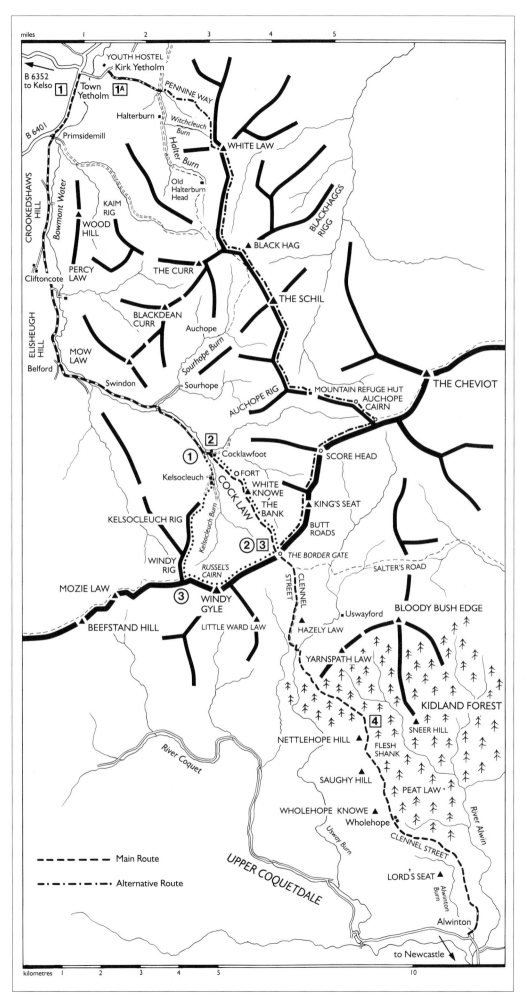

miles

YOUTH HOSTEL
Kirk Yetholm
B 6352 to Kelso ⬚1
Town Yetholm ⬚1ᴬ
PENNINE WAY
Halterburn
Witchcleuch Burn
WHITE LAW
B 6401
Primsidemill
Halter Burn
Old Halterburn Head
CROOKEDSHAWS HILL
BLACKHAGGS RIGG
Bowmont Water
KAIM RIG
WOOD HILL
BLACK HAG
PERCY LAW
THE CURR
Cliftoncote
THE SCHIL
ELISHEUGH HILL
BLACKDEAN CURR
Auchope
MOW LAW
Sourhope Burn
Belford
Swindon
Sourhope
AUCHOPE RIG
MOUNTAIN REFUGE HUT
AUCHOPE CAIRN
THE CHEVIOT
⬚2 Cocklawfoot
SCORE HEAD
①
Kelsocleuch
○ FORT
WHITE KNOWE
COCK LAW
THE BANK
KING'S SEAT
KELSOCLEUCH RIG
Kelsocleuch Burn
BUTT ROADS
②⬚3
THE BORDER GATE
SALTER'S ROAD
WINDY RIG
RUSSEL'S CAIRN
MOZIE LAW
③ WINDY GYLE
CLENNEL STREET
BLOODY BUSH EDGE
Uswayford
LITTLE WARD LAW
HAZELY LAW
BEEFSTAND HILL
YARNSPATH LAW
KIDLAND FOREST
⬚4 SNEER HILL
NETTLEHOPE HILL
FLESH SHANK
SAUGHY HILL
PEAT LAW
River Coquet
WHOLEHOPE KNOWE
Wholehope
River Alwin
Usway Burn
CLENNEL STREET
------ Main Route
—·—·— Alternative Route
UPPER COQUETDALE
LORD'S SEAT
Alwinton Burn
Alwinton
to Newcastle

kilometres

ALTERNATIVE ROUTE TO THE BORDER GATE VIA THE PENNINE WAY

This alternative increases the overall distance to 18¾ miles/ 30 kms. It is a well-defined and pleasant high-level walk.

Start Kirk Yetholm, OS 828283

1a Follow the lane going south-east from The Square at Kirk Yetholm, signposted Halterburn. At OS 840277, beyond a cattle grid, bear off left, signposted Pennine Way, and follow a path across the Halter Burn, then go uphill alongside a stone wall. Continue uphill to reach the high ground of Stob Hill. From here, the Pennine Way is clearly marked. The route leads south alongside the line of the border fence, across White Law and Steer Rig, to Black Hag, from where it continues to the summit of The Schil. Continue south, then east, past a refuge hut and over Auchope Rig, to where the line of the border turns sharply south-west at OS 896194. (The summit of The Cheviot at 2,674 feet/815 metres lies just over 1 mile/1.6 kms north-east of here.) Follow the border fence over Score Head and King's Seat to reach the Border Gate at OS 871160, *where the main route is joined.* (11 miles/17.7 kms)

CIRCULAR WALK
5½ miles/8.8kms

A pleasant walk that takes in the best of the Border hill country. There is a steep climb to start, but from the Border Gate the going is level, and then downhill. The route follows part of the Pennine Way, which is well-paved across wet ground. Walking boots and reliable weatherproof clothing are advised. A winter walk on the Border hills should be made only by those with winter hill-walking experience and with full winter clothing and equipment.

Start Cocklawfoot, OS 853186. There is informal, limited parking just before Cocklawfoot Farm.

1 Follow direction **2** on the main walk to reach the Border Gate.

2 Go through the Border Gate, then turn right to follow the large flagstones of the Pennine Way, south-west and alongside the border fence. Pass a large cairn, then continue to the cairn and trig point of Windy Gyle. Continue along the Pennine Way to Windy Rig.

3 Reach a gate, where a second wire fence leads off from the border fence. Go through a gate on the right and continue with the fence on your left for a short distance, then bear right down the broad back of Kelsocleuch Rig towards a plantation in the valley below. At the base of Kelsocleuch Rig, follow the track round right to reach a gate into the plantation, then continue through the plantation and go through a gate on its northern side. Follow a vestigial track across open ground to reach a fence corner, then descend to a broad track. Go left along the track, past the farm at Kelsocleuch, then continue to Cocklawfoot.

A Lead-Miners' Track
The Yorkshire Dales

Circular walk from Gunnerside 8 miles/12.8 kms

Parts of the Yorkshire Dales were mined for lead ore from the Roman period until early in the nineteenth century. The industry has left a wrecked and haunted landscape in the remote mining valleys that are known as 'gills'. This circular route explores the lead-mining country of Gunnerside Gill in Swaledale. It passes through a landscape that has been scarred by industrial exploitation, yet possesses raw beauty amidst its devastation.

Swaledale is as soft and supple as its name implies. Of all the Yorkshire Dales it is the most remote, the most enticing; it leads you on persuasively between low, swooping hills to where the softness and suppleness give way to the raw, bare moorland of the Pennines, with raw, bare names to match: Keld, Stonesdale, Ravenseat – true grit beneath the soft, viridescent skin.

Limestone may be the underlying rock of Swaledale, but gritstone forms the bare bones of this northern wilderness of peat moors and scoured valleys. The gritstone landscape makes a distinctive contrast to the limestone country of the Southern Dales, where the pale grey cliffs of Gordale, Malham and Kilnsey are the most spectacular outcroppings of the Great Scar, a vast reef of limestone that runs from Kingsdale in the west to Wharfedale in the east, and that gives the Yorkshire Dales their most famous features of crag, cave, pavement, waterspout, beck and gill.

The name Swale means 'swift and rushing', a name that matches the nature of the river that tumbles helter-skelter down the dale. It gathers its source tributaries from Winton Fell and Birkdale Common on the bleak flanks of the Pennines, drawing into itself the glittering threads of Great Sleddale Beck, Birkdale and Whitsundale Becks. Then the Swale tumbles through a tangle of falls and ravines that lie above and below the village of Keld, at Wain Wath Force, East Gill Force and Kisdon Force. The river tumbles southwards after these rites of passage, then runs through broad meadows between the steep slopes of North Gang Scar and Arn Gill Scar to Muker, where it is joined by the Straw Beck. Below Muker, the river flows due east; it passes beneath the elegant arch of Ivelet's seventeenth-century packhorse bridge, then runs past Gunnerside, to the place where the dale widens and the Swale becomes more stately in its progress towards Grinton and Reeth. Thereafter the 'swift, rushing' river glides less turbulently, in wide loops and quiet ripples through the green parishes of Ellerton, Stainton and Downholme on its wandering way to Richmond.

Throughout its length, Swaledale is a patchwork of intake meadows, stitched and buttoned with field walls and barns, the enduring motifs that define the overall texture of the Yorkshire Dales. The walls, especially, have great symmetry. They run in straight lines and outline precisely the meadows and green lanes. Yet there are reassuring divergences. Walls flex suddenly, to accommodate some territorial quirk or to avoid an immovable obstacle; they curve in great crescents here and there. Above the valley floor, they break away to climb the valley slopes onto the open fell, where they define the vast areas of rough land that were enclosed for grazing during the late eighteenth and early nineteenth centuries. Limestone rubble was used in the building of the walls and barns of Swaledale and, as is the way with natural material, the rough, random shapes of the limestone blocks have married style to function. The man-made structures seem rooted in the landscape; they are extensions of the underlying rock.

Limestone and Lead

Amongst the minerals common to limestone regions is lead, a metal that is both dense and heavy and that is easily smelted into malleable form. The lead of the Yorkshire Dales was injected like molten silver into the older rocks of the area about 100 million years ago. It is thought that lead solutions were formed within deep deposits of undersea mudstone, which had absorbed lead elements from salt water. As the mudstone deposits were compressed by the weight of fresh sediments, the lead-bearing liquid was squeezed out. Under pressure and at high temperature, this volatile solution was injected laterally, sometimes through many miles of intervening ground. It flooded into the fracture lines and cavities of the limestone rock of the Dales' area.

Lead exists mainly in the form of lead sulphide and is also known as 'galena'. It is often mixed with other minerals, including calcite, fluorite, silver and zinc. It can be found in thin layers that have been 'squinted' between beds of older rocks, or it may fill large cavities. The richest veins, or ore-bodies, can be up to 10 feet/3 metres wide; most veins are pitched vertically within the rock mass and may be up to 100 feet/30 metres deep and ½ mile/0.8 kms long. Extraction of lead-bearing ore, known as 'bouse', began in Roman times, as a simple digging out of ore from veins that were exposed on the steep sides of valleys. A rough but ready early method of exposing ore was known as 'hushing'; by which impounded water was released to scour the loosened slopes, exposing the lead vein and separating the heavier lead-bearing rock from lighter material. Early miners sank shafts on the open moor and then dug tunnels from their base for short distances on either side. In time, the shallow ore was worked out and deep-shaft mining developed. Deep shafts were often lined with masonry; descent was by toe-holds gouged in the wall, by ladder, or by a succession of 'stemples' – wooden battens jammed across the shaft. Ventilation was by means of 'windy kings', simple fans that were installed in each shaft and hand-driven by youngsters. Lifting gear at the top of the shaft was used for raising the ore to the surface, but it required water power, and then steam power, to make such deep mining profitable.

Another method of reaching the ore veins was by excavating a near-horizontal tunnel, known as an 'adit' or 'level', into the valley slope until it met a lead vein. This became the main method of mining in the nineteenth century. It gave access to the deeper parts of veins that shaft-mining could no longer exploit. Adits could be used for drainage, and narrow-gauge rails, on which ore wagons ran, were laid along them. Connections were made to other sites by driving 'cross-cut' tunnels between neighbouring adits. Along the north side of Swaledale, a 6-mile/9.6-km network of tunnels lies beneath the ground.

Roman Origins

Swaledale was the richest lead-bearing area in the Yorkshire Dales, and lead-mining in the dale dates back to Roman times. Verified records survive from the twelfth century, when Yorkshire lead was used in Norman churches and abbeys, and in great state buildings such as Windsor Castle. Swaledale lead was used at Waltham Abbey and at Clairvaulx Abbey in France, and there is an enduring legend that lead from the dale also graced the roofs of St Peter's in Rome. Dissolution of the monasteries during the sixteenth century led to a decline of this early industry, but by the end of the eighteenth century lead extraction was flourishing once more. The years of the late eighteenth and early nineteenth centuries formed the heyday of the Swaledale lead industry. However, it was all boom or bust. During the 1830s there was another decline in production, but yet again the industry recovered. The output of finished metal from Swaledale during the nineteenth century was between 2,000 and 4,000 ton(ne)s annually.

By the late nineteenth century, the industry was again moribund as British lead prices failed against competition from imported lead, which was cheaply produced as a by-product of American silver mines. In Swaledale, too, the richer veins were near exhaustion, and by the early 1900s lead-mining had all but ceased in the Dales. Soon, the mining areas were drained of their people. Those who did not leave resorted to farming as their main occupation. There was no further mining, or quarrying, in Swaledale, no exploiting of other minerals such as iron or fluorspar, as happened in other areas of the Dales. Because of this, there was some healing of the fractured earth and it is only in parts of Arkengarthdale and in the middle reaches of Gunnerside Gill that the gouged landscape still resembles an arid desert.

The eighteenth-century ideal of the picturesque placed great importance on visual harmony, even within a landscape of decay. But that decay had to be natural and regenerative. The devastation of

Gunnerside Gill is man-made. It negates the picturesque, and distorts our modern sense of what is 'scenic'. Yet in the bruised and wrecked landscape of the Gill there survives, somehow, a perverse beauty and an atmosphere of repose. Between the village of Gunnerside and the northern end of Gunnerside Gill, where the valley delves into the quaking mosses of Melbecks Moor, the evidence of lead-mining is everywhere. To walk along the miners' tracks that lead through the gill, amidst old workings and smelt-mills and below the wrenched hillsides, is to discover a topographical museum of Yorkshire lead-mining.

Gunnerside

Today, Gunnerside village delights the visitor with its vernacular architecture, the stone forms, which, like the limestone field walls, merge with the landscape that nurtured them. Gunnerside's name means 'Gunnar's Pasture' and relates, possibly, to a Norseman or Dane, one of the colonizers of the area in the years before the Norman Conquest. The village is like many of the hillside settlements of upper Swaledale. It seems set down precariously on the steep slope of the valley side. Seen from a distance, its lines of dark-walled houses resemble small, rocky escarpments.

In 1761 John Wesley found fertile ground for robust evangelism amongst the lead-miners of Gunnerside, just as he had amongst the tin-miners of Cornwall. Wesley is said to have sprained his thigh whilst walking on the steep fellside; undaunted, he inspired the 'earnest, loving, and simple people', who built a chapel that seated over 400 worshippers. Later they replaced it with the present chapel, a handsome building that is less severe in its sparse classicism than most Methodist architecture. It could hold 700 worshippers. This reflected the certainty of the blessed, and the well-fed. By 1900, when lead-mining had declined irretrievably, the population of Gunnerside had fallen to a mere 300. Swaledale was described as being 'dead alive with distress'. Workless miners and their families left for the wool and cotton mills of Lancashire and the West Riding, or for the emigrant ships. Today the population of Gunnerside numbers about 200.

Gunnerside Beck

There is a great threading of water through Gunnerside, where the walk begins. The River Swale tumbles past waterside meadows. The Gunnerside Beck runs between the houses to join the Swale at New Bridge, where the road swings steeply uphill towards Thwaite, Keld and the Dalehead. Gunnerside Beck passes beneath a sturdy little bridge near the King's Head Inn. It is from here that a well-surfaced path runs upstream to the old Gunnerside school building, which is now a private dwelling. A diversion leads up some steps to a path that runs behind the old school to the beckside, where the water threads its way across a bed of ragged boulders that have been washed down from far up the gill. There are small heaps of lead-spoil half-buried amidst the grass. On the banks of the gill wild flowers grow in profusion: primroses and violets amidst the glossy grass of the woods, pink marsh valerian and white bittercress on the damp banks. The path leads into Birbeck Wood, a relic of the acres of woodland that once covered the Dales and that were systematically denuded by human settlers. Now the wood is a mix of hawthorn and rowan, hazel and ash, with occasional bird cherry – a smaller version of wild cherry, but with its delicate white blossoms in single sprays.

Halfway through the trees, the path forks. A lower branch follows the stream to the far edge of the wood, while a higher path leads steeply uphill. Soon this higher path turns north-west to wind its way through small meadows, where walls snake across the landscape and sheep stumble in and out of the gaping doorways of old barns. In summer the meadows are filled with buttercups and white clover. The walls are punctuated by narrow squeeze-stiles, and by low-set gaps known as cripple holes or thirl holes, which allow sheep to pass through, but which restrain cattle. Soon the path drops down to join the lower route at the broad river flats and by the ruins of two ore-crushing mills, one to either side of the beck. These are the first substantial remains of lead works to be met. They processed the raw ore from an adit mine called the Sir Francis Level, which lies a short distance upstream on the west side of the beck.

The ore, or bouse, was placed in walled bays called 'bouse teams'. Fresh from the vein, it is a glittering silver colour that soon fades to a dull grey. The bouse teams survive and still contain heaps of graded ore. The bouse was first broken down with a hammer, called a 'bucker'. On this site a water-powered roller-crusher, like a huge mangle, was then used to reduce the ore even further. The lead 'galena' was then separated, in water, from the less dense and less heavy waste material, called 'gangue'. Separation was by use of sieves or devices called 'hotching tubs', or by means of a circular sluicing mechanism called a 'buddle'. The lead aggregate was then taken by pack-horse over the fells of Brownsey Moor to a smelting mill, the Surrender Mill, 3 miles/4.8 kms to the east.

Rich Veins

The Sir Francis Level was named after the son of a well-known mineral-rights owner, Sir George Denys. It was opened in the 1860s, in the hope of draining the lucrative ore-ground all the way up Gunnerside Gill and of exploiting the lower levels of rich veins. It took eight years to excavate the level through 550 fathoms (⅔ mile/1 km) of grudging rock. The tunnel was first cut by use of hand tools, then by drills powered by hydraulic pressure obtained from a water mill, and finally with the aid of dynamite. Large amounts of ore were mined from a number of veins along the Sir Francis Level.

In the green world above, the path runs on along the beckside, where sheds and water wheels, crushers and hotching tubs once stood amidst the noise and bustle of the dressing floors. Soon the path climbs away from the stream and runs below the escarpment of Winterings Scar. On the slopes to the west lies the old Silver Hill mine and, further north, the sisterly quartet of Barbara, Harriet, Priscilla and Dolly Levels. These lie to either side of the side-valley of Botcher Gill, above Botcher Gill Nook. Ahead the main valley opens out at the remarkable complex of the Lownathwaite and Bunton workings. This was an area of rich pickings, where the lead-rich veins of Old Rake, North Rake and the abundant Friarfold and Watersykes crossed each other.

Lownathwaite and Bunton Levels

Mining has shaken the land loose at Bunton. There is hardly a patch of ground undone. The vast, rock-peppered slopes plunge into the bottom of the valley, grey-faced and raddled, and latticed with tracks and pathways. In dull weather, the mood of desolation can be baleful; when the sun shines from a blue sky, there is a saving grace in the glitter of the beck water and the emerald mosaic of moor grass and sedges. On the eastern slopes lie the remains of the Friarfold, Merryfield and Old Rake Levels. On the west, just above the beck, is a building on top of a spoil-tip. Higher still lie the old Priscilla and Dolly Levels and the remains of the Lownathwaite smelt-mill. The most striking feature of the west side of the gill is the great gash of North Hush, a gutted ravine, crammed with the broken stone and rubble of the exposed lines of the Lownathwaite North and Middle Veins.

All the veins here were 'hushed' in the early years of lead-working. The name 'hush' belies the impact of this epic method of earth-movement. The Romans introduced hushing, but it was not until the eighteenth century that the device was used on a massive scale. The object was to expose the upper surface of the mineral vein. The miners first loosened the ground on the valley slope above the vein, using picks and metal spikes to turn the earth, and then built an embankment of rock and turf near the top of the slope. These turf dams were 100 feet/30 metres across. Behind them, drainage water was allowed to build up and, when the makeshift dam was broken, the torrential flood gouged its way down the slope, leaving behind rich pickings of galena amidst the shattered rock.

The deep gullies in the slopes of Gunnerside are the result of repeated hushing. It is a name to savour; a mere whisper, in comparison to the reality of all that roaring, tumbling water carrying down its tons of grinding and scouring rock. The deep hushes are tormented landscapes still, a teetering chaos of ragged shale and stone, amidst which few plants grow, and where it is dangerous underfoot. Hushing was eventually prohibited because of the danger of flooding to settlements on the valley floors. It belonged to a time, even before deep-mining, when brute exploitation of the environment was commonplace. Those old lead warriors stood on the high slopes, well clear of the hushing ground, and watched the brown, frothing torrent roar down the hillside, sending rocks, and dust, and great wings of water into the air. Their hearts must have lifted with the exhilaration of it all, when today we would be horrified by such environmental damage.

Shattered Landscape

The men who worked amidst this shattered landscape were a mixed breed. When the great age of Swaledale mining began during the late eighteenth century, the local workforce had to be supplemented with workers from neighbouring Cumbria and from as far away as Cornwall. These incomers brought with them hard-earned mining skills and an adventurous attitude that sustained Swaledale lead-mining for over 100 years. They helped shape the culture of Swaledale, and even contributed nuance and tone to the local dialect of the 'Swadlers', as the people of Swaledale were known. The lead-miners were a hard breed. They were inured to the most bruising work, but their wit and their spirit seem never to have failed them. They shared the ancient custom of nick-naming, or by-naming, in the way that Cornish fishermen still do. Swaledale nick-names reflected a sharp mix of affection and irony, and said much about such characters as Nettlebed Anty, Glowermore Tom, Splitmeat, Brag Tom, Screamer Tom and Kit Puke Jock. The miners had strange superstitions, again as fishermen do. Whistling inside a mine was forbidden, and it was bad luck to mention tailors or wild creatures.

This was all part of the culture of those who perform dangerous work, an antidote to uncertainty and to the random fate that shortened the lives of so many lead-miners. Mining was a baleful trade, in which the breaking and crushing of bodies from rock falls and slides were common. Lead-poisoning was endemic and was known locally as 'bellon', the lead 'colic'. It could kill a normally fit man by the time he was forty; it weighed him down with leaded blood that brought on terrible fatigue, muscle-wasting and stomach cramps. The death-mark was a blueness of the gums and of other parts of the body. Above ground, in the smelting mills, workers were poisoned by sulphur dioxide fumes and by lead vapour. Even pack-horses were muzzled to stop them eating grass that had become polluted with lead.

And all this within a landscape that today is cherished for its clean, invigorating air.

A Devastated Arena

At Bunton, that landscape now seems set in its ways. There can be no cleaning up here, no refurbishment or re-seeding of the devastated and rootless slopes. It is not until you are well past this great shattered arena that a natural greenness reasserts itself. Even so, the spoor of mining straggles along the ground all the way to the ruins of the Blakethwaite smelt-mill, at a junction with a steep little side valley called Blind Gill.

The Blakethwaite Mill was in production from the 1820s to the 1870s. It smelted lead ore from the main mines of the area. Today its ruins are impressive, although the stonework of the buildings has been vandalized. The fuel store, in which peat for the smelting hearths was kept, stands on the south bank of Blakethwaite Beck. It is a long, narrow building and has four openings on its west side, each with a finely set arch. The remains of the smelt-mill lie on the opposite bank. It contained two ore hearths and a roasting furnace, and the smoke and fumes were vented through flues that ran up the steep hillside to a chimney stack on the moor top.

Traditional smelting involved heating lead aggregate with peat, coal or coke in a blast-furnace. Air was supplied from a bellows powered by a water wheel. The smelted lead trickled from the furnace into a vessel called a 'sumpter pot', and was then cast into bars, or 'pigs'. This early method was straightforward, but wasteful. The lead was often impure and the slag residue of the blasting process retained up to 25 per cent lead, and needed further smelting. By the nineteenth century a more efficient method of smelting had been introduced. This involved an initial roasting of the lead ore in a sealed hearth made of sandstone. Hot gases were generated in a separate hearth and were blasted into the hearth containing the lead ore. The result was that lead particles separated cleanly from the waste rock and coagulated into more easily smelted lumps.

Today the Blakethwaite complex stands within a setting of green, silent hills, where the main gill becomes Blakethwaite Gill. Here, the stream is crossed by a huge slab-bridge, and from its north side a path leads up Blakethwaite Gill. Steep, rocky slopes close in, the floor of the gill is a scatter of loose stones, the beck tumbles over small sills of rock. Above lie the desolate fells; they are riddled with old workings and slashed with tracks and pathways, along which the miners trudged to their work. En route, they often knitted socks, Swaledale being a great centre of the hosiery trade at the time. If they felt like a rest, they sat down for as long as 'six-needles' worth'. The image is eccentric, but endearing. As those stocky, tough men and boys tramped through the dale, their rough, scarred fingers fluttered round the clicking needles. Other needles were used clandestinely to braid nets, which the miners used to catch grouse, when there were no gamekeepers about.

Blakethwaite Gill

The narrow, rocky path through Blakethwaite Gill leads to the breached rampart of the lower Blakethwaite Dam. There are two dams here, one behind the other. Water flowed to the catchment between them, along a leat from a reservoir at Moss Dams, 2 miles/3.2 kms to the south. It was then fed to the various mines and smelt-mills on the surrounding fells and in the gills. Today the surviving walls to either side of the lower dam sag alarmingly. Beyond the breach is the solid wall of the upper dam, its top crowned with massive slabs of cut stone. A tongue of silvery water pours down the face of the dam into what is now a strange grotto, lined with black moss and lichen, waterweed and ferns. Rowan trees, the mountain alders, frame the dark walls; their scarlet berries shine in the gloom of late autumn, beneath slate-grey skies.

It is like reaching the edge of the known land. There is no water impounded behind the upper dam, where moor grass and reeds sigh in the forlorn wind. Yet the causeway of rough stone that lies across the neck of the dam is like a harbour quay. To the north and west lies the waterlogged waste, bronze and flaxen-coloured and as featureless as the sea, except at the high points of Rogan's Seat and Water Crag. Three miles/4.8 kms to the north-west lies Tan Hill, with its famous pub and its surrounding scatter of abandoned coal-mines that once supplied fuel to the smelt-mills.

There is a mood of loneliness and regret at the dams, which seems to define the spirit of Gunnerside's lost generations of miners and their families, and of the ruined landscape itself. Yet the mood is oddly reassuring, perhaps because this man-made structure is the truest form of memorial that the miners could have, one that is being re-absorbed into the wilderness through a proper process of decay. It makes the return journey to the ruined Blakethwaite Mill a reflective one.

From the mill, a green track rises gently along the western side of Gunnerside Gill. It takes an unerring line to the high ground, where it crosses North Hush and leads to the head of Botcher Gill. Here the track joins a bulldozed estate road that runs along the charmingly named Jingle Pot Edge. This high-level return to Gunnerside is not as intriguing as the track along the valley floor. But it takes the walker from being knee-deep in mining remains to being conscious of the overview of Gunnerside Gill; an overview of the dramatic ruination that the winning of lead from the fragile fells has left as its compelling legacy to soft and supple Swaledale.

A Lead-Miners' Track
Information

Distance 8 miles/12.8 kms

Maps OS Outdoor Leisure 30 (Yorkshire Dales Northern & Central Areas)

Nature of walk A circular walk that is not too strenuous, though the going can be rough in places. Weatherproof clothing and sturdy footwear are advised. Conditions can change dramatically in the Yorkshire Dales and, in winter, can deteriorate quickly. *A number of mining ruins are visited. Mine adits (tunnels) can be extremely dangerous and should never be entered.*

Accommodation Hotels, guest houses, pubs and B&B at Reeth. Guest houses, pub and B&B at Gunnerside. Youth hostel at Grinton, near Reeth. Several Swaledale farms have seasonal camp sites.

Transport Rail connection to Darlington on London–Edinburgh line. Buses run from Darlington to Richmond, from where a daily bus service, Sundays excepted, runs to Gunnerside. For further information on local bus services, contact United Automobile Services Ltd, tel. (01325) 468771.

Further information Tourist Information Centre, Richmond, tel. (01748) 850252.

Start Gunnerside village

1 From the east side of Gunnerside Bridge, go north and follow the beck upstream for about 200 yards/183 metres. At the entrance gate to a converted schoolhouse, turn sharp right and go up some steps. Bear left above the building and then continue alongside the beck. Go through a squeeze-gate and into a wooded area. Soon go through another squeeze-gate and reach a fork in the path. (The lower path, sign-posted Woodland Walk, leads through Birbeck Wood, alongside the beck.) Follow the higher path steeply uphill and out of the trees, then bear left, signposted Gunnerside Gill. Continue across meadows and through narrow squeezes in stone walls. Rejoin the lower path at a squeeze-gate that leads to an area of flat ground, by the beck. (1 mile/1.6 kms)

2 Continue past the ruins of Sir Francis Mine, then cross a makeshift stile. Bear up right, away from the river, then continue alongside a stone wall. Follow the path high above the beck to reach a large area of workings at the site of the old Bunton Mine. Continue through the workings to reach a staggered crossing of paths, at the foot of a line of small crags and a rock-littered hush. Follow a path down left into the bottom of the gill, to reach the beck side at OS 940013. On the main route, continue northward alongside the beck to reach the Blakethwaite peat store and smelt-mill at the junction of the main gill with Blind Gill and Blakethwaite Gill.
(1¾ miles/2.8 kms) *From here, a return down the west side of Gunnerside Gill can be made; see direction* **4**.

3 To continue to the head of Gunnerside Gill, cross the fine slab-bridge that spans the beck, then follow the path uphill. Pass above Blakethwaite Force. Cross the stream just above the force, then continue on a path that rises above the east side of the beck to reach the broken wall of the lower Blakethwaite Dam. Return along the same route to the Blakethwaite peat store. (2¼ miles/3.6 kms)

4 From the slab-bridge at the peat store, follow the green track that runs due south and rises gently above Gunnerside Beck to the place where it merges with a bulldozed track at Botcher Gill Gate. Continue south, passing through a gate, then follow the track along the side of Jingle Pot Edge to where it bends sharply to the right, at a cairn. Leave the track at the cairn and keep south-east on a faint, grassy path that descends steadily towards Gunnerside. Pass a solitary hawthorn tree by a hollow, then continue ahead over the brow of the hill. Follow a faint track along a grassy spur above a line of hawthorns, then descend to a wall squeeze and gate above some houses. Continue downhill to reach the village centre.
(3 miles/4.8 kms)

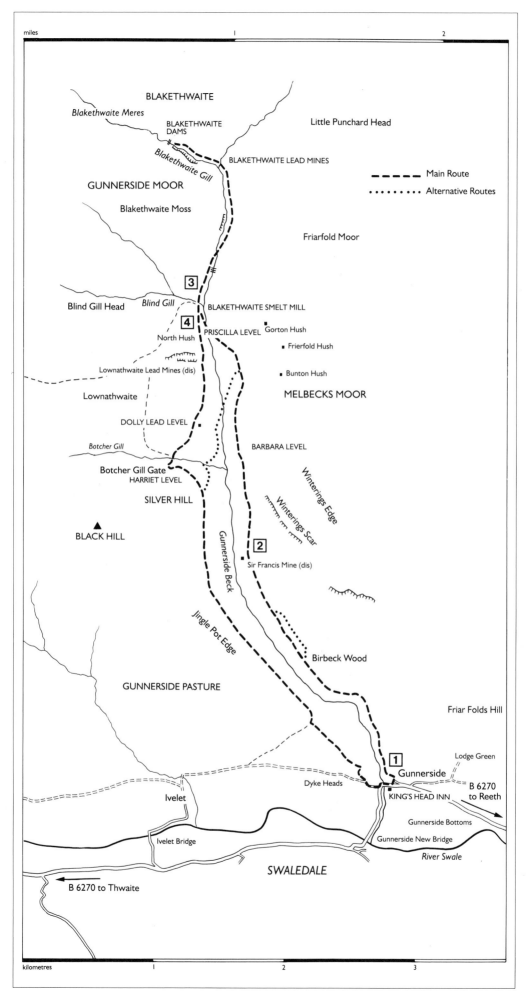

miles
1
2

BLAKETHWAITE

Blakethwaite Meres

Little Punchard Head

BLAKETHWAITE DAMS

BLAKETHWAITE LEAD MINES

Blakethwaite Gill

GUNNERSIDE MOOR

Blakethwaite Moss

Friarfold Moor

— — — Main Route

· · · · · · Alternative Routes

Blind Gill Head   *Blind Gill*

[3]

BLAKETHWAITE SMELT MILL

[4]

North Hush   PRISCILLA LEVEL   Gorton Hush

■ Frierfold Hush

Lownathwaite Lead Mines (dis)

■ Bunton Hush

Lownathwaite

MELBECKS MOOR

DOLLY LEAD LEVEL   ■

Botcher Gill   BARBARA LEVEL

Botcher Gill Gate
HARRIET LEVEL

Winterings Edge

Winterings Scar

SILVER HILL

▲
BLACK HILL

[2]

Sir Francis Mine (dis)

Gunnerside Beck

Jingle Pot Edge

Birbeck Wood

GUNNERSIDE PASTURE

Friar Folds Hill

[1]
Gunnerside   Lodge Green

Dyke Heads   B 6270
to Reeth

Ivelet   KING'S HEAD INN

Gunnerside Bottoms

Ivelet Bridge   Gunnerside New Bridge

River Swale

SWALEDALE

← B 6270 to Thwaite

kilometres
1
2
3

The Weavers' Trod
West Yorkshire

Hebden Bridge to Todmorden 8 miles/12.8 kms

The old parish of Halifax has been known as Calderdale since the early 1970s. The area was noted for textile manufacturing from medieval times until the industry's decline during the twentieth century. This walk leads between two of Calderdale's most famous cloth towns, Hebden Bridge and Todmorden. It follows ancient paved causeways along the mid-height terraces of the valley, through a landscape that has changed very little since the eighteenth century.

Calderdale is crammed with humanity, its machines, and its mess. It is as if people and their places have tumbled down from the terraced slopes of the dale and have fetched up cheek-by-jowl, all spaces taken. Road, rail, river and canal jostle with each other along the narrow trench of the valley. On sunny days, the light is bleached; there are shadows within shadows.

You drive, locked in line, between Hebden Bridge and Todmorden, eyes front, foot hovering over the brake pedal. At one point, however, between Charlestown and Eastwood, there is a fleeting glimpse of the famous monument that stands on the high moorland summit of Stoodley Pike. It is a glorious, momentary escape from the claustrophobia of the valley floor; distance is foreshortened, the curve of the hill is framed between dark buildings; a triumphant sun floods hill top and monument with a tawny light; the heart lifts. In that sudden contrast between moorland and machine world, Calderdale comes into focus – a compelling mix of the occasionally grim and the often glorious.

Upper Calderdale's distinctive topography of narrow gorge flanked by stepped terraces is a legacy of the Ice Ages. Successive glaciers ploughed a wide, shallow valley out of the gritstone and shale of the area. Then, during the final glacial period, a random tongue of ice pushed down from high ice-caps and gouged out a deeper trough within this shallow profile. As the ice melted, torrents of water cascaded down the huge drainage channel and deepened it further. The valley filled with meltwater, which became dammed behind plugs of glacial moraine. Side-streams carved out narrow ravines that survive today as wooded 'cloughs'. In time, the lakes disappeared and left Upper Calderdale as a valley within a valley, a narrow gorge with mid-height terraces.

The poorly drained, swampy floor of primeval Calderdale was dense with willow and alder trees. Oaks clothed the valley slopes and spilled across the terraces to mingle with moorland birch and pine. The first human settlers of the Neolithic period kept to the terraces, and it was here that cultivation began and settlement was confined for thousands of years. During the Roman period, Upper Calderdale was the last stronghold of Elmet, a pre-Roman British kingdom that once occupied most of Yorkshire. The Romans made little impact on the area, but during the post-Roman period, Elmet was overrun by Angles, Danes and Norsemen, a vigorous mix of races from which a native 'English' emerged. But neither human influence, nor the long adventure of Calderdale's subsequent history, has dissipated entirely the haunting spirit of Elmet. It is a spirit of lonely withdrawal that can still be felt today amidst the melancholy beauty of remote cloughs and on the margin of the dark fells.

Dispossessed

The English of Calderdale were dispossessed in their turn by Norman overlords, who first used the South Pennine area as a vast hunting estate. Then a later generation began to manage the land for gain. It was a move that stimulated the economic enterprise that was to make the name of West Yorkshire world-famous. By the fifteenth century cloth-making in the area had evolved from minor domestic production into a more commercial activity. The plentiful supply of soft water in Calderdale made the region suitable for fulling, the process by which loosely woven woollen cloth is felted and strengthened by immersion. Cloth-making in the area was stimulated further by the arrival of Flemish weavers and dyers, who were frustrated in their work by the guild restrictions imposed on the woollen industry of Yorkshire's east coast.

Calderdale's success in cloth-making may have been built on the energy of immigrant craft workers and on the area's plentiful supply of water. But the industry also flourished because of the readiness of local farmers and smallholders to diversify their activities. Farming was a hard business, and the land of the moorland edge was grudging. A rural woollen industry developed in tandem with farming, and there emerged in Calderdale a vigorous community of yeoman clothiers and cottage spinners and weavers. Farmers and cottagers on the marginal land of the valley terraces developed a dual economy; they cultivated small areas of ground and earned extra income from preparing and spinning wool, which was either passed on to the weaving sheds of clothiers or was woven by the 'outworkers' themselves.

The Pennine wool of the medieval period was of poor quality, and imported wool was traded through exchanges known as cloth halls. By the seventeenth century the main cloth hall of the Calderdale area was at Halifax, but as early as 1545 there was an important cloth hall at Heptonstall, above Hebden Bridge. Wool was delivered to the cottage outworkers, and the spun yarn and woven cloth that they produced was later collected for finishing and marketing. There were commercial pack-horse carriers who supplied transport, but cottagers often had their own pack-horses, which they used to carry goods to and from Heptonstall or Halifax. It was against this background of a domestic industry with a need to move materials quickly that a network of pack-horse routes known as 'causeys' or 'trods' became the transport system of the area. The trods kept to the mid-height terraces, descending only to cross intervening valleys. They were paved with gritstone slabs, to make travel easier across ground that was often wet and muddy, and to preserve the routes from erosion.

Industrialization

The machines that processed wool were easily converted to processing cotton and, by the 1780s, there were numerous cotton mills in Upper Calderdale. Many were located in the higher reaches of the cloughs, where even a small mill could harness enough water power to operate a few spinning frames. Today, in the densely wooded cloughs, the Gothic remains of these old mills give Calderdale some of its haunting appeal. Many were abandoned during the nineteenth century, when industrialization displaced the rural structure of domestic cloth-making.

Industrialization brought great wealth to Calderdale, but the wealth was not evenly distributed. It produced a change from a rural to an urban society, and it was accompanied by all the social abuses that attended Victorian capitalism. The valley floor became the main conduit of transport as advanced engineering cleared the way for road, rail and canal. Larger mills, more readily identified as factories, needed to be close to these revolutionary modes of transport; steam power supplanted water power; mills no longer needed to be located on high ground close to falling water.

During the nineteenth century there was a migration of workers to the valley floor from the terraces and the water-laced cloughs. It was a demographic shift that took place rapidly, and it left in the clear air of the high ground a landscape that retains, to this day, much of its medieval character. Along the mid-height terraces, the routes that were once followed by pack-horses still run through flower-filled meadows and by the wooded margins of the cloughs, past old cottages, ruined mills and clothiers' houses, the whole embedded within a matrix of sturdy gritstone walls. Today many of the old trods are part of a long-distance walking route, known as the Calderdale Way, which encircles much of the Calder valley. One of the most evocative sections of the route lies between Hebden Bridge and Todmorden; it passes through a richly textured landscape that retains much of the atmosphere and character of the old world of the West Riding.

Hebden Bridge

Hebden Bridge stands at the junction of the Hebden Water and the River Calder. Its tall buildings seem to reach for the sky. Many are four- or five-storeyed; they climb the lower slopes of the valley in tiers and, when a westering sun drenches their smoke-darkened stone with a bronze light, they resemble minor Georgian terraces, worthy of Bath. But only from a distance; this is Victorian factory architecture, after all.

The name, Hebden, derives from the Old English for *hep*, a wild rose, and *dene*, a valley. Once, when the Hebden and the Calder met amidst a quaking swamp called Black Pit Holme, human life in the area was confined to the high and dry ground of the valley terraces, and Hebden Bridge was insignificant as a settlement. Improved transport along the valley floor, and the growth of industrialization, transformed Hebden Bridge into a leading textile town. It became the manufacturing 'capital' of fustian, the collective name for such cotton cloths as corduroy, needlecord, twills and moleskin. Fustian-making was soon followed by the manufacture of hard-wearing work clothes for manual workers. The industry spawned many successful businesses engaged in all the processes of fustian-making. The famous Moss Bros originated as a Calderdale fustian-dyeing firm.

Hebden Bridge was also a centre of the nineteenth-century co-operative movement. Industrialization may have dismantled the social structure of rural cloth-making, but it did not dissipate the individuality and independence of the cottager, qualities that were vigorously expressed through Chartism, the working-class political movement of the mid-nineteenth century. Chartism developed out of anti-Poor Law agitation and campaigns for better factory conditions. It failed as a political force, but its pursuit of social reform led to expansion of the co-operative movement. Hebden Bridge became the focus of the movement, which was best expressed by the town's famous Nutclough Mill, the producer co-operative of the Hebden Bridge Fustian Manufacturing Society.

The Old Bridge

Hebden Bridge's eponymous Old Bridge is a Calderdale icon. It spans the Hebden River, a short distance from the latter's meeting with the River Calder. There have been pubs to either side of the bridge from its earliest days as an important river crossing on the Halifax to Burnley pack-horse route. Originally the bridge was made of wood, but by the early sixteenth century it had been rebuilt in stone. Contemporary records show that many of Hebden's great and good citizens were leaving workman-like legacies for improving a bridge that was a significant focus of the known world. Today's pubs confirm that it still is. One is called the White Swan, the other, The Hole in the Wall. They are not the original buildings, but both must have well-pickled heritage beyond compare.

Today, the Old Bridge is hemmed in by the modern world, though modern vehicles cannot cross it. It is made of the best Pennine stone, has an elegant hump – as only a pack-horse bridge can – and is three-arched. One of these arches is land-based, and once spanned a mill race or 'tail goyte' that served the adjacent Bridge Mill. Beyond the bridge, the old pack-horse route to Heptonstall leads steeply uphill on a splendid cobbled way known as The Buttress.

Heptonstall

It is a hard pull up The Buttress to the road above, then another steep flight of steps takes its toll before Heptonstall is reached, where neat cobbles begin. The village is a rare slice of Pennine 'heritage', and is frequently besieged by film-makers in pursuit of atmosphere. It is an outstanding period piece, a preserved medieval weavers' village that breathes authenticity as far as the true grit of its buildings go; an enchanting set, but without its original cast. Now, residents clatter off to their cars dressed in the smooth cloth of modern Moss Bros. Schoolchildren have that 'top o' th' hill' look about them in the generous morning light. There is not a parting out of place in Heptonstall these days, where once dung and blown straw were trampled into the creases of the cobbles of those maze-like alleys and courtyards, and where sunlight was filtered through a fibrous haze in dark doorways.

This was once the textile 'metropolis' of Upper Calderdale. Its cloth hall was Yorkshire's first textile exchange. The old Heptonstall Grammar School, near the churchyard, now houses an excellent local museum that portrays Heptonstall's past to great effect. The village has two churches; one is the roofless shell of St Thomas's, a medieval original. It was partly dismantled in 1854, when a new church was built nearby. The building of a new church seems to have been a lavish gesture and may have reflected the contemporary wealth of local factory owners, who were ever keen to advertise their piety. Between the beautiful, mottled ruin and its solid, meritorious Victorian replacement lies Heptonstall's old graveyard; a reef of recumbent headstones, irregular and rumpled; they jostle with each other for a Judgement Day awakening, as a good Yorkshire congregation should.

Beyond the church, a walled lane leads past a row of cottages known as West Laithe. A laithe was a medieval dwelling with a barn attached, and the name reflects Heptonstall's original rural nature. Beyond West Laithe, where fields once probably served as the 'tenter' ground on which cloth was stretched, a surfaced path leads through a modern estate of conspicuously upmarket houses. This is sunrise country, fresh-faced on the brink of Colden Clough, the deep, wooded valley that slices north from the main valley. The view reflects Calderdale's singular topography. From this airy terrace it excludes the valley floor, and is uninterrupted in its command of Stoodley Pike and the high ground to the south and west.

Colden Clough

Today, Colden Clough is a vast breath of fresh air, where once the dark and soot-laden smoke from coal-fired mills billowed up into the Pennine sky and fuelled the rain clouds with toxins. From the path, on the edge of a rim of crags, the view into the valley is blurred by a mass of trees through which the buildings of Mytholm, and the tall, imposing chimney of Mytholm Mill, protrude. The latter was built in 1789 as a cotton-spinning mill, and was later the first mill in the area to weave fustian.

The path along the rim of Colden Clough leads through Eaves Wood, a Gothic world of gnarled oak and beech trees, of heather banks and glossy boulders dappled with moss. In the early morning the air here is moist and sweet, the undergrowth heavy with dew. The woodland path ends at a narrow lane that slips down from Cross Hill above Heptonstall, past Lumb Bank House and into Colden Clough. The poet laureate Ted Hughes lived for a time at Lumb Bank. He was born at Mytholmroyd, to the east of Hebden Bridge, and his powerful, muscled language reverberates with the rhythms of the Calderdale landscape.

It is a subtle and layered landscape. The way through the misty woods has the same questing nature as the narrow lane; the tumbled boulders match the rough walls that flank the lane; the green glades of Eaves Wood are matched by the open meadows above Colden Clough. The rhythms change frequently. A short way down the lane into Colden Clough, a path bears off beneath tall trees and leads to a charming little corner at the centre of a web of walls. Beyond lie small meadows and sudden openness. There is a splendid view down into the wooded depths of Colden Clough. Directly below is the tall chimney of Bob Mill, one of the dozen or so mills that were once powered by the Colden Water.

From this corner, the way leads along a paved trod flanked by a sturdy field wall. The dished flagstones of the trod nestle amidst pale grass. The gritstone is dusky and mottled, and the field walls are like dark threads that run through the latticed countryside of meadows and green lanes. It was along these terraced meadows that generations of Calderdale people set up their homes; they did so wherever there was level ground, and wherever springs bubbled from the earth. The path leads along the edge of Bob Wood, passing behind an old building near which a spring oozes from a field wall.

Beyond, an unpaved track leads above a charming little garden that has been woven round a cluster of boulders. In early summer there is a riot of wild flowers here, and later in the year there are cushions of bilberries. The frothy yellow of lady's bedstraw is mixed with rusty-coloured sorrel and, above the rock garden, tall stands of pink-flowered rosebay willowherb grow by the path.

Pack-Horses

Along these tracks and paved causeways, the pack-horses trudged with their loads of raw wool, yarn and cloth. They would also have carried salt, lime and domestic supplies to the cottages and farms along the way. Even when water power gave way to steam, coal was carried by pack-horse to the mills that still operated in the cloughs. The lead ponies of the train were belled, to give warning of their approach, and the mellifluous chimes, and the clatter of hooves on the flagstones, must have made famous music.

The way passes into Foster Wood over a sturdy stile. Down to the left there is a little stone bridge over a gully, one of probably hundreds of such features that were a part of the causeway network. Huge, dished flagstones line the main trod where it leads beneath tall, gloomy beech trees; the flags are irregular, like the tumbled gravestones in Heptonstall churchyard; the dark stones are stained with powdery green lichen, and dappled with spangles of sunlight. Beyond the trees, the line of flags leads through a tangle of vegetation and across wet ground to the place where the path drops down to the Colden Water at Hebble Hole. Here the great national trail, the Pennine Way, merges briefly with the Calderdale Way for a crossing of Hebble Hole Bridge. The massive gritstone slabs of the bridge are reminiscent of the granite slabs of Dartmoor clapper-bridges.

Hebble Hole marks the top end of Colden Clough, where the valley grows shallow and wide and is absorbed into the broad, undulating fells. It is a delightful place, clouded with greenness in summer, its northern side dense with trees, the stream fringed with water plantain, bittercress, willowherb and valerian, the open south slope cushioned with heather and bilberry. Dippers and grey wagtails flit along the stony bed of the stream. A short distance below the bridge, a stone causeway crosses the stream. This crossing was probably used by pack-horses unless the stream was in spate, when the bridge would have been the safer way.

The path leads steeply uphill from Hebble Hole to a junction with a broad track. Here the Pennine Way breaks off to the south on a paved way between sturdy walls. The Calderdale Way turns north along a broad track, then climbs a grassy lane, where periwinkles create a splash of uncommon blue. The way leads off from the lane through farmland, where meadows have been left to grow naturally on the one hand, while others have been cropped by sheep. The contrast between the featureless turf of the sheep pasture and the long grass, meadowsweet, and buttercups of the hay meadows is startling.

Blackshaw Head

Beyond the meadows, the way reaches Blackshaw Head, a site that was occupied when a prehistoric route, known as the Long Causeway, linked the east coast of England with its western lands. Today Blackshaw Head stands on what is still known as the Long Causeway Road to Mereclough, at a junction with the road from Slack and the enticingly named New Delight. From Blackshaw Head, the Calderdale Way wriggles between houses and farm buildings to reach Hippins Bridge. Just before the bridge is the handsome Hippins Farm, dating probably from the seventeenth century, a period during which many of Calderdale's finest rural houses were built.

The rich texture of local stone has given an exquisite patina to these old buildings, and Hippins displays good features of its time. The house has numerous windows, whose mullions were chamfered in order to maximize the supply of light into rooms in which wool was often prepared and spun. Even the surrounding field walls are monumental; they are built of dressed grit and their rounded header blocks are as big as milestones. The name Hippins derives from an Old English word for stepping stones, and a line of such stones may once have crossed the beck where a road bridge now stands. To the south of Hippins is Jumble Hole Clough, an enchanting world of tumbling water, deep ravines and dense woods. At the head of the clough, just below Hippins, lie the Gothic ruins of Staups Mill, an early cotton-spinning mill.

At Hippins Bridge there is a sudden transition from fields and farm lanes to open moorland. A few yards beyond the bridge, a track leads off across Staups Moor. The colours here are dark and morbid, although the moor grass becomes bone-white late in the year. Black, lugubrious walls trail across the bleak landscape. In wild weather this is bruising, yet exhilarating country, especially when the wind is 'wuthering' from the high ground. Haworth lies just 8 miles/13 kms to the north. When you are whipped by the icy sting of Pennine rain, it is easy to identify with the bitter-sweet romanticism of those Brontë minds.

Great Rock

On the brow of Staups Moor, the track is funnelled between sturdy walls. Framed ahead, on the distant southern edge of Calderdale, the Stoodley Pike Monument crowns its bare hillside above a latticework of small fields. The original monument commemorated the Peace of Ghent and the end of the Napoleonic Wars in 1814. It was damaged by lightning in 1856 and rebuilt in its present form. The monument stays in view as the track descends to a minor road by Great Rock, a massive carbuncle of gritstone, which thrusts from the brow of the hill. The south face of the rock is fluted with water-worn channels, its rough hide is scarred by graffiti. Great Rock should really stand in isolation on some high, lonely fell, far from human contact. Yet even here, on its roadside anchorage, it is a powerful presence.

From Great Rock the route leads west along the road to its junction with a lane that drops south to Todmorden. A short distance down this lane, the Calderdale Way breaks off along a green track, which curves round the slope of the hill between walled fields and then dwindles into a rough path. For the next mile or two, the path wanders over patches of rough moorland and small fields, past Higher Birks and Killup Farm. It crosses sunken lanes and tumbled walls, to reach finally a surfaced lane by West Hey Head Farm. These are lonely corners of the South Pennines. The meadows and lanes rise northward from here into the strange, melancholy fells of Stansfield Moor, Stiperden and Hoar Side Moor.

The Hey Head lane is followed south for a short distance to where a path leads off alongside a golf course, on the raw, high ground of the ominously named Hanging Field. The path stumbles on through low broken walls and scrubby ground to the broad track of Scraper Lane, above Wickenberry Clough. From Wickenberry, at the very edge of the valley terrace above Todmorden, the main route of the Calderdale Way leads west over a bridge and then on towards Whirlaw Common. But the descent to Todmorden keeps to the south along dark loops of muddy track, shrouded by trees. It passes below a ragged quarry face draped with dark ferns and from which a huge sycamore tree protrudes, supported by its tangled roots.

Todmorden

Below the quarry, the track twists and turns to the spot where the steep, narrow lane of Meadow Bottom Road is reached. From here it is a foot-bracing descent to the Burnley Road and into Todmorden, where the economic and cultural history of Calderdale's textile industry is expressed in a remarkable mix of buildings. They include the seventeenth-century Todmorden Hall, the eighteenth-century Golden Lion Inn and the Victorian, neo-classical Town Hall. The latter has an elaborate, yet unfussy façade of Corinthian columns, which support a bold pediment thronged with symbolic statuary.

At one time Todmorden's Town Hall stood half in Yorkshire, half in Lancashire, until a late nineteenth-century reorganization of county boundaries placed the town entirely in Yorkshire. The statuary of the building's pediment symbolizes the two counties, and the motifs represent cotton, engineering and agriculture. The rounded apse-like back of the Town Hall is every bit as impressive as the front. From an island site at the heart of Todmorden, the building lords it rather grandly over its surroundings. It is overlooked only by the ubiquitous Stoodley Pike Monument and by the high ground of the valley terraces, along which the history of Calderdale is expressed, perhaps most powerfully by the rough stones of field wall and weaver's cottage, and by the old pack-horse trods that still wander between them.

The Weavers' Trod
Information

Distance 8 miles/12.8 kms

Maps OS Outdoor Leisure 21 (South Pennines)

Nature of walk A high-level walk through delightful Pennine countryside above the Upper Calderdale Valley. The walk follows part of the Calderdale Way, a 50-mile/80-km route encircling Calderdale, which was opened in 1978 after fruitful co-operation between a number of official and voluntary bodies. There is a steep climb at the start, but the walk is mainly level. Weatherproof clothing should be carried and waterproof footwear worn. The walk is signposted at intervals by the Calderdale Way logo, a cleverly designed clover-leaf symbol.

Accommodation Guest houses and B&B at Hebden Bridge and Todmorden. Seasonal camp sites in the vicinity of Hebden Bridge. Further details from Hebden Bridge and Todmorden TICs.

Transport Rail connections to Hebden Bridge and Todmorden from main centres. Rail and bus connections between Hebden Bridge and Todmorden. For further information on trains and buses, tel. (0113 245) 7676.

Further information Tourist Information Centre, Hebden Bridge, tel. (01422) 843831; Tourist Information Centre, Todmorden, tel. (01706) 818181.

Start Hebden Old Bridge, Bridge Gate

1 Cross the Old Bridge to Old Gate, then go diagonally left to the start of the steep, cobbled Buttress, signposted Heptonstall. *The way is very steep for the next ½ mile/ 0.8 kms. The cobbles of The Buttress can be very slippery when wet.* Reach a road and go right for a short distance, until opposite some steps. Cross with care, then go up steps to reach a higher road. Go right and uphill to enter Heptonstall. Just before the Red Lion Inn, turn left beneath an archway, signposted Museum. Follow a flagstone path past the old church and graveyard, then bear right to pass the north porch of the Victorian church. Go through

the church gate, then turn left and follow a walled lane round to the left. Turn right at West Laithe. Cross a road, then follow a track round right, signposted 'Public Footpath to Colden'. Follow a walkway between houses, cross a drive, then continue to a path at the top of crags above Colden Clough. (1 mile/1.6 kms)

2 Go right and follow the winding path along the edge of crags, and then on through the trees of Eaves Wood. Reach a lane at OS 982284, turn left, then after about 100 yards/91 metres bear off right along a path beneath trees. Reach a junction of paths by a telegraph pole and a seat. Follow the paved trod ahead and pass behind a ruined building. Just beyond the building, at a junction, go down left, then turn right, to pass above a walled area with planted trees and scattered rocks. Follow the paved trod alongside walls on the right and through squeeze-gaps, to reach a gate. Just beyond the gate, turn sharp left and go through a narrow squeeze that is made awkward by a central pole. Turn right and follow a paved trod across a meadow to enter a short wooded section. Beyond the trees, follow a paved trod to pass a junction with the Pennine Way, then reach Hebble Hole Bridge. (1½ miles/2.4 kms)

3 Beyond the bridge, follow the path left and up some steps, then turn right along a track. At a junction, turn sharp left and uphill for a short distance. Where the track bends sharply left by a house, keep straight ahead and follow a rough lane between stone walls. In 200 yards/183 metres, go right and through a field gate, which is painted bright yellow on its far side. Climb diagonally left across a meadow to a stile. Continue through meadows and over stiles to reach a lane. *Blackshaw Head and pub are just up to the right.* Cross diagonally right, then go left down a lane between buildings. Keep right of a house, then go over a stile and continue between a wire fence and a wall. Go through a kissing-gate, then follow a sunken trod to another kissing-gate. Bear round left to reach a stile by a house. Continue to the next stile, then go through a squeeze into a lane by a water stoup, at Apple Tree Farm. Follow a rough track ahead to reach a big wall-squeeze. Continue between old barns, on past Hippins Farm and down a drive, to the public road at Hippins Bridge. (1½ miles/2.4 kms)

4 Turn left and cross the bridge, then go up right and off the road to climb a short, rocky path onto open moorland. Keep ahead across the moor, with a wall on the left at first, to reach a walled lane. Follow this lane to reach the road by Great Rock. Turn right and follow the road for about 200 yards/183 metres to where a lane leads off left. Turn left down this lane for a short distance, then bear off right along a green lane. After ¼ mile/ 0.4 kms, go down left, then right. Pass above Higher Birks Farm, cross a stream, then continue through a heathery dip to a big wooden stile. *This section is often very muddy.* Keep alongside a tumbled wall, and then a fence, to reach a wall-squeeze into a green lane. Go right, then up left and through a squeeze. Walk through rough

ground, cross another sunken lane, then continue across fields to pass behind farm buildings. Follow the farm track to reach a road at OS 945257. (2¼ miles/3.6 kms)

5 Go left down the road, then just after a left-hand bend, turn right and off the road at the corner of a golf course. Follow a path alongside the golf course, passing through gates and squeezes, to reach a junction with a walled track. Go down right towards the bridge at Wickenberry Clough, then turn down left past a rocky outcrop on the left. Continue down a wide muddy lane amidst trees. At a junction turn left, pass a house, then at another junction turn right and down Meadow Bottom Road. At a junction with Fielden Terrace, go right and follow the road round left under a railway bridge. Continue down Victoria Road to its junction with Burnley Road. Turn left and continue to Todmorden

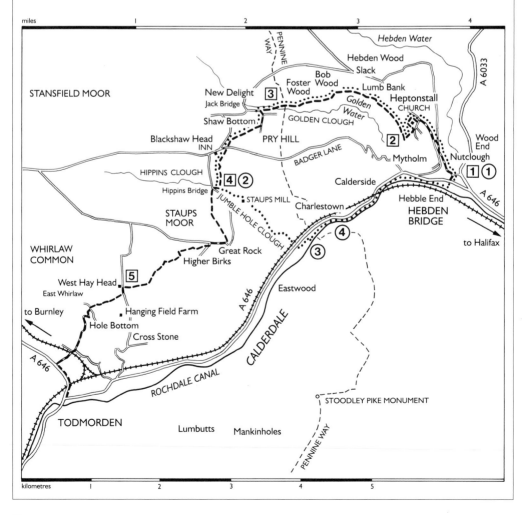

Town Hall. The railway station is up to the right of the Town Hall. (1¾ miles/2.8 kms)

CIRCULAR WALK
5 miles/8 kms

A walk that follows part of the Calderdale Way. The route passes through Heptonstall and then diverts down the delightful Jumble Hole Clough, returning finally to Hebden Bridge along the towpath of the Rochdale Canal.

Start Hebden Old Bridge, Bridge Gate

1 Follow directions **1**, **2** and **3** on the main walk to reach Hippins Farm.

2 Do not continue beyond Hippins Farm. Instead, turn left just before the house, go through a kissing-gate, then continue alongside a wall as far as a stile. Bear down right from here to pass a flat-topped boulder. Descend some steps, cross a bridge, then descend more steps to pass above the ruined Staups Mill. Follow a path uphill to a junction with another path. *Dogs should be kept on leads throughout this section.* Go left, cross a stile, then follow the path, high above the valley, to reach a gate. Continue to another gate, then drop down to join a cobbled track on a steep bend. Go down the track, past an old millpond, then bear sharply left and cross a bridge over the stream. Go through a gate and turn right. Continue down the track, keeping straight ahead at junctions and passing between the buildings of Jumble Hole, then go under a railway viaduct to reach the A646.

3 Go left for about 250 yards/230 metres, then cross the road, with care. Turn right and away from the road and cross a bridge. Just before a second bridge over the canal, bear left across some waste ground, then go through a gap in a wooden fence to reach the canal bank. Turn left along the canal.

4 Follow the canal towpath to the Black Pit Aqueduct and then on to Black Pit Lock, from where Holme Street leads to the centre of Hebden Bridge.

The Water Way
Clwyd

Llantysilio to Chirk 9 miles/14.4 kms

The Llangollen branch of the Shropshire Union Canal has no locks between its source at Horseshoe Falls, near Llantysilio, and the town of Chirk. But between Trevor and Froncysyllte, the canal is carried over the River Dee on Thomas Telford's spectacular Pontcysyllte Aqueduct. This walk follows the towpath of the canal through the delightful countryside of the Vale of Llangollen, and then across the aqueduct and on to Chirk.

Thomas Telford's Pontcysyllte Aqueduct is certainly of 'sure, solid and permanent utility'. But it has also the lightness and elegance of classical architecture. Viewed from the west, from the Cysylltau Bridge over the River Dee, part of its central section is visible within a framework of trees. It makes such a graceful skyline arcade that it seems as if the Romans rather than a late eighteenth-century engineer must have been responsible for such simple, confident design. In 1862 the Scottish writer and social reformer Samuel Smiles said of Telford, 'with his head full of bridges and viaducts, he thus kept his heart open to the influence of beauty in life and nature'. Telford's Pontcysyllte is one of those engineered works that does not overpower the landscape. And the slow, stately progress of narrowboats across the aqueduct adds to its elegance.

Canals were the main mode of commercial transport in Britain between the late eighteenth century and the middle of the nineteenth century, a time when existing roads could not cope with the increase in commercial traffic brought on by industrialization, and when the railway system was in its infancy. By the 1830s, however, the railway was beginning to dominate transport at the expense of canals.

Commercial use of canals continued throughout the rest of the nineteenth century and well into the twentieth century. But by the 1920s road improvements and the emergence of the motor lorry spelled a further decline for the canal system. Soon many canals stagnated, in every sense, until they enjoyed a renaissance as leisure amenities. Today over 2,000 miles/3,218 kms of waterways thread their way across England and Wales, and in the sedate progress they still afford to traditional narrowboats there is preserved something of the measured pace of a less frantic age.

Rivers have been used for travel and transport since the first hunter-gatherers launched a hollowed-out tree trunk onto water. The Romans were the first to build artificial waterways in Britain. They created a number of aqueducts, such as the Car Dyke between Peterborough and Lincoln, and the Foss Dyke, which linked the Rivers Witham and Trent. These Roman 'canals' were used for drainage while others, such as the aqueduct in the valley of the River Frome in Dorset, supplied water to Roman cities, in that case Dorchester. But for many centuries thereafter rivers were the favoured means of waterborne transport.

Adventures

In 1761 England's first industrial canal was opened by the Duke of Bridgewater as an outlet for his coal mines at Worsley near Manchester. The success of the Bridgewater Canal prompted other adventures in canal-building. The Staffordshire and Worcestershire Canal was opened in 1770 and the Trent and Mersey in 1777. Canal-building was a brute process. The courses were dug out by hand and the contractors employed teams of itinerant workmen, or 'navigators', who gave the word 'navvie' to the English language and who spawned a folk culture that was sustained through railway- and road-building up to the present day.

The Bridgewater Canal was designed by a remarkable self-taught engineer called James Brindley, who set the design proportions of English canals by establishing a uniform width of under 10 feet/3 metres. Brindley's calculation was based on keeping down the costs of canal-building and on the knowledge that a narrow course meant a more efficient regulation of water supply. It was Brindley's standard that produced the characteristic narrowboat of the English canal system, with its limitation on load to 30 ton(ne)s. Ironically Brindley's standardization ensured the demise of the canal system in the twentieth century, when payloads of 30 ton(ne)s became uneconomic.

In the late eighteenth century, however, canals were a revolutionary form of transport, and during the early 1790s 'canal mania' emerged. Between 1790 and 1795 the main canal routes of England were established. With the opening of the Kennet and Avon Canal, and the extension across the Pennines of the Leeds and Liverpool Canal, both accomplished during the first years of the nineteenth century, the main English network was complete. The English countryside was opened up to manufacturing, to commerce and to influences that transformed, and in many ways destroyed, the regional textures of towns and villages. Today we lament the urbanization of the countryside by concrete. But the Canal Age first brought alien slate and brick to remote backwaters of thatch and cob, and then revolutionized farming and stimulated rural industry. Canals were the true arteries of industrialization.

Thomas Telford

Canal-building stimulated also the ambitions and genius of such engineers as John Rennie and Thomas Telford. The experience these men gained from canal-building gave them the confidence and skills for great works of civil engineering and set the scene for later road and rail developments. Telford was the great name of early civil engineering. A sober Scot, the son of a Lowland shepherd, he began work as a stone mason. His genius was nurtured by practical experience, but his career reflected the shrewdness and attention to detail of the canniest of men. Telford absorbed all available information about engineering and kept meticulous notes of even the most minor experiment. He learned French, simply to enable him to read French manuals of engineering. The French were more advanced in engineering than the British, mainly because French transport systems were under the collective control of the state, whereas Britain's entrepreneurial philosophy promoted a wasteful culture of competition, secrecy and obstructiveness in canal speculation. Telford cut through all that with his genius, and with his independence of outlook. He was involved in canal-, road-, bridge- and harbour-building throughout the whole of Britain. His greatest works included the Menai Suspension Bridge, St Katherine's Dock in London and the rebuilding of the Holyhead to London road. Of his canal work, the Pontcysyllte Aqueduct is the most outstanding feature.

Pontcysyllte was a key element of the proposed Ellesmere Canal, a venture that sought to link the ports of Bristol and Liverpool by canal and to exploit the rich agricultural lands and iron and coal districts of the Welsh Borders. The favoured route proposed a link from Chester to Ruabon, south of Wrexham, and then across the Dee Valley from Trevor and south towards Shrewsbury. It was the challenge of crossing the Dee Valley that produced the Pontcysyllte Aqueduct.

The Ellesmere Canal
The dream of linking the Mersey and the Severn by canal was never realized. The plan for the Ruabon to Chester link, with its massive series of locks, tunnels and embankments, was abandoned as being too complex and expensive. The link south to Shrewsbury never materialized, after rival companies developed local canals in the Shrewsbury area. Ultimately the Ellesmere Canal became a regional waterway linked to the general network through connections to the Shropshire Union. But the dream was still fresh when work started on various sections of the proposed canal in 1793.

The section south from Trevor was started under the control of William Jessop, a Devon man. Jessop was a disciple of the great maritime engineer John Smeaton, and was highly respected as an engineer. He was soon to be eclipsed by Telford, however, who was taken on as part of his team, and there is a suggestion that Jessop was usurped by Telford. Records seem to indicate that it was Jessop who proposed the revolutionary use of a cast-iron trough on stone piers for the Pontcysyllte Aqueduct, although Telford later claimed credit for the idea in his autobiography.

In the event, it was Telford who designed and built the aqueduct. The foundation stone was laid in 1795, but the aqueduct was not finally opened until 1805. In truth, it was a major work that went nowhere, once the Ruabon continuation to Chester was abandoned.

But the aqueduct was given some justification when a canal feeder-line was built from Trevor to Llangollen and Llantysilio. The line drew a regular supply of water from the River Dee at Horseshoe Falls, Llantysilio. This supply fed the eventual 'Ellesmere Canal', which ran for over 40 miles/64 kms from Llangollen through Chirk and Whitchurch to Hurleston, and to an eventual connection with the old Chester Canal and the main Midlands network. The system later became part of the Shropshire Union.

The Ellesmere Canal thrived for most of the nineteenth century. During its commercial heyday, a variety of goods and materials was carried. These included coal, coke, limestone and iron ore, lead, bricks, tiles, gravel and timber, malt, grain and flour. Domestic goods and farm produce were also staple cargoes, and in later years Trevor Basin handled chemicals and pottery produced by adjacent factories.

By the 1870s concern was being expressed about the lack of use of the Ellesmere Canal's western section and there were unresolved plans to turn the branch from Llangollen to Weston, near Ellesmere, into a narrow-gauge railway. By the beginning of the twentieth century the western branch was in serious decline, although limestone – or fluxingstone as it was called – was still being carried from Trevor. After the First World War commercial traffic all but ceased, and from the 1920s onwards the canal became weed-bound and silted. But use of the canal as a feeder of the Hurlestone Reservoir ensured some maintenance, and the canal's picturesque surroundings made it suitable for the leisure cruising that developed after the Second World War. By the 1950s cruising on the canal was becoming popular and the name 'Llangollen Canal' had been adopted in place of 'Ellesmere' by the British Transport Waterways, forerunner of British Waterways. Today the Llangollen is one of the most popular cruising lines in Britain. The nature of the countryside through which it passes in its higher reaches also makes it a delight to walk along, especially from its source at Llantysilio's Horseshoe Falls.

Horseshoe Falls
Horseshoe Falls are a touch disappointing. The name makes it sound as though the falls should roar, rather than pour. But pour is the right word to describe the steady overspill of the pent-up River Dee as it drains from the semi-circular weir below Llantysilio. The weir was built by Telford to create a head of water to feed the canal. Horseshoe Falls is a serene place, shaded by trees and flanked by fields. The falls pour ceaselessly in a shallow necklace of glittering water slung between light and shade. Llantysilio church stands above the falls in quiet seclusion.

The Llangollen Canal starts demurely to the east of the falls, where the water is drawn off at a small sluice. The line was opened in 1808 and the water flowed without check. Since the 1940s it has been metered through a small gauging house that stands at the canal head. The daily outlet is six million gallons over twenty-seven million litres. To the west, the rain-gathering Llantysilio Mountains and the Berwyn Range ensure a steady supply. The canal is narrow here, and shaded by beech and oak trees. It drifts sedately beneath gloomy rock walls on its northern side. Dark, glossy ferns sprout from the rock face; the shallow water is crystal-clear; mallards bob and glide above the flickering water weed.

Just below Horseshoe Falls, the canal passes beneath King's Bridge, where the main road crosses canal and river. Beyond King's Bridge the canal drifts past the rear of the Chain Bridge Hotel. The famous Chain Bridge spans the River Dee on the south side of the hotel. The original bridge was built in 1814 by a local businessman with the formidable name of Exsuperious Pickering. On the opposite side of the valley is the refurbished Berwyn Station, a popular halt on the Llangollen Railway.

This was eighteenth- and nineteenth-century excursion country – scenic, romantic and recreational, though in the more literal, restrained meaning of the word. The wealthy came here to indulge in the fashionable romanticism of the age. There is still a flavour of the picturesque: the narrow frame of the wooded valley, the railway clinging to one side, the canal to the other. Below, the tumultuous river gorge known as the Serpent's Tail adds to the picture. Beyond the Chain Bridge Hotel, the canal is river-like, but without rapids, where it curves to the south, sandwiched between the River Dee and the main road. To the north lie the ruins of Valle Crucis Abbey, a twelfth-century Cistercian foundation. The abbey was partially dismantled after the Dissolution of the monasteries, though much of the stone-robbing seems to have taken place during the nineteenth century. At Pentrefelin there was a slate works during the 1850s. The slate was carried down to the canal bank from the nearby Oernant Quarry. It was cut and dressed on-site, then sent off in narrowboats. This was the most westerly industrial enterprise on the canal.

Today tourists enjoy trips on horse-drawn barges from Llangollen to Pentrefelin, a trade that began in the 1880s after the end of slate-carrying and at a time when commercial use of the canal was declining. Photographs of the early 1900s show a pleasure boat full of passengers, at ease beneath a canopy. For a short stretch below Pentrefelin, the canal runs between the road and the railway, then veers off beneath the road at Tower Bridge to run along the valley slope. Soon it passes the winding hole south of Pen-y-ddol Bridge, the last turning point for narrowboats, and then reaches the wharf at Llangollen, where modern tourism has transformed the old working wharf into an attractive amenity.

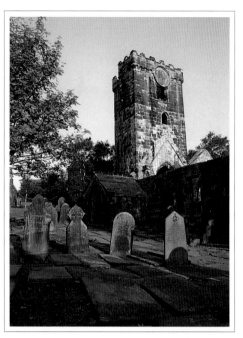

The Weavers' Trod: West Yorkshire
TOP LEFT Foster Wood, Colden Clough
TOP RIGHT The ruin of St. Thomas's Church, Heptonstall
BELOW Hebble Hole Bridge

The Water Way: Clwyd
TOP Pontcysyllte Aqueduct, Vale of Llangollen
BELOW Traditional narrowboat on the Llangollen Canal

The Celtic Fringe: North Pembrokeshire
TOP LEFT Pwllstrodur, near Abercastle
TOP RIGHT The Church of St. Gwyndaf, Llanwnda
BELOW Carreg Samson, near Trefin
OVERLEAF Coetan Arthur, St. David's Head

The Castle Road: The Welsh Borders
TOP Near Lade, Skenfrith
BELOW Skenfrith Castle
OVERLEAF Hollow Way, north of White Castle

A Painters' Way: Essex and Suffolk
TOP Near Fen Bridge, Dedham
BELOW Flatford Mill
OVERLEAF Church of St. Peter, Boxted

The Ladies of Llangollen

Llangollen lies to the south of the canal. The town is situated amidst 'the beautifullest country in the world', according to its most famous past residents, the Ladies of Llangollen, Lady Eleanor Butler and Miss Sarah Ponsonby. These two Irish eccentrics moved to Llangollen in 1789 and lived for most of the next fifty years at the lovely house of Plas Newydd on the southern outskirts of the town. The Ladies were adored by the Enlightenment society of pre-Victorian England. They lived a rich social life, and were treated with curiosity and affection by local people. They were devoted companions, of whom leading poets and essayists of the day wrote arch appreciations, but were more often treated with fond respect. Both ladies dressed always in riding habits and wore tall beaver hats over their cropped, mannish hair. Today Plas Newydd is an exquisite memorial to their 'life of sweet and delicious retirement'.

Despite its inevitable submission to traffic, modern Llangollen retains some of the serenity and grace that so attracted the Ladies. On certain days it is besieged by tour coaches and seethes with curious humanity. There is a venerable precedent for this. Llangollen was on the famous 'Dublin Road' from London to Holyhead, and during the eighteenth century it became a popular halt on the coaching route, and later on the rail route. The River Dee and the handsome fourteenth-century bridge set off Llangollen amidst its cradling hills, and the town's fame is further enhanced by its annual staging of the International Musical Eisteddfod. To the north, Llangollen is dominated by the elegant conical hill of Dinas Bran, on which stands the rough ruin of an early thirteenth-century castle.

Llangollen Wharf

Llangollen Wharf seems to mark a change in the nature of the canal. There is tourist bustle here, and a sense of serious waterway business as cruise boats come and go. Yet the canal remains narrow beyond the wharf, where it is barely 9 feet/2.75 metres wide. Trees overshadow the water and lend intimacy to the gloom. The north bank is a line of low, ragged crags where the rock was blasted out to accommodate the canal. Oak trees grow on the perilous edge of the crags, their exposed roots grotesquely twisted, like Medusan locks.

Narrowboats line the water's edge on temporary moorings. They have intriguing names, as all boats do; but there is a canal nomenclature that reflects the measured pace of cruising on fair water, rather than on rough seas. Narrowboats would break their backs offshore. Here, the boats are fondly named: *Water Music, Coster Road, Reflections, Roma, Tara, Wiglet, Mr Pip, Tick Tock Tuppence* and the wonderful *Puddle Jumper*. Many are hire boats, and are dull and plain in their paintwork. But a proud ownership is displayed on individual boats by flamboyant decoration: gleaming brasswork; Saracen's head knots; the vivid primary colours of traditional narrowboat painting on artefacts such as Buckby water cans, stools and hand-crafted goods for sale. Narrowboat painting has its own gypsy-like style, with its motifs of playing-card symbols, roses, castles, moons and geometric shapes. It was a style that emerged only during the latter part of the nineteenth century, when entire families began to live on their boats and a domestic canal culture evolved. Working boats were plain and unadorned until then, their bodywork stained and scarred by hard use. By decorating their boats so lavishly, the last of the canal people were defining themselves, as their way of life declined. The decorative symbols had meaning, too, and born-and-bred canal people had their own esoteric language.

The canal is wider by the moorings, but soon narrows once more and drifts on through crowding trees that muffle the rumble of traffic on the road below. Soon the canal swings to the north and passes a modern lift bridge, one of those weighted platforms that can be lowered by simple leverage and just as easily raised again. The canal contours the hillside and passes beneath the attractive Llandyn Bridge by a charming waterside cottage. At Wenffrwd Bridge it turns south and passes under the main road.

There is not much pressure on the canal walker. The pace is as serene as the pace of the narrowboats that drift occasionally into view, and then churn past, an exchange of relaxed greetings fading on the air. Yet the journey along the unchallenging towpath does not pall. The walker is freed of mapwork and of anxiety about the nature of the route ahead. From necessity, canals run a plain course. The towpaths were built for the plod of straining horses. In the early days of towing, teams of men often bent to the ropes. But horses were the great engines of canal transport, until first steam, and then diesel power, became the norm.

From the canal path near Sun Trevor Bridge there are fine views of Dinas Bran and the limestone escarpment of Eglwyseg. Limestone from the escarpment's Trevor Rocks, and from nearby quarries, was carried down on tramways to be loaded onto boats here. For the next mile or so the canal runs through peaceful countryside, passing beneath little bridges at Bryn Howel, Bryn Ceirch and the prosaic Millar's. Then, suddenly, the great Pontcysyllte Aqueduct comes into view, with the ugly chemical factory that has dominated the area for decades silhouetted behind it. For the last mile/1.6 kms to Trevor Basin, the canal runs between trees and the view of the aqueduct is lost.

Pontcysyllte Aqueduct

At Trevor Basin, the canal takes on a more workaday character. It was from here that the Ruabon arm was planned as a connection with Chester and the Mersey. The basin was promised a great future.

Wharves were built and a dry dock installed, and in truth the complex flourished, even though it was at the far end of a branch line. The basin became the centre of an industrial hinterland, where tram lines from quarries and coal fields converged. During the 1880s a chemical production plant was established nearby. Half the world supply of carbolic acid was produced here, and narrowboats brought in coal tar and carried away refined chemicals. The trade in chemicals continued until well into the twentieth century, not least because such carriage was forbidden at the time on road and rail.

Today Trevor Basin is brisk with the business of leisure cruising. Narrowboats queue to cross the aqueduct; their crews peer anxiously along the razor-sharp perspective to the far side, a mere pin-prick in the distance. There is no organized system of regulating the traffic. Boats from either direction need to judge if the line is clear before they set off. Somehow, it all works. Northbound boats disgorge from the narrow trough of the aqueduct into the open water of the basin. There is room to manoeuvre here, although the 90-degree turn into the narrow mouth of the Llangollen feeder can throw amateur boat-handlers into chaos, made all the more entertaining by the basin being a very public arena. Narrowboats do not bend, but they may crunch, humiliatingly. In the old dry dock on the south side of the basin, the gaunt hulk of a narrowboat slumps amidst the weeds. Aptly its name is *Symbol* and there are plans to restore it to its due glory.

There are those who have great difficulty in simply walking across Telford's sky-high stream. The statistics are unnerving enough. The aqueduct has eighteen piers, the central ones rising 126 feet/38 metres from the valley floor. The iron trough that carries the water is over 100 feet/30 metres long and about 12 feet/3.6 metres wide. It is just over 5 feet/1.5 metres deep. The trough is alarmingly exposed to the mighty drop into the valley. There is no protecting rail and the deck of a narrowboat is level with the exposed edge. Cruising manuals warn that children and pets should be closeted below for the trip. It crosses the mind that a sudden rise in water level might place a new meaning on the word overspill. But the boats have a strait gate here. They steal across and, when seen from below, in convoy, are like small pavilions in the sky. The towpath is protected on its outside edge by sturdy railings, but there is still a *frisson* of exposure. A glance downwards is dizzying. In the old days, horses would often panic on the metal-plated towpath. One horse broke loose, plunged into the canal and swam the rest of the way.

The exhilarating exposure of the aqueduct is dissipated instantly on the south side exit, where southbound boats and walkers are drawn into a comforting cloak of trees. From here the canal loses some of the pastoral charm that is so evident in the Vale of Llangollen. Canal and towpath wind on relentlessly at the same measured pace. The towpath is a wide, dusty track, along which vehicles sometimes drive. The track veers off at Pentre, where the canal turns to the south-east and the towpath narrows.

Chirk

Now the way is through a sometimes eerie world of beetling trees and turgid water. Just past Bryn-yr-Eos, the canal slides beneath the A5 and into the Whitehouses Tunnel. The eeriness intensifies; far ahead, the southern exit glows faintly, like a silver coin. The towpath is irregular underfoot and, though there is a hand-rail, a torch is a comfort. To have a narrowboat glide past you in this Stygian darkness is to feel the faintest bat-squeak of nightmare.

For a few seconds the emergence into daylight at the tunnel exit is like a re-birth, but the trees crowd in once more, until the openness of Chirk Marina and golf course clears the air on the opposite bank. The marina's docks are crammed full of narrowboats and the whole complex lends a peculiarly maritime air to the landscape. Again, the canal becomes overwhelmingly gloomy beneath its rain-forest canopy of trees. At any minute you expect the snout of an alligator to break surface. The edges of the canal are crumbling away in places, and the towpath is stony and awkward underfoot. Ugly drainage pipes protrude from the bank; red and white warning poles mark invisible obstructions in the menacing water. The railway flanks the canal here and a rash of factories looms beyond the straggling trees. The air is thick with the astringent smell of glue from a huge chipboard factory, and the thud and clatter of heavy work echo all around. More than anywhere else along the canal, there are sharp reminders here that the great network of nineteenth-century waterways carried industry afloat.

Just before the black hole of Chirk Tunnel there is a line of moorings. The side of the towpath is flanked, rather bizarrely, by sturdy display panels advertising everything from the nearby Chirk Castle, to Chirk's local Indian restaurant. An escape can be made here onto the road that leads east into Chirk, but for those who lean towards the dark, Chirk Tunnel beckons up ahead. It is double the length of Whitehouses, and the same delicious eeriness applies. Think not on the ghosts of great horses coming the other way. Beyond the tunnel lies the Chirk Aqueduct, another splendid piece of engineering, this time a co-operation between Telford and Jessop. Though not as grand as Pontcysyllte, the Chirk Aqueduct has a classic style in its ten tall piers and arches. The structure is flanked by the higher railway aqueduct of 1848, and the whole symbolizes in many ways the outstanding engineering achievements of the Canal and Railway Age. Stepping out onto the modern A5 on the way to Chirk is something of an historical anticlimax.

The Water Way
Information

Distance 9 miles/14.4 kms

Maps OS Landranger 117 (Chester & Wrexham); OS Landranger 126 (Shrewsbury)

Nature of walk A level walk along a canal towpath, which is generally dry underfoot. The route passes through a long tunnel at one point, where use of a torch is advised. *NOTE: The towpath described here is not a public right of way. Canal towpaths, in general, are not public rights of way. Most are on land owned by British Waterways and may be walked by the public because of British Waterways' open-access policy. Walkers are asked to respect the towpath and its surroundings.*

Accommodation Hotels, guest houses and B&B at Llangollen. Youth hostel just outside Llangollen. Seasonal camp sites in vicinity of Llangollen. Further details from Llangollen TIC.

Transport Rail connections to Chirk and Ruabon. Buses to Llangollen. For further information on trains and buses, tel. (01824) 706968.

Further information Tourist Information Centre, Llangollen, tel. (01978) 860828.

Start Llantysilio Church, OS 195435. Reached by bus from Llangollen.

1 Go through the church lych-gate, then follow a path down a field (*dogs on leads, please*). Continue through two kissing-gates, then pass alongside Horseshoe Falls to reach the beginning of the Llangollen Canal, sign-posted Llangollen, at a sluice-gate and small brick-built gauging house. Follow the canal towpath past the rear of the Chain Bridge Hotel, then continue along a broad drive alongside the canal. Where the drive goes left and over a bridge, keep straight ahead along the towpath, then continue to Llangollen Wharf. (2 miles/3.2 kms)

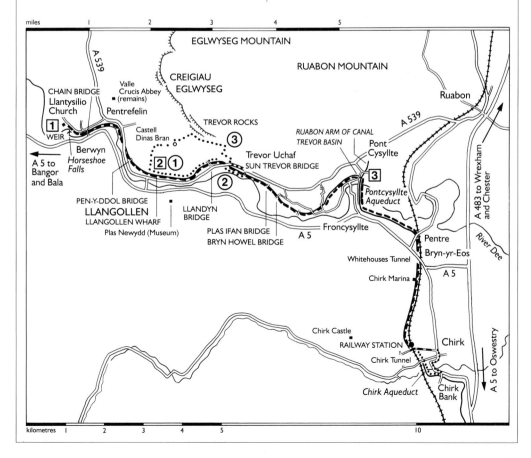

85

2 Follow the towpath to reach the A539 at Trevor. Cross, with care, to reach Trevor Basin, where there is a shop/café and a nearby pub, and toilets in the adjoining car park. (4 miles/6.4 kms)

3 Cross the basin by a footbridge, then turn right to the start of the Pontcysyllte Aqueduct. Cross the aqueduct, then continue along the towpath past Froncysyllte. In about 2 miles/3.2 kms you reach Whitehouses Tunnel. The tunnel is 191 yards/175 metres long. *It is very dark, and the towpath surface is uneven in places. Use of a torch is advised.* Once through the tunnel, continue along the towpath, passing opposite Chirk Marina, to reach Chirk Tunnel. Just before the tunnel entrance, bear up left to reach a road. Turn left and follow the road into Chirk. (3 miles/4.8 kms) *NOTE: The continuation through Chirk Tunnel and across Chirk Aqueduct can be followed to Monk's Bridge at Chirk Bank. The A5 is reached by turning left here; a left turn along the A5 leads into Chirk. (1 mile/1.6 kms)*

CIRCULAR WALK
3½ miles/5.6 kms

A walk along the Llangollen Canal as far as Wenffrwd Bridge, from where a steep lane leads to the Panorama Walk road. From here, the summit of Castle Dinas Bran is reached and a return made to Llangollen.

Start Llangollen

1 From Llangollen, cross the Bishop Trevor Bridge over the River Dee, then cross the busy Abbey Road, with care. Go left for a few yards/metres, then turn off right, along a passageway, then head up steep steps to reach Llangollen Wharf. Turn right and follow the canal towpath for 1½ miles/2.4 kms as far as Wenffrwd Bridge, where the canal passes beneath the A539, at OS 237425.

2 Go up to the main road and follow it to the east for a short distance. Take the lane on the left and continue steeply uphill to reach a T-junction with a road. Turn left and soon merge with the Panorama Walk road. Continue for ¼ mile/0.4 kms

to reach a junction with a lane going off left, below the summit of Castle Dinas Bran.

3 Go left along the lane for a short distance, then turn off right, over a stile, and follow the clear path to the summit of Castle Dinas Bran. From the south-west corner of the castle ruin, follow a path that zigzags downhill (*do not descend directly, as this increases erosion to the slope*). At a junction with a track, turn left and continue downhill past Tirionfa. Keep straight ahead at junctions and then, just past a school, reach a T-junction with a lane. Go straight across and then down right to Llangollen Wharf, then retrace your steps to Llangollen.

The Celtic Fringe
North Pembrokeshire

Fishguard to St David's 27 miles/43.4 kms

South-west Wales is a land where change in the landscape has been slow and where the tangible evidence of ancient cultures survives in the remains of Bronze Age burial sites and Iron Age promontory forts. These relics, which some may call Celtic, but which are inspiring by any name, punctuate the route of this walk along the magnificent coast path of north Pembrokeshire.

A line of ancient burial sites spans the broad waist of the Pen Caer Peninsula like a beaded belt. They are not spectacular, these low, stony ruins – they are mottled with lichen and stained with salty dampness – but their survival establishes the antiquity of this most ancient corner of wild Wales, where the northern edge of the Celtic Sea breaks on a shattered coastline, and where the west wind is out of Celtic Ireland, too.

You should not look for Welsh Wales on this old nose of north Pembrokeshire. Political Welshness, with its overt nationalism, is too intense for words – English words especially. It is ancient Wales that beckons, with its memorials of Bronze Age and Iron Age Britain, which lie embedded within the misty landscape of a dead culture – though modern 'Celts' would tear out your tongue for this last aspersion.

There is too much wishful thinking in the Celtic mist. You blow it away at your peril, so fierce is the sense of Celtic identity wielded by those who believe they have inherited the potency of a lost race of romantic heroes; a race that they believe was suppressed, but never eradicated, by the brutish Saxons. Sceptics argue that the Celts were never an identifiable race; they suggest that the term 'Celtic' emerged as a casual epithet for a fragmented and declining Iron Age society, which clung to the periphery of Europe's dominant cultures during the last centuries BC and was finally absorbed by those cultures. The inheritance of the Celtic Iron Age claimed by modern romantics is 'folk memory', rather than genetic lineage. A cultural sentimentality has stitched up the Celtic Fringe.

The Greek historian Herodotus knew what was in a name. In the fifth century BC he labelled Europe's northern tribespeople *keltoi*, a word that may derive from early Indo-European terms for 'foreigner' or 'enemy'. Herodotus's tone was pejorative and prejudiced; it was applied randomly to anyone whom the classical world saw as being the 'other' – those beyond the pale of Mediterranean civilization. The Roman commentator Diodorus was equally waspish about the Celtic hierarchy. He described how the nobles 'shave their cheeks, but let the moustache grow freely so that it covers the mouth. And so when they are eating, the moustache becomes entangled in the food, and when they are drinking the drink passes, as it were, through a sort of strainer.'

As ye eat, so shall ye be judged. This fastidious disdain for the Celtic 'other' reflects xenophobia and a north–south divide of classical proportions; the sensuous heat of the Mediterranean on the one hand, the dank chill of northern Europe on the other; the elegance of the villa and the wine cellar, compared with the smoky cages of hides and oak branches within which the Celts boasted of their prowess in all departments, and drank themselves into a stupor to prove it.

It is unlikely that the Iron Age tribes of the north, who 'dwelt beyond the Pillars of Hercules', called themselves 'Celts'. In spite of Diodorus's sarcasm, the people of the cultures known as La Tene and Hallstadt were the inheritors of sub-classical art forms, of subtle oriental themes and of abstract symbolism; all of this was expressed in their exquisite metalwork, with its enrichments of enamel, filigree and amber. They numbered many tribes and confederations, comprising people with a common culture, and whose restless influence threatened the Mediterranean hegemony of the Greeks, and then of the Romans. For us to refer to them as 'Celts' is simply a historical convenience.

Mythical Nation

Today, we may cherish the idea of the noble Celt as ancestor, and we may use the word Celtic as a useful label for a race of mythical Arthurian heroes, but there never was a Celtic nation. Rather, the so-called Celts of the Iron Age were partly the descendants of Bronze Age and Neolithic peoples who colonized Britain centuries before the assumed Celtic period, and whose burial chambers lie sprawled and ruined on the high, remote places of the Celtic Fringe. Elements of these pre-Roman cultures survived longest on the periphery of north-west Europe: in Gaul, and for much longer in Britain and Ireland. Here, later commentators applied to these cultures the term 'Celtic' rather than the more accurate term 'British', which derived from the unexplained Gaulish word *Pritani* and, significantly, was used by Roman commentators as a matter of course.

In the coastal areas of west Wales, in what is now Dyfed, life for these ancient Britons changed slowly during the pre-Roman period. Competition for land seems to have increased throughout the final millennium BC. This was probably due to an increase in population, to the new technology of the Iron Age, and to the strictures of a climate that had become less amenable than that of previous centuries. The land became more grudging. The people of the Late Neolithic/Bronze Age period had already devalued the natural environment through the wasteful practice of 'slash and burn', which had destroyed large areas of woodland. Life for the prehistoric farmer became more difficult and more anxious. Territorialism brought with it a need for greater civil cohesion and for more organized defence against potential aggressors. It was during this period that the hill forts and promontory forts were established, most spectacularly on the rugged sea coast of north Pembrokeshire.

One possibility is that each fort served an individual tribe and was the place to which that tribe retreated with its goods and animals in time of inter-tribal warfare or seaborne invasion. Many of the hill forts and cliff castles contain the remains of stone houses, indicating long-term residence. Some authorities are less certain that the forts were wholly defensive; they suggest that they may have been commercial and cultural sites, the civic centres of a large tribal community. The forts may have been selectively abandoned during the Roman occupation, in favour of more open settlement.

Confederation

At the time of the Roman invasion, most of Dyfed was occupied by a post-Iron Age tribal confederation known as the Demetae, who seem to have accepted the titular Roman presence without demur. Rome's influence on the western parts of Wales was superficial. The Roman presence was more of a holding action at the limits of military strength, and the Demetae seem to have lived through the three and a half centuries of Roman occupation without much change to their way of life. At a time when sea transport was the quickest and most efficient way of travelling, west Wales was always more strongly influenced by Ireland. The people of Dyfed were as much 'Irish' as 'Welsh', and Irish influence increased during the post-Roman period, when there may have been a re-occupation of the promontory forts.

Today, the relics of wild Wales may be old heaps of stone, but on the lonely, sea-washed headlands of north Pembrokeshire they can still make your head whirl with romantic nonsense and then grow still with the cool certainty that there lived on this crenellated coastline a remarkable people. Their lives could be truly desperate, yet they were always vigorous and, at times, inspired. Whether we call them Celts or not is irrelevant. These 'ancient' Britons are far beyond our living memory and we can have only tenuous genetic claims to their existence. Only the Welsh, Gaelic and Irish languages are a tangible link with their ancient tongue and offer the most persuasive evidence of the 'separateness' of the Celtic Fringe today. The place names of Welsh Wales will always celebrate that separateness. But the most dramatic evidence of pre-Roman Wales still lies amidst the blurred remains of the ancient burial grounds and fortifications that can be visited today on a convenient pilgrimage from Fishguard to St David's.

Prehistoric Pen Caer

At Fishguard there is little evidence of antiquity. It is a matter-of-fact place; forward-looking, if not entirely modernized. The monuments of Celtic Wales, the raw, broken stones of prehistoric Pen Caer have little relevance to Fishguard today, where local interests merge seamlessly at times with those of the larger world. There is nothing Welsh, or even English, about supermarket packaging, standardized services and the evening news. Fishguard is busy with honest, everyday life. It is only on the outskirts of the adjoining village of Goodwick that the ancient map of the landscape unfolds, beyond the uneasy mingling of suburban housing and the dull fields of Penrhiw Fach.

Pen Caer rattles with bones, ancient and modern. On the high ground north of Goodwick, at Garn Wen, there is a line of three Neolithic burial chambers dating from the fourth to third millennium BC. They are within shouting distance of the houses and close to the natural rock outcrop of Garn Wen. Gorse and bracken swamp the massive capstones of the chambers. A short distance west lies another chamber tomb of the same period; its capstone was re-erected on three uprights in recent years. Just west again a conventional cemetery lies marooned amidst quiet countryside by the lane that leads to the hamlet of Llanwnda. The cemetery is overlooked by the rocky knuckle of the hill of Garn Wnda, on which there is yet another Neolithic chamber tomb, its capstone still supported by precarious uprights. All these ancient tombs pre-dated the so-called Celtic period by nearly 3,000 years.

The roadside cemetery is part of Llanwnda churchtown, where the grouping of the little church and farm buildings has a pleasing naturalness about it. Llanwnda is typical of very old settlements, where buildings accommodate the lie of the land. Such naturalness imparts authenticity and, at the still heart of a place, a cool serenity. The Church of St Gwyndaf at Llanwnda was restored during the latter part of the nineteenth century. Its rough plainness has not been sacrificed to Victorian domesticity. Ancient wooden beams still support the nave; the interior is simple, its details sparse. The incense in the air is the raw odour of dampness and non-conformity. There was probably a fifth-century monastic cell on this site, and before that – before the Christianizing of Romano-British society – a pagan shrine. The early Christianity of the Britons survived the Roman withdrawal and then developed its own peculiarly British identity, its roots still embedded in paganism.

This old Christianity was satisfyingly troublesome. It was at odds with the more sophisticated Roman faith and there were fierce disputes over such bizarre matters as the style of the monastic tonsure, and the date of Easter. The true reason for schism was, as always, political – a cultural resistance to perceived foreignness, the old Celtic – Latin conflict. It reflected a clash of cultures rather than of religions. The Christianity of the Britons had a strong flavour of pantheism about it; there were closer ties to the natural, elemental world of sea, sky and mountain than to a Roman ceremonial that was more sophisticated and more political.

Welsh and Irish Christian 'saints' built their altars in the fields; meditation was matched by a sense of place – and by a good view. From the little church at Llanwnda, the great sloping shelf of the Pen Caer Peninsula swoops down towards the distant sea and to the finger-like promontories of Pen Anglas, Y Penrhyn, Penfathach, the broad headlands of Carregwastad and Pen Capel Degan, and to Strumble Head itself; this last, a pronounced relief for English speakers. Those rough-skinned Welsh names are swallowed like lumps of dry bread.

Garn Fawr

From Llanwnda, a green path leads westward. It winds along the edge of the high ground above sloping fields, on past Pontiago – more Spanish than Welsh in the melodious sound of its name – then over the shoulder of Garn Gilfach, the site of another Neolithic chamber tomb, where rock-strewn slopes spill down from the hill's ragged crest amidst a tangled mass of bracken and saffron gorse. To the north, the column of Strumble lighthouse gleams bone-white on its dolerite island of Ynys Meicel. The fields that fill the broad lap of Pen Caer display a mosaic of Iron Age development in the pattern of their random boundaries. Beyond the greenness lies the glittering sea, fretted with white, when wind and tide meet head-on. In fresh, windy weather, ribbons of white cloud stream in from the sea across a cool, cobalt sky.

The size of the great hill fort of Garn Fawr is not at first obvious from the east. Its adjoining hill of Garn Fechan is difficult to distinguish against the main mass of the higher hill. But soon the individual rocky summits become distinct. Garn Fawr dates from the late first millennium BC. It had big outer walls of dry-stone construction that were covered with earth and turf, and linked to natural outcrops, thus enclosing the fort within formidable ramparts. The subsidiary fort, on the adjoining summit of Garn Fechan, and a promontory fort on the narrow headland of Dinas Mawr, due west of Garn Fawr, indicate the strategic importance of the Pen Caer area during the Iron Age and Romano-British period. Those old tribes bound themselves tightly to the Celtic Fringe.

Penbwchdy

The coast path is joined below Garn Fawr. Nearby is a trim memorial stone to the Welsh poet, Dewi Emrys. The inscription is taken from the final line of one of his poems and reads: 'Such are the thoughts that come to you as you sit above Pwll Deri.' The tone is gloomy, yet persuasive, and is Celtic sentimentality at its lachrymose best. Pwll Deri is a thought-provoking place, and the poet's words are a reminder that, within the Welsh language, there is a genuinely ancient resonance. Individual words and phrases may seem rough and lumpen to the philistine, but in full flow the language swirls about the mouth.

The great cliffs that run south-west from Garn Fawr to the distant point of Penbwchdy plunge steeply from the rounded summits of blunt headlands. At their feet, the sea can be as smooth as silk in the sheltered bay of Pwll Deri, the 'Pool of the Oak', where the silken heads of seals break surface in the cool of the evening. From Penbwchdy, the coast path winds high and low past several coves, where shale cliffs rise from narrow, rock-studded beaches that are stained green at the tide-line. These cliffs are loose and uneasy; the shale is mottled grey and rusty-red, below dripping cornices of green sedge. On summer evenings, the light from the setting sun turns the cliff faces to a fiery red, which fades like glowing embers as the light dies.

At Aber Bach and Aber Mawr, great banks of pebbles have been storm-swept into the mouth of the valleys. These are the Celtic *abers*, the stream mouths, where early Britons, and their Irish neighbours, drew up their boats from the sea roads that served them best for transport. On the northern arm of Aber Bach, on Carreg Golchfa, there is the site of an Iron Age fortification with sketchy ramparts. Beyond Aber Mawr the path snakes along the teetering edge of Mynydd Morfa, where wind and weather are eroding the cliff edge. On Penmorfa there is another cliff castle, which is approached across the narrow neck of the headland.

Abercastle

The coast path winds on along the cliffs. West of Pwllstrodur, the way feels precarious. This is a stretch of spectacular coast, where the cliffs send ragged spines of rock spilling into the sea. At the base of the cliffs there is a chaos of pinnacles and small sea stacks that thrust from the water like dragon's teeth. The pinnacles are stained with yellow lichen on their upper sections and are jet-black where the sea sucks and swirls about their feet. The top of the cliffs is composed of friable clay, which glows like old gold in the sun and matches the gold of the lichen. In hard weather, the sea boils white round these cliffs; it overwhelms the pinnacles and sends great wings of spray halfway up the main face.

Beyond this point, the path descends to the sheltered inlet of Abercastle across a headland that has a huge cave at its heart. Abercastle was a trading harbour, probably from Bronze Age times until the last century. Once ships were built here, and there is an old lime kiln at the edge of the beach. The roofs of old cottages are warped and crusted from years of cement-washing. Boats are moored on ropes slung from side to side of the inlet, and old cannons are embedded in the turf along the shore. They served as mooring bollards for the

Victorian trading sloops that came here from Bristol and Liverpool carrying limestone and culm.

Just beyond Abercastle, a side path leads inland through Cwm Badau, the 'Valley of the Boats', to the impressive Carreg Samson, a Neolithic artefact of six upright stones with a massive capstone resting on three of them. The stones comprised the core of a burial chamber and were originally covered with earth and turf, through which an entrance passage led to the inner chamber, where cremated remains were found. Carreg Samson dates from the fourth to the early third millennium BC. The chamber was constructed within a pit and there are suggestions that the capstone may have been naturally in place and that the pit was excavated around it. This suggests opportunism on the part of the builders rather than a selective choice of site. A mile west along the coast lies the promontory fort of Castell Coch, the 'Red Castle', a name that has been attached to several promontory forts along the Welsh coast. Carreg Samson and Castell Coch belong to periods that are over 2,000 years apart – the same number of years that separates Castell Coch from the twentieth century. Our own monuments may not prove so resilient.

Aber Draw

The coast beyond Castell Coch takes a great gulp inland. The cliff here has slipped in places and is riven with fissures. In summer, the landward banks and walls are bright with cushions of pink thrift and the creamy bells of sea campion. The path runs above a vast gulf in the cliffs, which breeds its own windy thermals where blunt-headed fulmars glide silently to and fro. Soon the path leads alongside wide fields and drops to Aber Draw, where there is the ruin of an old grist mill, complete with millstones still in place. The quiet little village of Trefin is a short distance inland.

A mile/1.6 kms west along the coast path from Trefin is Porthgain, one of those industrialized coastal sites that are as striking for their ruins as they are for their natural beauty. In 1878 Porthgain Village Industries was established, in order to extract and market building stone from the dolerite quarries of nearby St Bride's. The fortress-like walls that dominate the harbour are the remains of storage hoppers, where crushed stone was kept. For many years, stone-carrying vessels sailed from Porthgain to London and Bristol, but the industry declined after the First World War.

The path from Porthgain winds along the cliff top through the fractured landscape of the quarries. The next headland of Penclegyr has a needle's eye sea-cave running through its neck. Beyond two more headlands lies the fine beach of Traeth Llyfn, from where the cliffs run west to Trwyncastell, the 'Castle Cape', the site of what is thought to have been another Iron Age fortification, now crowned by the ruin of an old tower. The tower was possibly a nineteenth-century signal station used for guiding the ships that once traded here onto the broad beach of Abereiddy below. There is an abandoned slate quarry; it was gouged out of the dark cliffs and, when work ceased, a breach was made to the sea and a small harbour created for use by local fishermen. It is called the Blue Lagoon, because of the sky-reflected colour of its milky water in bright weather. On the loose, and dangerous, seaward edge of the quarry, a stark wall of wind-eroded slates rises like a black honeycomb from smooth boulders.

A mile/1.6 kms west of Abereiddy is Caerau, where there are two linked promontory forts of the late first millennium BC. Caerau is a complex structure of ramparts and ditches, with remnants of the original stone facings. A mile/1.6 kms west again is another promontory fort known as Castell Coch. It stands above a tangle of reefs and rocky islands. From here on the underlying rocks are igneous and the cliffs take on a stonier texture than those of the soft shales.

St David's Head

Ahead, the craggy summit of Carn Penberry dominates the view. A steady climb leads over its seaward flank below slabby rocks, then the path rises and falls to pass Carreg yr Afr. From here to St David's Head, the landscape is a splendid wilderness of rocky heathland. No road or buildings intrude between the coastal shelf and the spine of rocky outcrops that runs parallel to the shore. The habitat of this stretch of Pembrokeshire coast is typical maritime heath, with a carpet of heather and wind-clipped gorse and a colourful flora of pink thrift, bright yellow kidney vetch and the sweetly scented wild carrot. The rocks are bearded with sea-ivory lichen and starred with white stonecrop.

The path becomes rockier and its surroundings more pleasingly desolate towards St David's Head and its scatter of broken boulders. The head was the site of a promontory fort as substantial as that of Garn Fawr; the surviving ramparts are impressive still. They are known as Clawdd y Milwyr, the 'Warriors' Dyke'. Inside the ramparts lie the remains of eight hut circles. The original Iron Age walls were much higher, and wooden posts supported a brushwood or turf roof. Victorian excavators found flint utensils, spindles, pottery and glass beads here. Along the base of the inland hills of Carn Hen and Carn Llidi there are traces of extensive Iron Age field systems, and it is likely that similar huts lay scattered between these hills and the sea. The hut cluster within the promontory fort may have been a chief's settlement for an Iron Age metropolis, here at the farthest point of ancient Wales.

The antiquity of the site is confirmed by the presence, outside the Iron Age ramparts, of the scant remains of a Neolithic burial chamber of the same date as Carreg Samson. It is called Coetan Arthur, probably a gratuitous reference to the legendary Celtic king, just as Carreg Samson is to the medieval Irish St Samson. The stones are scattered now, but a narrow capstone survives. It rests precariously on a single upright against a background of crouching boulders, and of skies that are often turbulent, especially towards dusk. Even a Celtic sunset is overwhelming.

The view to seaward from St David's Head is reminiscent of the Hebrides and of the Isles of Scilly. Ramsey Island neatly encloses Whitesands Bay and the narrow Ramsey Sound. In the western distance are the offlying islands and reefs of the Bishops and Clerks, 'the eight perils' described by Ptolemy in the second century AD. There is a lighthouse on South Bishop; its gleaming light pulses through the hostile dark. In rosy sunsets and in the mellow summer's dusk, the atmosphere at the farthest tip of St David's Head is serene. But during westerly gales, the sea roars into the mouth of the bay and massive waves thud into the cliffs. Then, the buffeting wind sends you scurrying along the well-worn path to Whitesands Bay.

The great beach at Whitesands must have seen a steady traffic of Bronze Age and Iron Age sea trade. It was a landing point on the seaway that took Dark Age Irish and Welsh merchants and missionaries through Cornwall to Brittany, and on to Rome. St David is said to have been born on the nearby clifftops, where a chapel dedicated to his mother, St Non, now stands. He founded a sixth-century monastery on the site of the present cathedral, a location that represents the progress of post-Iron Age ritual towards a more passive and sophisticated form. The subsequent history of the foundation was not entirely peaceful, however. Repeatedly, during the tenth and eleventh centuries, Viking longships grounded on the shining sands of the bays and their rapacious warriors laid waste to the neighbourhood and to its religious sites. These were brutal traumas that diminished the Celtic provenance, yet added to the potency of history and of race. By the Norman period, Welsh Christianity had lost its independence, but St David's status as the site of a cathedral, and as a focus of pilgrimage, was assured.

From Whitesands Bay, dull roads lead to the charming little 'city' of St David's, a village in non-ecclesiastical terms, and to the splendour of the cathedral, a fitting place to end a coastal pilgrimage. The colours of the cliffs and their rough forms are replicated in the cathedral's exquisite mauve sandstone and in its elegant mix of Romanesque and Gothic architecture, which, in spite of its sophistication, represents the same cultural imperatives as did the lonely promontory forts and burial chambers of the Celtic Fringe.

The Celtic Fringe
Information

Distance 27 miles/43.4 kms

Maps OS Landranger 157 (St David's & Haverfordwest)

Nature of walk An exhilarating walk along Pembrokeshire's wild north coast, passing numerous ancient sites. The going is varied and there are a few steep sections. Generally dry underfoot. Strong footwear and weatherproof clothing essential. *Winds on this coast can be very strong and some sections of the path are close to the cliff edge.*

Accommodation At Fishguard, Goodwick and St David's. B&B accommodation available along the route, although this may require a detour inland. Youth hostels at Pwll Deri, Trefin and Llaethdy (near St David's). Camp sites outside Fishguard and at Trefin, and around St David's.

Transport Rail connections to Fishguard from main centres. Bus connections to Fishguard and St David's from main centres. Local bus service between Fishguard and St David's via Trefin.

Further information Tourist Information Centre, Fishguard, tel. (01348) 873484; Tourist Information Centre, St David's, tel. (01437) 720392.

Start Fishguard

1 Reach Goodwick on foot, or by bus. From the roundabout at OS 946381 keep ahead across a bridge over the railway to reach a T-junction. Turn left, then, after a few yards, cross the road and go obliquely right up New Hill. At the top of the hill, bear left at a junction just before a telephone box. Follow a narrow lane onto a rough track. At Penrhiw Farm

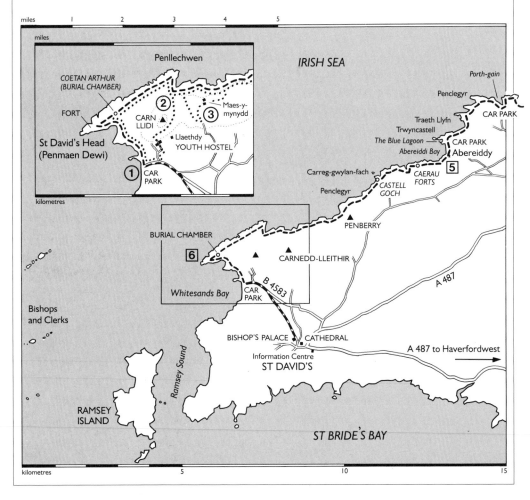

go straight ahead, quietly, through the yard and go over a block stile. Follow a track round left, then right, to reach a road junction. Keep ahead past a graveyard and reach Llanwnda. (2¾ miles/4.4 kms)

2 At a grassy open area just before St Gwyndaf's Church, go left along a lane signposted 'Unsuitable for Motors'. Where the track bends right, keep ahead through a gate by a Public Footpath sign and continue along a green lane. Cross a road and go along a grassy track past a house. Go through a gate and follow the right-hand field edge to reach a road at OS 920387. Go along the road and, at a broad opening on the right opposite Penysgwarne Farm, go right up a track. Just past a house, join an overgrown path through scrub. At a junction of paths, keep left and follow a rough track to reach a gate. Turn left beyond the gate and follow a hedged path round

right to reach a road. Turn left up the road. At a car park, turn right and climb to the summit of Garn Fawr. (3 miles/4.8 kms)

3 From Garn Fawr, follow a rocky path downhill to a stile by some houses. Go left down a surfaced drive to reach a road by the youth hostel at Pwll Deri. Turn left, pass the Dewi Emrys memorial stone, then go off right to join the coast path, which is well signposted and obvious underfoot. *There are some steep sections along this stretch. Care is required where the path runs close to the cliff edge round Mynydd Morfa at OS 870345, at Pwllstrodur, OS 865337 and at Castell Coch, OS 843337.* Follow the coast path to Aber Draw at OS 833326. (The village of Trefin (shop, pub, toilets) can be reached by following the road to the left for ⅓ mile/0.5 kms.) (8½ miles/13.6 kms)

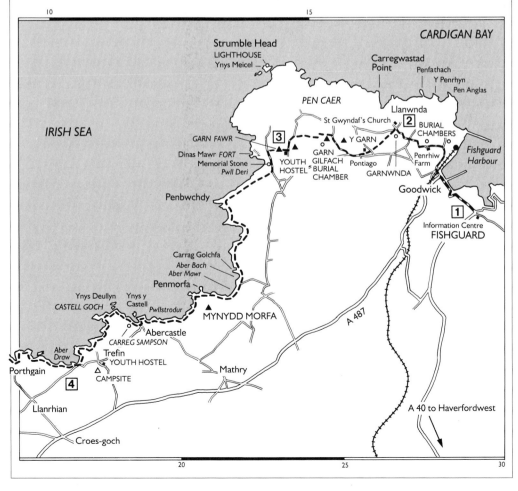

97

4 From Aber Draw, go right along the road for 200 yards/183 metres, then turn right at a signpost by a house. Follow the coast path to Porthgain (pub, restaurant, toilets) and then on to Abereiddy. (4 miles/6.4 kms)

5 From the beach at Abereiddy, go up the road, then branch down right on a side road. After a few yards, turn off right opposite a house to rejoin the coast path at the National Trust property of Pwll Caerog. Continue to St David's Head. (5¾ miles/9.2 kms)

6 From the tip of the headland, follow the broad track east, then south, to the car park above Whitesands Bay. Go up the B4583, and at OS 741268 bear off right down a lane to St David's. (3 miles/4.8 kms)

CIRCULAR WALK
4½ miles/7.2 kms

Start Car park above Whitesands Bay, OS 734273

1 Go up the road from the car park and take the second turning on the left, by some caravans, to reach Upper Porthmawr Farm. Follow the signposted lane through the farm, to a gate and stile. A few yards ahead, turn off right, signposted Youth Hostel. At the path junction above the youth hostel, go left and follow a path over the shoulder of Carn Llidi to reach the coast path.

2 Turn right and follow the coast path for a short distance, then at a signpost go right and uphill on a path. At the top of the slope, at another signpost, turn left and follow a path over a stile to pass by the ruined buildings of Maes-y-mynydd.

3 From Maes-y-mynydd, continue to a T-junction with a broad track. Turn left and descend to join the coast path. Turn left again and follow the coast path to St David's Head and then to the car park, as in direction **6** of the main walk.

The Castle Road
The Welsh Borders

Circular walk from Skenfrith Castle 18 miles/28.9 kms

'[The Normans were] a harsh and violent race, they were the closest of all western people to the Barbarian strain in the continental order.'

Sir Frank Stenton, *Anglo-Saxon England,* 1943

When the Normans consolidated their 'conquest' of England in the years after 1066, they built many castles throughout the Welsh–English Border. From these they set about the difficult task of subduing Wales. Three of the most famous of the Border castles commanded an area near Monmouth and Abergavenny and were known as 'The Three Castles' or 'The Trilateral'. Today, they are linked by a circular walk known as the Three Castles Walk.

In the years after Hastings, the Normans bludgeoned most of England into sullen submission. In time, they took over entirely the mechanisms and framework of English governance and landholding. Around 10,000 Normans may have entered England after the Conquest, measured against an indigenous 'English' population of approximately two million. Yet, by the end of the eleventh century, only a handful of the 200 or so major landholders in the country were English. In Scotland, Norman influence increased during the early twelfth century through the grace and favour of the Norman-educated Scottish king, David I. The Normans also made significant inroads to Wales during the first hundred years after 1066, but conquest of Wales by 'England' was not achieved until a post-Norman king, Edward I, gained control of Gwynedd in 1283.

Wales of the eleventh century was a land of disparate native kingdoms. Conquest of the country was therefore piecemeal and Norman advances were often reversed. The semi-independent Norman barons, who thronged the Welsh Borders, lacked the power of a national Norman army, with which to co-ordinate their territorial adventures. It was the Normans' uneasy relationship with Welsh Wales that prompted them to establish a chain of formidable castles across the neck of the country. Of these, the evocative ruins of Skenfrith, Grosmont and White Castle, the Three Castles of The Trilateral, are outstanding survivors.

In the late twelfth century stone buildings were constructed on the sites of the original earth and wood castles of the Welsh Borders, including those of The Trilateral. These early stone castles comprised square keeps that were surrounded by a plain curtain wall, with a single entrance and simple gate towers. Within twenty-five years many Border castles were again reconstructed, this time in what we recognize as typical medieval form. Round keeps supplanted the square originals; curtain walls were equipped with protruding corner towers. And the towers were pierced with vertical and cruciform arrow-slits, through which the walls could be covered by longbow and crossbow fire.

During the Norman and post-Norman period, the Three Castles passed into the control of successive lordships, including that of the future King Edward I. All three castles were the focus of agricultural estates; they were busy, bustling places to which successive repairs and refurbishments were carried out. But their military purpose remained paramount and the Three Castles, and especially White Castle, were prepared for war in the 1260s when the Welsh Prince of Gwynedd, Llywelyn ap Gruffudd, brought the fire of Welsh nationhood to the walls of Abergavenny. Llywelyn got no further, but his vigorous campaign placed the Three Castles in a war-zone once more. White Castle was refurbished and extended in response to the Welsh threat.

The House of Lancaster

In 1267, the Three Castles came into the hands of the House of Lancaster, an association that lasted until the nineteenth century. By the late thirteenth century, however, independent Wales had succumbed to the relentless pressure of Anglo-Norman ambition, and the military role of the Three Castles declined. They saw military use one last time, during the uprising, in 1404–5, of the great Welsh hero Owain Glyndwr. Owain's son, Gruffudd, laid siege – unsuccessfully – to Grosmont. After the failure of Glyndwr's rebellion, the Three Castles became administrative and domestic units once more.

By the 1530s each of the Three Castles had been abandoned. And by 1613 all three were described as being 'ruynous and decayed, tyme out of the memory of man'. They remained thus for the next 300 years until, in the early 1920s, White Castle and Grosmont came into the care of Welsh Historic Monuments, the predecessor of CADW. Skenfrith eventually came into the hands of the National Trust and is now maintained, on behalf of the Trust, also by CADW. Today the Three Castles are linked by a circular walking route that was established by Monmouthshire County Council. The walk can be started from any of the Three Castles, but the route described here begins at Skenfrith.

Skenfrith Castle

Skenfrith Castle stands on a flat grassy space within the small village of Skenfrith. Once the castle was moated; the ditch enclosed all but its east side, where it was joined to a leat diverted from the River Monnow. An original earthwork of pre-Conquest date was levelled when Skenfrith was rebuilt to its present plan between 1219 and 1232. The new castle comprised a circular keep and domestic buildings, the whole surrounded by a semi-rectangular curtain wall with corner towers.

Today Skenfrith seems less elevated than Grosmont or White Castle, but its river-fed moat must have made it an easily defended site. Its circular keep survives, though it is partly ruinous, and dominates the ragged walls of the enclosure. The top of the keep was crowned with a wooden 'hourd', a roofed palisade that was peppered with arrow-slits. Skenfrith seems a good place to start the Three Castles Walk, as it is the most easterly castle of The Trilateral. The modern border between Wales and England lies a mere ½ mile/0.8 kms to the east, the meander of the River Monnow being given over to Wales entirely at Skenfrith. The walk west belongs to Wales.

There are more twists and turns on the Three Castles Walk than there are in a ball of wool. The first mile of the route sets the pattern, as it threads its way in and out of adjoining fields, an arrangement that avoids too much road-walking and the usual slipstream of dust and exhaust fumes. Just beyond a junction with the Monmouth road, an escape is made into deep countryside where field paths unwind across rolling hills. This is a steeplechasing landscape interspersed with walls, hedgerows, fences, ditches, tracks and spinneys.

From the roadside, the way lies alongside a deep ditch, which is dust-dry in summer. Hawthorns and oaks line the edge of the ditch and at one point there is a tumbled pile of uprooted tree-trunks, huge and scaly, like the chopped-off limbs of some woodland dinosaur. The going is easy, but numerous stiles break the rhythm until Lade Farm, a cluster of buildings amidst a web of fields. The track that leads south from Lade rises steeply at first, then levels out on the brow of the hill into more open country.

Coach Road

The track ends at a junction with the Monmouth road and a minor road that is followed west to a sharp bend. This corner was once a famous stop on the old coaching route between London and Aberystwyth. Embedded in the wall on the inside of the bend is a milestone indicating 'The Travellers' Seat'. The blurred inscription is dated 1780 and records distances to such places as Brecon, Ross and Gloucester.

The modern road is left here, and a track followed to the west, into a hollow-way that leads to the edge of the small, steep-sided valley of the Llymon Brook. The line of the coach road descends past a ruined building and into the valley bottom, where another ruin, said to be the site of the Travellers' Rest Inn, stands amidst a thick scribble of trees. Horses were changed here and their needs attended to in the stables and in the nearby smithy, the broken walls of which lie amidst thick undergrowth. The bed of the Llymon Brook is a scatter of stones that at one time may have formed a cobbled way across the muddy stream. Today this hidden corner is gloomy and faintly menacing at dusk, when the air is heavy with the odour of dank old age.

The line of the coach road continues over the high ground of Wayne Green, but the Three Castles Walk veers south and leads through quiet fields to Great Llan-llwydd Farm. There are views from here to the butte-like hills of The Skirrid and Blorenge, and to the

Black Mountains in the hazy distance. The way ahead follows a sinuous route through more fields and wooded valley bottoms, and along narrow lanes and twisting paths that dip in and out of hidden corners, until the impressive hilltop site of White Castle is reached.

White Castle

White Castle was originally called Llantilio Castle, after the nearby village of Llantilio Crossenny. The name White Castle was first recorded in the thirteenth century and referred to the white mortar that covered the castle's walls. Our cherished image of the 'bare ruined towers' of natural stone, so typical of old castles, is entirely modern. Most medieval stone buildings, including Norman churches, were rendered, colour-washed and clad in parts with wood; the towers and curtain walls of castles were roofed with lead.

White Castle, in its thirteenth-century form, was the grandest of The Trilateral. It comprised three earthwork enclosures; an elliptical inner ward surrounded by a moat, within which the main structure lay. Its walls and towers rose from a sloping revetment that was clad in stone. This inner ward was protected to the south by a crescent-shaped hornwork, which guarded the original twelfth-century entrance, and which itself was surrounded by a moat-like ditch. Attached to the northern side of the main enclosure was a third enclosure, the outer ward. This was a large open space, possibly intended as a sanctuary for field armies. Sometime during the thirteenth century, when the stone structures were built, a new entranceway from the north was opened through the outer ward.

Today White Castle retains the bare bones of its original forms. There is a lack of detail in most ruins of this type; the less enduring materials have long since wasted away and what is left to us is a medieval X-ray picture. Once, these inner walls were lined with domestic buildings of mainly wooden construction, but resting on stone foundations. They included kitchen, brewhouse, hall, and a west-facing solar or sitting room. The gatehouse towers had four storeys, the perimeter towers two.

Towards Grosmont

From White Castle, a lane is followed to a junction with the B4521 Skenfrith–Abergavenny road. A short distance to the east of the junction, a grassy path leads off north into an ancient hollow-way that is roofed with the branches of flanking trees. This is one of those forgotten thoroughfares, abandoned in favour of alternative routes and never 'improved'. Judging by its alignment on the map, it may have been part of the original direct route between White Castle and Grosmont. The bed of the track is deeply rutted; the high banks to either side are peppered with exposed stones and webbed with the twisted roots of trees. After heavy rain, water drains from the adjacent fields and gushes down the bed of the track. The leaves of the interlocked trees drip incessantly in the green undersea light, and the rich, pungent smell of damp earth and leaf mould fills the air. Ahead, the leafy tunnel runs into the distance towards a beckoning gleam of light, where the trees end and the countryside opens out once more.

The next section of the route to Grosmont climbs onto high ground by a series of increasingly steep inclines. The way skirts past the withdrawn little church of St Mary's at Llanfair Cilcoed, where the path runs through the church's detached graveyard, but with discretion. It then leads on through fields, towards the swelling heights of Graig Syfyrddin, the high ridge-like hill that dominates the approach to Grosmont. A narrow lane contours round the western side of the Graig to Grosmont, but the best route rises through the steep fields to the wooded crown of the hill. It is a punishing climb, but near the top, at the edge of the trees, there is a solid wooden seat from which there are exhilarating views into the heart of Wales. On the high, broad back of Graig Syfyrddin, easy walking leads along forestry tracks between stands of dense conifers that rustle with the occasional passage of roe deer and fat, red foxes. Beyond the trees a rough lane runs downhill beneath ancient beeches and into the valley of the Tresenny Brook, from where a short, steep climb leads to the Church of St Nicholas and to Grosmont Castle.

Grosmont Castle

Grosmont, by name and by nature, was probably an entirely Norman settlement. The village stands on a suitable height of land above the River Monnow. It has a restrained charm that belies its medieval stature as a busy and important borough.

The Church of St Nicholas has a thirteenth-century nave that was left untouched by Victorian restoration. It is an impressive place, unfurnished, undecorated, poorly lit and resembling a shadowy crypt, rather than the original nave that it was. It is sealed off from the chancel of the modern church by an oak screen and doorway, where once the rood-screen stood. Screen and doorway are inset with small glass lights. The effect can be disorientating. Peering through into the brightly-lit, furnished chancel, you get the eerie impression that you are looking at a reflection and that the dark, bare space behind you has been somehow magically transformed into a well-lit church.

Grosmont is doubly blessed with its church and castle. The latter was the most lavish of The Trilateral. When rebuilt in the early thirteenth century the former rectangular hall-block was retained and a trapezoidal curtain wall with corner towers was added. The plan was the same one that survives in today's ruin. The surrounding castle ditch also survives, as does a handsome fourteenth-century chimney, complete with a gabled and coroneted top, the lavishness of which reflects the fashionable domesticity of later Lancastrian occupants. The oldest part of Grosmont, the south-west hall-block, has suffered most from erosion and decay. The internal walls are also decayed, although the rubble sandstone has weathered to an attractive texture. In late summer, monkey-flower plants sprout from high ledges, their yellow and red colours vivid against the red sandstone. When light from the setting sun strikes the western wall of the hall-block, it casts a huge, menacing shadow, like an armed knight, across the grassy floor.

Graig Syfyrddin

The way from Grosmont involves a reprise of the steep initial climb to the summit ridge of Graig Syfyrddin. The Skenfrith road is followed south into the valley of the meandering Monnow, then field paths are traced steeply towards the wooded crest of Upper Graig. Here the conifers are darker and denser, but the gloomy way through the woods is enlivened in spring by the white splash of wood anemones, and by the surprising gold of the daffodils that bloom amidst the damp understorey of the trees.

Beyond the woods, field paths lead once more through an intricate mosaic of farmland on the edge of high ground, where the fields echo, in spring, to the plaintive chorus of lambs. A short, steep descent leads back to the Skenfrith road at White House Farm, and from here the final lap wanders through Box Farm and Trevonny. Throughout this circular tour of the Three Castles, the minuscule forms of the Border landscape merge with each other, the pattern repeated endlessly: small meadows nestle amidst coiled hedgerows, isolated spinneys crown the tops of hills, sparse streams glitter in tiny valleys, farms are linked to each other by narrow lanes that wind between fields of ox-blood earth. In summer, the air is sweet with the scent of bruised grass and flowers; the heat can be torrid. In winter, the landscape is still dense, its vegetation withered; but the air is raw and damp.

From Box Farm, a further descent is made into the valley of the River Monnow. Beyond the river the high ground of Garway rises steeply above Cockshoot Wood. Soon the path skirts a meander of the river and continues through Birch Hill to where a farm track climbs over the slope. The track soon merges with a surfaced lane that leads past Drybridge House to a junction with the lane that leads to Skenfrith. This lane passes the Church of St Bridget, a sturdy building with a thirteenth-century pagoda-like tower, solid-walled and capped with a dovecote. Its dual purpose was as church tower and makeshift fortress, indicating that churches served also as potential 'castles' in the uncertain world of a medieval Welsh borderland that had been set alight by the 'harsh and violent' Normans.

The Castle Road
Information

Distance 18 miles/28.9 kms

Maps OS Landranger 161 (Abergavenny & The Black Mountains)

Nature of walk A long and very enjoyable circular walk created and maintained by Monmouthshire County Council. The route is quite complicated, and will take experienced walkers a full day to complete. It leads through a complex landscape of fields, woods and quiet country lanes. Directions are, of necessity, very detailed. The route is well signposted through use of the Three Castles title, but close attention to the detail of the directions is required. Parts of the route are along permissive paths. *Visitors are asked to take great care when passing through farmland, and should keep dogs under strict control at all times.*

Accommodation Hotels, guest houses and B&Bs at Monmouth. Some B&B accommodation in the area of all three castles, but enquiries are advised through local TICs. Seasonal camping at Lower Tresenny Farm, Grosmont.

Transport Mainline rail connection to Abergavenny from Hereford, and from Newport. Bus services throughout the Three Castles area are sparse, and what services there are may be subject to seasonal change. Further information from Abergavenny and Monmouth TICs.

Further information Tourist Information Centre, Abergavenny, tel. (01873) 857588; Tourist Information Centre, Monmouth, tel. (01600) 713899.

Start Skenfrith Castle, OS 457203

1 From the castle, walk down to the B4521. Turn right and follow the road past a stile on the left, then reach a second stile, signposted Three Castles Walk. Go over this stile into a field, then turn right, along the field edge. Continue for about ½ mile/0.8 kms, alternating between fields and roadside until you reach the old school house at Norton. Continue along the B4521, past a staggered junction, signposted Grosmont and Monmouth. A short way past the Monmouth turning, go left over a stile, signposted Three Castles Walk. Pass to the left of a Dutch barn, then follow the edge of a dried-up stream bed to a stile. Continue through fields and over stiles to reach Lade Farm. Pass to the right of the farm buildings, then bear right up a steep track and over the brow of the hill. Descend to a gate, then continue along the track to the B4347 Monmouth road at its junction with a minor road on a sharp corner. Turn right and follow the minor road for about 1 mile/1.6 kms until it bends sharply right at the Travellers' Seat. (3 miles/4.8 kms)

2 Go down the track that leads west from the road corner. Pass several houses, then continue down a tree-shaded hollow-way to a stile into a sloping field. Bear down to the right, past a ruined building, to reach two other ruins. Cross the stream, go over a stile, then go left across a narrow footbridge and up to a stile into a field. Cross the field bottom to a Three Castles Walk signpost, then turn up right. Pass a solitary oak tree and reach a stile. Bear up right, then, at the field corner, go right and over a stile, then walk along a surfaced lane, past some farm buildings. A few yards ahead, go left over a stile and into a field. Continue straight over the brow of the field and down to a fence by a waymark on a post. Descend alongside a line of elder trees and dogrose bushes, then go right and over a stile, and bear left down the field to a wire fence. *Do not go over the stile in the fence.* Instead, go left and follow the fence to a stile by a gate. Cross this stile, then bear left and downhill alongside a small valley, to the edge of a wood. Go through the wood and cross a narrow bridge. Bear round left and cross a stile by a riding gate, then go right and into a field. Go right, alongside the edge of trees, to another stile. Descend to a farm track, and follow this track. Just before a building, bear right and go over a stile into a lane. (2 miles/3.2 kms)

3 Turn right and follow the lane for about ½ mile/0.8 kms. Pass the converted barn on your left and the stile just beyond. Go left over a stile

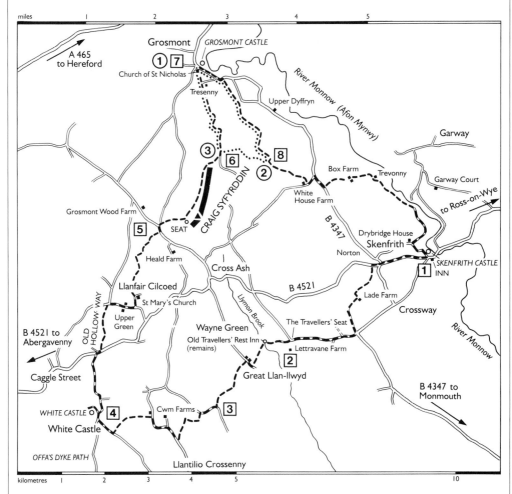

and into a field. Keep alongside a hedge and follow it round to the right, then go through a gap beside an oak tree. Go straight down the next field and cross a narrow bridge over a stream. Go diagonally left across a field, to a stile by some electricity pylons. Continue down the edge of the next two fields to reach a road by a brick building. Turn right and follow the road for about ½ mile/0.8 kms, passing Lower and Middle Cwm Farms. At the top of a rise, go left through two gates at a waymark on a post. Keep alongside a fence and down a field to a signpost at a fence. Go right and between some trees, then follow the fence uphill to a stile. Go left over the stile, then keep straight ahead across an open field and past a tree, to reach another stile in a wire fence. Continue across the next field, aiming for a small wooden post. Continue to a second post, then bear left alongside a hedge to a final post. Descend to a narrow bridge, then go left across

the bottom corner of a field to a footbridge. Go over a stile, then go left and up the field edge to a stile into a paddock. Cross the bottom of the paddock, then go over a stile. Go right and along the edge of the next paddock to reach steps down to a narrow lane. Turn right, then follow the lane steeply uphill to a junction. White Castle can be reached by following the left-hand junction for a short distance. (2 miles/3.2 kms)

4 From the junction mentioned above, go right and follow the road, ignoring a right-hand branch on the way, to reach a T-junction with the B4521, signposted Ross. Turn right for about 50 yards/46 metres, then, just before a house, bear off left onto a grassy, muddy lane. Cross a narrow bridge, then continue along a shaded hollow-way, to reach a road at OS 384191. Turn right and follow the road, keeping straight ahead at a junction, signposted Cross Ash. Just beyond

Upper Green Farm, turn left down a surfaced road, which leads to St Mary's Church, Llanfair Cilcoed. Just before the church, at a graveyard, go left through the graveyard gate, on through the next gate and into a field. Keep right, alongside the field edge, go right and through a gate, then continue past a brick building to reach a stile. Cross the next field to a stile in its far left-hand corner, then go down the next field, to cross a muddy dip and a small stream. Continue uphill, for a few yards, then go right, over a stile by an oak tree. Go through an orchard to another stile, then continue across a field to a fence above a stream. Go left alongside the stream to reach a footbridge. Cross the bridge, then continue, steeply up the next field alongside a line of trees, to a stile. Go up the next field to another stile onto a road. (3 miles/4.8 kms)

5 Turn left along the road, then turn right, signposted Grosmont. A few yards along the road, turn right and go over a stile. Climb steeply uphill to another stile, then continue diagonally left and uphill to reach the tree-line at a sturdy seat. Go over a stile and climb steeply up wooden steps to a T-junction with a forestry track. Turn left and follow the track through pines, keeping straight ahead where the track merges with another track. Emerge from the trees and, at a junction with a surfaced lane, turn left. After about 200 yards/183 metres, reach a stile by a gate at OS 409225. (1¼ miles/2.8 kms)

6 Go over the stile, then follow a rough track through hawthorn trees. Continue downhill towards Grosmont. The track becomes surfaced and, near the valley bottom, go through a gate, then turn left to cross a footbridge over a stream and continue steeply uphill to emerge by St Nicholas Church. Grosmont Castle is reached by a lane opposite the church entrance. There is a shop and a pub, The Angel, at Grosmont. (1¼ miles/2 kms)

7 Leave Grosmont by walking south along the B4347. Cross a bridge over the Tresenny Brook and pass Lower Tresenny Farm. Just beyond the farm go off right and over a stile. Follow the track up to a stile by a gate. Keep the edge of the field

on your right and go over another stile by a gate, then follow the hedge on your right to reach a narrow footbridge over a stream. Beyond the bridge, ignore the steps ahead. Instead go left through some trees, then along the field edge to pass behind an old barn. Beyond the trees, bear up right to a stile, go left behind a cottage, continue along the field edge, then bear right across a field to a stile. Continue to another stile by a gateway. Cross the next field to a stile in the top left-hand corner, then go up diagonally left to the edge of the wood. Follow, with careful attention, a signposted path through the trees. Pass a big moss-covered rock, and later reach a stile into a field. Go up the field, with the fence to your right, then at a field corner go left for 50 yards/46 metres, then cross a stile on the right. Go left alongside this fence for a few yards, then bear right down a rutted field track. Go right at a junction with another track and pass above a field barn. Reach a junction with another track above a murky pool at OS 421222. (1¾ miles/2.8 kms)

8 Go left along the rutted track to a stile above a gate into a field. Continue alongside the right-hand edge of this field to a gate and stile by hawthorn trees. Cross the stile and follow the fence on your right until a track bears off to the right and down to a stile by a gate. Go over the stile then continue, beneath the trees, to a gate. Just before the gate, bear down right to a stile. Pass some quarried rock outcrops on the left, then follow a line of trees downhill, bearing right to reach a stile onto the road by White House Farm. Go left along the road to a T-junction with the B4347. Turn right, then, after about 300 yards/274 metres, turn off left along the drive to Box Farm. At the farm buildings keep left between barns and continue along the track to a gate. Follow the track towards Trevonny Farm. Before reaching the buildings, follow the waymarks and cross a stile by a gate. Having passed in front of the farmhouse, follow the waymarks through the field to another gate, then keep straight ahead through two more gateways. Head towards another gate. *Do not go through this gate.* Instead, continue with the fence on your left, then keep alongside a hedge. Cross a ditch to a boardwalk and stile on the right. Beyond this stile, follow a

hedge on your left and then cross to a stile beside
a gate. Continue past Birch Hill Farm to another
stile beside a gate, then go on to yet another stile.
Join the farm drive and go left. Follow the drive,
which soon becomes a surfaced lane, to reach a
junction with a lane at Dry Bridge House. Turn
left and follow the lane to Skenfrith Castle.
(3¼ miles/5.2 kms)

CIRCULAR WALK
4 miles/6.4 kms

A pleasant walk that can include a visit to
Grosmont Castle and St Nicholas Church. The
route incorporates part of the main Three Castles
Walk. There is a steep section at the beginning.

Start There is very limited street parking in
Grosmont and the needs of residents should be
considered. There is informal parking in a lay-by
alongside the B4347, south-east of Grosmont, at
OS 413242.

I If starting from Grosmont, follow direction **7** on
the main walk. If starting from the lay-by at
OS 413242, walk back towards Grosmont for about
200 yards/183 metres, to reach a stile into a field on
the left, at OS 409241 and just before Lower
Tresenny Farm; then follow direction **7** on the
main walk to reach the pool at OS 421222.

2 At the pool, turn right along a rutted track and
continue to a gate. Beyond the gate, continue along
a winding field track. Reach two gates, side-by-side.
Go through the right-hand gate and head for a line
of hawthorns that starts partway up the field. Follow
the edge of the hawthorns to a stile onto a field
track. Turn left along the track. Go through a gate
and continue. Reach a junction of tracks and a gate
and stile, at OS 409225, as described in direction **5**
of the main walk.

3 Turn right over the stile, then follow direction **6**
on the main walk to Grosmont. Continue along
the B4347, if you have parked in the lay-by.

A Painter's Way
Essex and Suffolk

Bures to Manningtree 16 miles/25.6 kms

'Landscape is my mistress – 'tis to her I look for fame, and all that the warmth of imagination renders dear to man.'

John Constable, 1812

A walk along the valley of the River Stour, from the village of Bures to Manningtree on the Stour Estuary. The route passes several secluded churches and takes in the area round Dedham and Flatford Mill, made famous by the paintings of John Constable.

John Constable was born in 1776 at East Bergholt, Suffolk. His father, Golding Constable, was a prosperous miller and businessman, who had the lease of Flatford Mill on the River Stour, near Dedham, as well as on other mills in the area. He was also a boat-builder and ship-owner, and was involved in the river traffic that once carried bricks, malt and flour between Sudbury, 20 miles/32 kms inland, and Mistley on the Stour Estuary, for transfer to seagoing ships. The Constables were thus deeply rooted in the life of the Stour Valley, and the young John Constable was brought up at close quarters with rural industry, as well as with Nature. The result seems to have saved Constable from being overly 'romantic' in his view of Nature and of life itself. His brother, Abram, said of his work, 'When I look at a painting of a mill by John, I see that it will go round, which is not always the case with other artists.' This was as fine an accolade as any artist might wish for.

Constable's intuitive theory of art sprang from his perception of the reality, rather than the idealization, of Nature. Idealism was the legacy of the picturesque tradition and, although Constable first drew on the formal style of such impeccable classicists as Claude Lorrain, he believed that he should paint what he saw, rather than what his imagination *chose* to see. Such honesty and directness in landscape painting earned him the criticism, and at times the contempt, of the contemporary art world.

English Shores
Constable travelled very little. He never left English shores, except for a month spent at sea in a clipper ship, a trip that resulted in his 1806 Academy watercolour *His Majesty's Ship Victory*, a fashionable piece commemorating the Battle of Trafalgar and aimed, perhaps, at presenting Constable as a 'public' artist to match the stature of his rival J. M.W. Turner. But his *Victory* was a seascape that could not quite match Turner's great, salty, storm-wracked marine paintings. Nor did Constable's foray into the raw landscape of the Lake District produce much great painting. He seems to have been intimidated by the scale and ruggedness of mountain scenery, though he produced some fine studies, including his 1806 *Langdale Pikes*. Instead it was rural landscape on a human scale, and with human associations, that was Constable's *métier*; and it was the water world of Flatford and Dedham Vale that inspired his greatest works; 'the sound of water escaping from mill-dams, willows, old rotten planks . . . I love such things,' was how he defined his devotion to home ground.

Golding Constable disapproved of his son's ambition to become a painter. His reasons were pragmatic, as befitted a shrewd businessman, and were based on the conviction that a decent living could not be made from painting. But when Constable had worked for a time in the milling trade, Golding relented and allowed his gifted son to live permanently in London, and even provided him with a small allowance. Constable duly enrolled at the Royal Academy Schools and devoted himself to painting.

In 1802 Constable painted a view of the Stour countryside and called it *Dedham Vale*. It was a seminal piece, its subject to be repeated in numerous, more famous paintings, and it became the model for a much larger painting of the same scene carried out twenty years later. During the next dozen or so years, Constable worked steadily at his art, exhibiting regularly at the Royal Academy. His critics accused him of a 'want of finish' in his paintings, and his work was openly scorned by some. But Constable followed the lonely star that shone above Dedham Vale.

Marriage

Constable's painting entered a new and powerful phase after his marriage in 1816 to his childhood friend Maria Bicknell. Their courtship was a difficult one, due mainly to the Bicknell family's disdain of Constable's mercantile background and of his dubious financial status as a painter. It was only when Golding Constable died and left John part of his estate that Maria Bicknell's family relented. In the years after his marriage Constable produced his 'six-footers', the famous large paintings so loved today. These included his famous *The Haywain*, called originally *Landscape: Noon*, which was well received at the Academy exhibition of 1821. It was followed in 1822 by *A View on the Stour near Dedham*. Such paintings came from the very core of Constable's being. They captured the everyday activities of country people against the rich background of river and trees. In all of these, the languid, yet muscular world of the Stour is brilliantly portrayed; the eye explores the density, colour and texture of trees and water, as much as of paint; the nose may even twitch at the thick smell of watery decay and scented green things.

During 1823 and 1824 Constable visited Brighton in the hope of improving Maria's fragile health. He was not comfortable with Brighton – the sea was not his element, and it made him uneasy in the same way that the Lake District mountains had intimidated him. But he did produce some fine seascapes, including the oil-on-paper studies, *Brighton Beach with Colliers* and *The Chain Pier, Brighton*. Seaside forays apart, he always stayed true to his theme of English country landscape and to his inspirational Dedham Vale. In 1824 he produced *A Boat Passing a Lock*, followed in 1825 by *The Leaping Horse*, both based on Flatford, and with the ubiquitous tower of

Dedham Church in the background. In 1826 he exhibited *The Cornfield*, at first called *The Drinking Boy*, one of the most popular of English landscape paintings, perhaps because of cultural sentimentality rather than artistic merit, but worthy of its fame all the same. Again the venue was Dedham Vale, this time Fen Lane, on the route followed by Constable as a schoolboy between East Bergholt and Dedham. There could be no prouder expression of a sense of place.

Devastation

In 1828 Maria Constable, never robust and worn out by seven pregnancies in twelve years, died, aged just forty-one. Constable was devastated, and his life from then on was weighed down by unhappiness. His tardy election as a Royal Academician in 1829 must have been cold comfort, it seemed so grudging. Constable was then fifty-three; Turner had been elected to the Academy at twenty-seven. Constable continued to paint, but with a heavy heart and a heavy hand. Late works, such as *Fording the River, Showery Weather*, displayed dark skies and funereal trees. But he continued to produce great works for the Academy, including the 1836 watercolour *Stonehenge* and the last painting before his death, *Arundel Mill and Castle*, which was hung at the Royal Academy in 1837. On 31 March 1837 Constable died, probably of a heart attack.

Constable's great contribution to European, as well as to English, art was to introduce the principle that what is directly seen is what should be painted. This approach included grappling with the challenge of changing weather and of changing light. It was an approach that inspired the later *en plein air* school of painting. Soon after his death, his ideas were taken up by a group of artists, including Millet and Courbet, who settled in Barbizon in France and who developed a movement of 'Realism' in art. They were the precursors of the Impressionism of Manet, Monet and Renoir, who also studied Constable's work. Most of this new wave of European painters followed the custom of painting in the open air, as Constable had done in his bid to 'preserve God's Almighty daylight'. It was an artistic legacy that Constable might have welcomed more readily than the popular, sentimental acclaim that some of his work now commands.

Today, Constable's country – the compact, riparian world of the River Stour at Dedham and Flatford Mill – is in the grip of cultural tourism as never before. However, in the careful hands of the National Trust, which shares the upkeep of the several buildings with the Field Studies Council, Flatford has been spared overt development and there is still an atmosphere of repose here, early and late in the day. At busy times, of course, the immediate approach to Flatford can be a crowded canvas. A satisfying alternative approach is a long walk by the Stour from the village of Bures far to the west.

Bures

Bures is two-in-one, yet suffers no confusion over its duality. The village stands on either side of the River Stour: Bures Hamlet is in Essex, Bures St Mary's in Suffolk. Bures St Mary's is the older of the two, and boasts a grand, eponymous church and several handsome buildings. Bures Hamlet is more residential. The railway line from Colchester to Sudbury flits past its western edge. The tiny rail-halt has a wooden shelter with just enough room for the handful of commuters who travel to the outside world. St Mary's Church has a fourteenth-century north porch that is also of wood; but this is a splendid piece of work. The main arch is shaped from a pair of oak timbers, as if for a ship's hull. Cusped barge-boards and open tracery add finesse; age has given a satisfyingly rugged patina to the whole.

The way east from St Mary's Church leads through Church Square, and then along the arrow-straight Nayland Road. A field path is taken where the road bends north-east at Clicket Hill. The path runs alongside the River Stour and past a wooded mere, then on through fields to Smallbridge Farm. To the south is the moated Smallbridge Hall, built in the sixteenth century by the Waldegrave family and rebuilt in 1874. Its panelled rooms welcomed Queen Elizabeth I on at least two occasions.

Beyond Smallbridge, the Stour is followed once more. Thickly reeded banks diminish the presence of the river as it flows sluggishly through the flat countryside. On fine, breezy days, huge white clouds process across the sky; they seem to press down on the muted landscape, accentuating its flatness. Where the ground rises away from the river, the Nayland road is followed for a short distance until paths lead down towards the river once again. At first the path winds through a narrow ride, flanked by wind-whispering woods that include fruitful apple trees amongst the hawthorns, elders and holly.

St Mary's, Wissington

Paths lead to Wissington (or Wiston for local flavour) and to the Church of St Mary, a building whose great charm has been compromised only slightly by restoration. St Mary's is still essentially a Norman building. It stands upon a once-moated enclosure amidst thickets of trees and gravestones. Its nave, chancel and apse are all Norman in design, although the apse is a Victorian replacement. The weatherboarded bell-turret has a pyramid roof, and the walls of the church are rendered and painted in the medieval fashion. The south door has splendid carvings; one lintel sports two medieval scratch-dials, originally used to indicate the time of services.

Inside St Mary's there be dragons – or rather one splendid specimen, a painted depiction of the fabled sea-monster, the kraken, that swirls across the north wall. Other paintings illustrate events in the life of Christ and of St Nicholas and St Margaret, the beheading of John the Baptist, St Francis's sermon to the birds and, lest we forget, a faded devil above the north doorway. All are believed to date from the late fourteenth or early fifteenth centuries and are probably painted over earlier motifs.

From St Mary's, the way leads in front of the late eighteenth-century Wiston Hall, a subdued red-brick building with classical details. The entire complex of buildings at Wissington may once have been moated, and some sections of the larger moat survive. The water is green and viscous; thick reeds and dense foliage crowd round the pools, where giant carp may still lurk amidst the gloom. A short distance ahead, the grassy track runs close to the River Stour. The river is broader here. It is lined with drooping willows and its mirrored surface reflects the drifting clouds. Now the field paths follow a straight course; they lead past the entrance to old Wiston Mill and onto the busy main road at Nayland, and a crossing into Essex. Just before Nayland, the Stour divides and sends a northern branch to the village, where it divides a second time. At this point there is a pretty weir; lush willows hang over the stream. On the north bank flower-filled gardens run down to the river from attractive houses.

Nayland

Because of the river diversions, Nayland lies within an islanded site. Its name derives from the Old English *Eiland*, meaning island. Nayland was a wool-manufacturing centre during the medieval period, and the manipulation of the river was probably geared to the fulling and dyeing that attended cloth-making. The village prospered and rich, self-satisfied clothiers contributed to Nayland's architectural charm. There are fine, timber-framed and jettied houses and the streets have a pleasing irregularity. The impressive Church of St James reflects the early wealth of Nayland. John Constable's aunt lived in Nayland and in 1810 she asked him to paint an altar piece for St James's. The result was *Christ Blessing the Sacraments*, a fairly dull piece, but with special provenance.

From Nayland, riverside paths lead through corn fields that seem plucked from the French countryside. Beyond the fields, a steep road is followed to where farm tracks and paths lead to Boxted's delightful Church of St Peter, which stands within a peaceful enclave of trees. The sturdy eleventh-century tower is built of ironstone, pebbles and old Roman bricks, the whole tightly webbed with mortar. The rest of the church is brick and rubblestone and the overall mix of materials creates a pleasing mosaic.

The countryside through which the way now leads to Langham's Church of St Mary has lost much of its complexity and texture since Constable's time. But it is still serene and peaceful, and satisfyingly remote. In hot, sunny weather, the air is heavy with the stupor of summer; the colours are dry and rich; fields are ochre, saffron, faded green; hedgerows and spinneys are dark and speckled with pink campion and dog rose, with bone-white stitchwort and bramble. Thick, creamy clouds fill in the Constable sky with ease.

St Mary's, Langham

The area round Langham Church is 'Constable country' of special significance. Here, the painter is said to have had secret meetings with his beloved Maria Bicknell prior to their marriage. The pair are said to have met at the church and at the nearby farmhouse. The church has a tall, proud tower of rubblestone and ironstone with limestone dressings. In the porch there is a charming plaque inscribed with an appeal for kindness to animals, 'The Dumb Animals' Humble Petition'.

From St Mary's it is a short distance to Stratford Bridge and a crossing of the River Stour into Suffolk. The river sets the mood of this sweetly passive landscape and of the route through it. Now, there are no inclines; the path follows the north bank of the tree-shaded Stour; broad, flat fields lie to the left. At dawn, pale mist rises from the water and lies pooled along the north side of the hedgerows. There is great sense of repose, as if rough winds rarely disturb such passivity. Yet the North Sea is not too distant, and harsh weather still ruffles the feathery willows; on winter mornings, an aching frost bites into the earth. Ahead lies Dedham, its church tower a repeated motif of so many of Constable's paintings.

The path leads to Dedham Bridge. From here the town can be reached, through Essex now, by following Mill Lane past Dedham Mill. Dedham was a prosperous centre of the wool trade from the fourteenth century until the end of the seventeenth century, when East Anglian cloth-making began to decline. The High Street is a splendid open space, reflecting its original status as a market place. It is flanked on its south side by the Church of St Mary the Virgin, a handsome example of fifteenth-century perpendicular architecture that exhibits, in its parochial grandeur, the generosity of the medieval clothiers who paid for its construction. Dedham played host to other well-known painters, including the robustly eccentric Alfred Munnings – like Constable, the Suffolk-born son of a miller. Munnings was noted for his paintings of horses and of sporting events. He moved to Dedham in 1920 and bought Castle House at Castle Hill. The house is now a museum and gallery of Munnings' paintings and memorabilia. In the late 1930s Dedham also became home to a group of modernist painters led by Cedric Morris. Their work was anathema to the anti-modernist Munnings, but the group included such outstanding artists as Lucian Freud and Joan Warburton. Dedham Vale is not entirely Constable's country after all.

Constable Country

Between Dedham and Flatford Mill lies the true 'Constable country', however. Constable said of the area, 'I love every stile and stump and lane . . . these scenes made me a painter and I am grateful.' The lineaments of this inspirational countryside survive, but the inspiration is perhaps shared by too many of us now. There is a feeling that the spirit of Constable has slipped quietly upriver. At Flatford, the mill, Willy Lott's house, the boat-building yard, the medieval Valley Farm, the carefully reproduced bridge over the Stour seem too much like domestic motifs. Samplers and saucers, place-mats and postcards now define the work of one of England's greatest landscape artists – until you stand before the originals.

Life still goes on in Dedham Vale. On summer evenings, groups of youngsters gather on the old towpath alongside the mill pool. This is the precise location of Constable's painting, *Landscape, Boys Fishing*, his principal Royal Academy exhibit of 1813. Today's youngsters still cast fishing lines into the duck-dappled water. They smoke, and they jostle each other, and they brag and bully, much as the river children of Constable's day must have done, though there is a different slant on what may pass for innocence today. On the east side of the mill complex, by Willy Lott's house, visitors make their leisured, hushed way. Painting classes are held *en plein air* on the forecourt of the mill before the living frame of Constable's *Willy Lott's Farm* and *The Mill Stream*. The light of a summer's sunset is outrageously beautiful, though it fades to a smoky dusk on the east side, as the sun sinks and the blue shadows deepen.

Beyond Flatford, the Stour is followed for just under 1 mile/1.6 kms into the broad, bleak estuary flats, where great earth embankments protect the river meadows from flooding. Here, the Stour loses its enclosed charm. The flatness of the landscape is captured in Constable's *The Stour Estuary*, painted in 1804, in which there is a feeling that he wished to go no further. A concrete dam is passed where the Dedham Old River edges towards the estuary; then, where the embankment runs close to the river, tracks lead east between high bushes, to pass under the railway line and on to Manningtree Station. Beyond lies a world where industry and commerce have ringed the estuary banks with everyday life, and where the sharp reek from the mudflats tells of the not-too-distant sea, a world away from Constable's 'safe and calm retreat' of Dedham Vale.

A Painter's Way
Information

Distance 16 miles/25.7 kms

Maps OS Landranger 155 (Bury St Edmunds & Sudbury); OS Landranger 168 (Colchester & The Blackwater); OS Landranger 169 (Ipswich & The Naze)

Nature of walk A riverside route through farmland and villages, with very few inclines. A full day's walking should be allowed, however. Field paths may be muddy in wet weather. Weatherproof clothing and footwear should be carried. Parts of the route follow sections of the designated Essex Way, and of the Stour Valley Walk.

Accommodation Guest houses and B&Bs at Bures, Nayland, Dedham and Manningtree.

Transport Train connections to Manningtree from Colchester and Ipswich. Train connection between Colchester and Bures, via Marks Tey. It is possible to park at Manningtree Station and then to reach Bures by carefully calculated connections via Colchester.

Further information Tourist Information Centre, Sudbury, tel. (01787) 881320; Tourist Information Centre, Dedham, tel. (01206) 323447.

Start Bures Station

1 Turn left outside the station and walk down The Paddocks, then turn right to reach Colchester Road. Cross, with care, then keep straight ahead, signposted Sudbury, to cross the bridge over the River Stour. Continue along Bridge Street past the Church of St Mary, then, at the junction with High Street, turn right. Follow the road round left into Church Square, then continue round to the right into Nayland Road. Follow the road for about ½ mile/0.8 kms to reach a sharp left-hand bend. (1 mile/1.6 kms)

2 Leave the road by a public footpath sign, and follow field paths to Smallbridge Farm. Just before the farmyard, bear slightly left, then go over a stile. Cross a farm track, then continue over a series of stiles onto a surfaced drive, to reach a junction with the drive to Smallbridge Hall. Cross over, then, at a signpost, go diagonally left across a field to reach a road. Turn right for a short distance to reach a bridge over the Stour, then turn left and follow a path alongside a choked drainage channel, and then alongside the Stour itself. After ⅓ mile/0.5 kms, at a ditch and fence, go sharp left and away from the river for about 100 yards/91 metres, then turn right across a footbridge. *Dogs should be kept on leads throughout this area.* Follow the field edge to reach a road. (1¾ miles/2.8 kms)

3 Turn right and follow the road for just over 1 mile/1.6 kms. Just beyond two red-brick houses, and opposite the entrance to Rushbanks Farm, turn right at a signpost, follow a broad track downhill for a short distance, then go left over a stile. Cross a grassy meadow, go over two more stiles, then follow a track through dense woodland, finally emerging into meadows and reaching St Mary's Church at Wissington. (1¼ miles/2 kms)

4 Leave the churchyard by its eastern right-hand gate. The right of way crosses in front of Wiston Hall. Follow a grassy track along the left bank of the River Stour, with open fields to the left. Pass the entrance to Wiston Mill, then continue along a field path for about ¼ mile/0.4 kms. Cross a footbridge over a ditch, then follow the right-hand edge of a field alongside a reedy ditch. Cross a stile and a wooden footbridge (*dogs should be kept on leads throughout this area*), then continue through meadows and over stiles to reach a road. (1½ miles/2.4 kms)

5 Turn right to reach the A134. Cross, with care, then turn right and walk down the grass verge. Cross a bridge over the Stour, then go down left, signposted Circular Walk/Stour Valley Walk. Follow a path alongside the river and past a weir to reach some steps up to a road. (*Nayland village can be reached by going left past the Anchor Inn. There are several general shops, a post office and two pubs.*) Cross the road to a picnic site with seats. Go over a footbridge, then turn left along the river bank. Continue alongside the river until

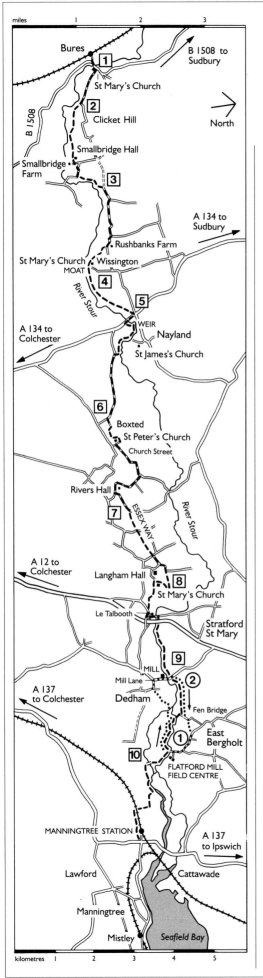

abreast of a stout wooden bridge. Bear right across the field, go over a wooden footbridge and on through woodland to reach a minor road. Turn left and follow the road for 1 mile/1.6 kms. (2 miles/3.2 kms)

6 At the top of Burnt Dick Hill, and just beyond a cottage, turn left down the 'goods entrance' to Boxted Hall Farm, signposted Essex Way. Follow the track round to the right, still signposted Essex Way, past a solitary tree. Just by a bungalow on the right, turn sharp left and follow the path down the side of a field to reach a lane by Boxted's St Peter's Church. Turn left down the lane, then right. Continue along Church Lane for ½ mile/ 0.8 kms until abreast of some old barns. Turn right, signposted Essex Way, and follow a wide track downhill. Just past a deep pond, on the right, bear left and then right and go steeply uphill past an attractive house. Just before the barns of a large farm complex, go sharp right, still signposted Essex Way. Go through a few trees, then keep straight ahead with a barn on your left. Go left behind the barn, then keep straight ahead in front of a small building (office). Turn left beyond another building signposted Public Footpath. Reach a surfaced drive and turn right to reach a minor road on a sharp bend. (1¾ miles/2.8 kms)

7 Turn left and follow the road for ½ mile/0.8 kms and then, on a bend, go up right and over a fence, signposted Essex Way. Follow a faint track diagonally left across a field towards the corner of a wood. Keep alongside the wood to reach a gap just past Plumb's Farm. Turn left through the gap, then turn right and follow the track to a road. Turn left for a short distance, then go up right into a field. Keep straight ahead through several fields to reach another road. Cross the road and follow a track opposite a junction. Go left for a short distance, then go right over two stiles and into a field. Cross the field, bearing slightly left towards the corner of a wood. Cross a stile and a plank bridge, then continue alongside trees. At the far edge of the trees continue with the hedge on your left to reach a junction with a broad track. Turn sharply right and uphill and continue to St Mary the Virgin Church at Langham. (2 miles/3.2 kms)

8 Just beyond the church go left, again signposted Essex Way, and follow a surfaced drive to reach a road by a lodge entrance with handsome gold and black wrought-iron gates. Go left down the road, with care, bearing left at a junction to pass Le Talbooth Restaurant. Cross the River Stour into Suffolk, then go right and through a kissing-gate. Pass through a tunnel under the main road, then go through another kissing-gate into a riverside field. Follow the river bank for just under 1 mile/1.6 kms to reach the B1029 by Dedham Mill (*Dedham can be reached by turning right*). (1¾ miles/2.8 kms)

9 Cross the road, with care, then continue along the river bank for about 300 yards/274 metres to reach a gap in a hawthorn hedge. Bear off left away from the river and along a well-worn path to reach a kissing-gate. Go through the gate, then follow a tree-shaded path to a junction with Fen Lane. Turn right, then cross Fen Bridge. Go left along the river bank to reach Flatford Mill. (1¼ miles/2 kms)

10 Keep right at the bridge over the Stour, to pass abreast of Flatford Mill. Continue along a gravelly track to reach an old weir by a National Trust sign for Lower Barn Farm. Climb over the metal gate-steps provided, then, where the weir ends, go up left and over a stile. Continue along a raised bank, crossing several stiles. Pass to the left of a pylon, then, where the river bends, reach another stile. Beyond here, go right along the path, away from the river. Cross another stile, then continue between bushes. Follow the track left, then right. Go under a railway bridge, then turn left and follow a wide track. Abreast of Manningtree Railway Station, go left to reach the station car park. (1¾ miles/2.8 kms)

CIRCULAR WALK
3 miles/4.8 kms

A pleasant walk that takes in Flatford Mill, Dedham and the River Stour, the essential 'Constable country'.

Start Car park for Flatford Mill at OS 075336

1 Follow the footpath down to Flatford. Cross the bridge over the Stour, then follow the riverside path for just under 1 mile/1.6 kms, to reach Fen Bridge. Continue on the south bank of the river and go across a gated bridge. Veer off left, away from the river, along a field path. Continue to a wide track by a National Trust sign for Dedham Hall Farm. Keep ahead along the track, then bear round left at some buildings. When almost at the main road, go sharp left over a stile, then right to reach the B1029. Turn right into Dedham. Turn down Mill Lane opposite the Church of St Mary. Pass Dedham Mill on the left, then cross the River Stour. Turn right through a gate onto a riverside path.

2 Follow direction **9** on the main walk to the junction with Fen Lane. Turn left at this junction. Follow a gravelly track, then cross a bridge. Just beyond the bridge, go over a stile on the right and into a field. Go diagonally right up the field, crossing a shallow ditch midway, then bear right towards the top of the field to reach a metal stile into a lane. Cross to the other side of the lane, then go right to follow a path that runs parallel to the lane. Follow the road for a final short section to reach the Flatford Mill car park.

The Circle Road
Wiltshire

Circular walk from Avebury 17 miles/27.3 kms

'The place is alive with the dead. . .'
Richard Jefferies, *The Story of My Heart*

The ancient stones and earthworks of Avebury lie at the heart of the Marlborough Downs, a landscape that has been shaped by human activity for thousands of years. This long circular walk begins and ends at Avebury and links a number of remarkable ancient sites, which reflect that activity.

Avebury is alive now with the leisured living, though they may not be too lively. The midsummer sightseers, who wander at will amidst Avebury's surviving crop of standing stones, seem weary and a little bewildered at times. Jefferies's ancient dead are long gone; their bones have been picked over by Victorian antiquarians; more than three-quarters of the great megaliths have been destroyed. What remains are sparse memorials of an ancient culture that we barely understand.

The forms of Avebury's circles and avenues are over 4,000 years old. They date from the Neolithic, Old Stone Age period and were constructed between the years 2800 and 2100 BC. Their purpose was probably ceremonial, but the site was also the 'civic' centre of the Neolithic communities of southern England. Avebury was Britain's most complex prehistoric site of which archaeologists are aware. The stone circles are the largest of their kind known in Britain, and the circular embankment, or 'henge', that surrounds the site is the third largest of its kind in the country.

The henge encloses an area of about 28 acres/11 hectares. Its inner side was lined with 100 megaliths. The circles, and the other arrangements inside the henge, were composed of 166 large stones, some as tall as 20 feet/6 metres. Near the centre of the henge were two large circles, north and south, and within these were other settings; the whole, a giant stone bagatelle. An additional 200 megaliths formed the parallel lines of the 1-mile/1.6-km-long West Kennet Avenue, which led south-east from Avebury's main enclosure to the site of a circular building on Overton Hill, now known as The Sanctuary. A second avenue of megaliths, the Beckhampton Avenue, led westward from the Avebury henge, though little has survived of its features. A mile/1.6 km south of the henge lies Silbury Hill, the largest man-made earth structure in Europe. This huge symmetrical mound is 130 feet/40 metres high, and covers an area of 5.5 acres/2.2 hectares.

Such hefty statistics indicate that Neolithic Avebury was a public arena every bit as awe-inspiring as modern stadia and concert halls. Silbury Hill was constructed 100 or so years before the building of the great henge. Its purpose has never been understood and it may simply have been a triumphant expression of identity by early Neolithic communities. The henge and its stone circles have a more familiar theme. They belong to a period of economic, political and social change, when greater use of the land by an agrarian community may have prompted the 'religious' appeasement of nature.

Ceremonial and Practical Uses

Sacrificial rites were probably carried out at Avebury amidst the billowing smoke of ceremonial fire and the reek of the charnel house. The complex is emphatically open-air and sky-worshipping. Did these ancient people offer homage to the sky from which nurture came; to the Sun God and the Rain Maker? We are still sky-worshippers today, though we have disengaged from nature in the raw. Many of our own ceremonies and feasts still relate to the same seasonal changes that dominated the lives of Neolithic farmers. To such people, Avebury must have been cathedral and camp, court and community centre.

But Neolithic Avebury had more practical purposes, too. It was a market for produce and a commercial centre, where tools and household goods, animals and crops were traded. During the Late Neolithic period it is estimated that 10,000 people lived within the area of the Marlborough Downs, while 50,000 occupied the larger area of Wessex. Avebury was their Mecca, their Canterbury, their London market, and the heart of a vibrant, naturalistic culture.

The great henge measured 50 feet/15 metres from the top of the bank to the base of the ditch. Its construction seems to have been systematic, as if carried out by disciplined teams. Tools were fashioned out of antlers and the shoulder-blades of oxen; spades were made from wood; wicker baskets were used to carry the chalk rubble. So much for the material at hand. Transporting and handling the great stones was more of a challenge. They lay scattered across the neighbouring downland, fragments of the sheets of sandstone that once covered the area. They weighed up to 60 ton(ne)s and were moved on wooden rollers by teams of workers yoked to them by leather ropes. On-site, the stones were levered upright into pits, then packed round the base with chalk rubble.

It is estimated that 1.5 million work hours went into building the Avebury henge and its stone settings. Did the workers volunteer – out of faith, or community spirit? Were they forced into such back-breaking labour by a class of priests or shamans? Were they slaves? Or were they paid for their efforts, grumbling and shirking, wrenching muscles and breaking bones, yet proud to be part of the making of this monumental public arena?

Superstition

The builders of Avebury were certainly respectful of their creation. Their descendants were less so. By the Late Bronze Age, some 1,500 years after its final phase of construction, Avebury seems to have been abandoned as a significant public site. The Romans bypassed Avebury, although evidence shows that it was visited during the Roman period, probably as a 'primitive' curiosity. There were Saxon settlements at Avebury after AD 600; the remains of Saxon longhouses have been found inside the henge and beneath the modern car park. These early inheritors of Neolithic Avebury seem to have had no cultural or spiritual association with the stones, yet they may have revered them, and seem to have respected them. It was a later society, distanced in time from Avebury's creators, gripped by superstition and then by greed, that vandalized this magnificent monument.

The Saxons built a Christian church at Avebury and, by the late twelfth century, a Benedictine priory and oratory were established. Significantly, these Christian buildings were all built outside the henge. By the early medieval period a Christian culture had demonized the stones by attaching 'satanic' names to them. Here were the Devil's Chair, the Devil's Brandirons and the Devil's Den. Fear and superstition promoted crude reactions, as the medieval Church struggled to erase the old values and to destroy the symbols of paganism. Many of Avebury's great megaliths were toppled during this time. They were buried where they fell, and the site was allowed to become overgrown.

In 1649 Avebury was 'discovered' by the antiquarian writer John Aubrey, who rode past while out hunting. Aubrey was captivated by the drama and mystery of the site. Later he accompanied Charles II to Avebury. The king instructed him to 'dig for bones', but Aubrey never did so, although he recorded details of the site. Sixty years after Aubrey's visits, the antiquarian, William Stukeley, began a study of Avebury. He described it as 'that stupendous temple . . . the most august work at this day upon the globe of the earth'. But Stukeley was lauding an already desecrated 'temple'.

By Stukeley's time, there was a village at Avebury. Part of it lay inside the henge and, from the late seventeenth century onwards, the stones were quarried for building material. A less superstitious age than that of the medieval period now sought to profit from the past. Local people dug pits at the base of a stone, and then lit fierce fires in the pits; cold water was thrown over the heated stone, which fractured and was then smashed up into manageable blocks. Scores of megaliths were destroyed in this way. The first one to be broken up was incorporated into the end wall of the village inn some time during the 1690s. Stukeley objected to the destruction of the stones, but could not halt it. He consoled himself with dreamy fantasizing about Druids.

Respect

After Stukeley, academic interest in Avebury grew, and with it came investigation and a growing respect for ancient artefacts. By the early years of the twentieth century, archaeologists such as Harold St George were drawing thoughtful conclusions as to Avebury's Neolithic provenance. But the cherishing, and the refurbishment of Avebury, came with the arrival of the remarkable Scottish businessman and amateur archaeologist, Alexander Keiller. Keiller bought the central site of Avebury and part of the West Kennet Avenue in the early 1930s. His enthusiasm was fuelled by his disgust at the way in which the site had become a squalid tip. As well as the rubbish that filled the encircling ditch and swamped the surviving stones, the interior of the henge was a tumble of old cottages, ramshackle sheds, allotments and scrubby orchards. The 'outstanding archaeological disgrace of Britain' was Keiller's brusque summation.

Within five years he had cleared the site and restored many of Avebury's buried stones. He located numerous burning pits, where stones had been broken up. Above each one he placed small concrete plinths, which stand today alongside surviving megaliths as uneasy cenotaphs to the past. Keiller used lifting sheers and block-and-tackle hoists to re-erect the massive stones. His methods were innovative, and would have fascinated the Neolithic 'engineers' of Avebury. Most of the set-piece stones we admire at Avebury today are those resurrected by Keiller; and the excellent Keiller Museum, behind the parish church at Avebury, displays artefacts from the main site and from nearby Windmill Hill.

Spirit of Place

Today, the emergence of Avebury as a tourist attraction has elbowed out the spirit of place. Pale shades of Avebury's ghosts may linger at night, but all have stolen away by the bright noonday. The stones remain as curiosities for the diversion of a very different type of pilgrim from those of the Neolithic period. The images of the stones have been sucked onto miles of film. The more sentimental visitors *commune* with the Avebury megaliths. They conduct little ceremonies; they meditate within measured patterns of ley lines and alignments; they are scornful of the mere 'sightseer'. The hopelessly sentimental hug the stones; some may even bang their heads against them; most prowl self-consciously, as they reflect on one of southern England's most inspiring ancient sites, through which subsequent cultures have driven more than just a coach and horses.

The eager, self-conscious culture of our times has handled the ancient complex with some measure of dignity, however. Avebury is a World Heritage Site. It is in the fastidious care of the National Trust and has been spared the more lurid trappings of theme-park fashion. Discreet marketing and low-level interpretation continues, probably in much the same way as Neolithic people traded goods against the outer bank of the great chalk henge and instructed visiting tribes-people in the sacred rituals. The massive stones are left to speak, mutely, for themselves. The spirit of place is thus not entirely ousted. Yet there is still a sense of relief on quitting the milling heart of midsummer Avebury, to take the walking route north towards Windmill Hill.

Seeking Summits

The Marlborough Downs are great billowing sweeps of land desperately seeking summits. At high points, such as Windmill Hill, the green swell barely interrupts the flow. This is ground that bends easily to the plough. Where there are few barriers to such thorough cultivation, the price is a bland smoothing out of the landscape. This is not the garden of England; nor is it England's allotment, stitched together by colourful threads of species-rich flora, as it should be. In spring there seem to be few wild flowers upon these disciplined acres, where detail and colour have lost out to the broad brushstrokes of winter corn and the head-splitting yellowness of rape. The way to Windmill Hill leads through a landscape that is flat in every sense. Field corners and belts of woodland take on a richer significance in this one-dimensional countryside. The eye focuses, with relief, on untidy corners. At Windmill Hill itself, there is some sense of escape from the dull plain. The broad summit has a refreshing airiness and the hill is well named; in brisk weather, huge banks of clouds go windmilling by.

The low mounds that barely interrupt the smooth curve of the hill today are Bronze Age burial sites. But Windmill Hill was in use long before the Bronze Age. It was the first Neolithic causewayed site to be excavated in southern England and the term 'Windmill Hill Culture' is now applied to the general life of the period. The evidence points to an early Neolithic settlement of 3700 BC, and suggests that Windmill Hill may have been a communal centre of trade and ceremony, a forerunner of the Avebury henge itself.

Vast Fields

A long field track leads to the A4 from below the western edge of Windmill Hill. The track runs between vast fields, upon which tractors make hour-long, arrow-straight journeys. Beyond the angry buzz of the A4, at Knoll Down, the landscape becomes more interesting. The shallow amphitheatre of land to the south looks as if it belongs to battles; an arena for the massed movements of cavalry. Oldbury rears up from the crown of Cherhill Down, a 'mountain' amidst the low hills. From the road a track leads west along the scarp of an ancient earthwork. Below, in the green saucer of the Downs, svelte horses are exercised along broad gallops. They flow across the cropped grass, one behind the other like mobile silhouettes. The track leads along dusty chalk treads to a junction with a hollowed way that winds up to the grassy summit of Oldbury. 'Softer to walk upon than a Turky [sic] carpet,' said William Stukeley.

Oldbury 'castle' is a fortified site that was probably first used as such during the Neolithic/Bronze Age period. It evolved into a major hill fort during the Iron Age. This was Avebury elevated – Iron Age people lived in more threatening times; they guarded their backs from high places. Oldbury lacks the drama of Maiden Castle in Dorset, or of Somerset's Cadbury Castle, but it is impressive still. The flat summit is given strong focus by the Lansdowne Monument, a triumphalist Victorian gesture. The giant obelisk thrusts skyward from its monolithic base; it is bereft of the natural style of even the smallest of Avebury's stones, but is endearing in its huge blatancy. It was designed by Sir Charles Barry, and was built in 1845 by the third Marquis of Lansdowne in memory of his seventeenth-century ancestor, Sir William Petty, the 'first' English statistician and founder member of the Royal Society. The monument was repaired in 1990 by the National Trust, which owns Oldbury Castle.

On the western flank of Oldbury is the outline of the Cherhill White Horse. It dates from the late eighteenth century, when there seems to have been a fashion for such monumental gestures. The Cherhill Horse was the creation of a Dr Alsop of nearby Calne. From a vantage point on the roadside, the eccentric doctor used a megaphone to direct workmen as they cut the outline on the hill's slope. The eye of the horse was filled with inverted bottles to make a honeycomb of glittering glass, but vandals soon robbed the eye of its facets. Today, a rather ragged Cherhill Horse still canters engagingly across the scooped slope below the Lansdowne Monument.

From all quarters of Oldbury lies the palimpsest that has been made of this great sweep of Middle England. North lies Swindon, across a sea of scrubbed acres. South lies the slow fall of the Downs towards the Vale of Pewsey. On Oldbury itself, the fleecy white clouds of fine weather windjam across a blue sky that fades into a pale, hazy fog of bleached air upon the distant arc of the horizon. Sheep wander contentedly across the stamping ground of the Iron Age fort; the breeze is scented with the fresh smell of bruised grass; the distant whine of traffic is unthreatening when heard from this small, green skylight of a hill. It is tempting to linger. But the path that drops south from Oldbury needs to be followed through a plantation of attractive hawthorn trees on Calstone Down. It leads to a junction with the emphatic line of the Roman road that linked Marlborough to Bath.

The Roman road leads south-west across North Down along the edge of a precise stand of trees. In spring, the fields to the east shimmer with the yellow of bobbing rape flowers; their sickly, sweet scent is naggingly unpleasant. The track soon leads to a junction with Wansdyke, a much more intriguing earthwork of the post-Roman period, which in its great length doubled as means of defence and as ancient highway.

Wansdyke

Wansdyke is typical of the earthworks that were thrown up by the people of the post-Roman period, after they had been left without the protection of Rome's regular army. The Romano-Britons of the south-west resisted Anglo-Saxon and Danish influences from the north and east of their beleaguered country by erecting ramparts of earth across the landscape. The line of Wansdyke ran from near Inkpen on the Hampshire border across the Marlborough Downs, then on to Bath and to the Bristol Channel coast near modern Portishead.

Wansdyke may have been built by the Romano-British leader Ambrosius, who, with his kinsman, the historical Arthur, resisted Anglo-Saxon influence. It is unlikely that the dyke was defended throughout its length. Rather, it may have been the physical symbol of a territorial agreement between native British and encroaching Saxons. 'Thus far, and no further' may have been the implied message.

The Wansdyke path is followed for miles along the crested and dimpled surface of the Downs. Occasionally field tracks breach the high banks. To either side the Downs are peppered with tumuli and burial barrows, but many are now insignificant features in the managed landscape. It is pleasant walking here; like travelling along a mountain ridge without the troublesome climb required to reach it.

The view to the north is across Bishop's Canning, Easton, Horton and Allington Downs. Along the broad-backed ridges that run to the north there are more gallops. South of the dyke the land rises to the escarpment edges of Easton Hill and Tan Hill above the Vale of Pewsey. Uncropped fields expose the white, flinty earth of the chalk downland. This is the raw material of Wansdyke. Long before a green pelt cloaked the great embankment, the dyke must have lain like a white, slashed ribbon across the countryside.

On Tan Hill, where a field track cuts through Wansdyke, a broad track is followed to the north-east along the crest of Allington Down. Soon the way descends to the low ground, where a tortuous right of way leads first to the east, and then back west along the banks of the River Kennet to where it skirts the West Kennet Long Barrow. A subsidiary path leads uphill to this magnificent burial chamber.

West Kennet Long Barrow

The West Kennet Long Barrow is one of the finest examples of its kind in Europe. It pre-dates Avebury and was in use from about 3700 BC until the Late Neolithic/Early Bronze Age of 2000 BC, when the use of such chamber tombs seems to have ended. Over forty people were interred in the stone-lined chambers, and there may be many more remains in the unexcavated mound that comprises most of the 328 feet/100 metres length of the barrow and which dates from the earliest Neolithic period.

John Aubrey recorded details of the West Kennet Long Barrow in 1665, and both he and William Stukeley noted that a Dr Took, or Toope, had pillaged the 'Golgotha' of human bones, with which to make 'medicine'. Neglect of the barrow, and damage from turf-cutting and stone-gathering, continued until the late nineteenth century when West Kennet and the nearby Silbury Hill became protected legally by the first Ancient Monuments Act. The stone chambers were restored during the 1950s.

The entrance to the long barrow is spanned by a massive shield of rock. The interior is composed of a central passage flanked by side chambers. The passage ends at a main chamber. The interior of the barrow is like the belly of some huge stone animal; and its proboscis of stone pays homage to the rising sun. On occasions, in the terminal chamber, there is the lingering odour of burnt joss; bruised wild flowers often litter the beaten earth where some modern acolyte has communed. As with Avebury's bare megaliths, the belly of this ancient burial chamber encourages all manner of therapeutic fantasies and fads. Devotees say that they have felt the great mass of the long barrow shudder at sunrise and sunset. You may feel yourself shudder certainly, as the light fades from the mouth of the barrow and a death-like chill rises from the packed earth; the massive, shrouding stones at the entrance entrap the icy air.

Silbury Hill

Across the A4 from West Kennet lies the mysterious Silbury Hill, Avebury's greatest enigma. It squats by the side of the modern mayhem of the A4. Silbury was built in three stages during the early centuries of the third millennium BC. No internal chambers, nor any significant artefacts, have ever been found inside the hill. Only the carefully engineered layers define its human construction. Five miles/ 8 kms to the east lie the scant remains of a similar, though smaller, mound in the grounds of Marlborough College. Today, the fragmented countryside surrounding Silbury Hill – the fences, hedgerows, trees and telegraph poles, the blurred patchwork of fields, the constant stream of traffic – detracts from the powerful visual impact that may have been the hill's only purpose. In the same way, the Egyptian pyramids exhibited a triumphalism that was not far removed from southern England's Neolithic self-awareness.

Beyond Silbury Hill, a pleasant streamside path leads back to Avebury and to those entrancing stones, which were ancient when the Romans passed by and when the Wansdyke was being built. And still the people come and go, amidst their encircling shadows.

The Circle Road
Information

Distance 17 miles/27.3 kms

Maps OS Landranger 173 (Swindon, Devizes & Surrounding Area)

Nature of walk This circular route links a number of prehistoric sites in the Wiltshire countryside and follows long sections of ancient earthworks, including Wansdyke.

Accommodation Hotel, guest house and B&B accommodation in surrounding towns and villages. Camp sites at Marlborough and Calne.

Transport Train connection from main centres to Chippenham. Bus services to Avebury from Chippenham and Marlborough. Further information from Avebury TIC.

Further information Tourist Information Centre, Avebury, tel. (01672) 539425.

Start Avebury car park, OS 099697

1 Walk into Avebury from the car park and, on reaching the High Street, turn left. Follow the street to its end, then go right, between some houses. Follow the lane round to the left. Cross a bridge over a stream, then bear right at a fork. After a few yards, go over a stile on the right into a field. A few yards ahead, go right over a wooden footbridge, then turn left, alongside the stream. Continue over stiles to reach a cross-junction with a broad track. Turn left, signposted Bridleway, then climb steadily up to the summit of Windmill Hill. (2 miles/3.2 kms)

2 Walk across the flat top of Windmill Hill, between the tumuli (no path), then bear right to where the belt of trees ends. Go through a gate, then turn left along a broad track, keeping right at a fork. Continue for about 2 miles/3.2 kms to reach the A4. Turn left and walk along the verge of the A4, with care, for about ⅓ mile/0.5 kms, then cross the road, with care, to a car-parking area. Turn right and follow a path through tall trees on Knoll Down, to reach the line of a prominent earthwork. (2½ miles/4 kms)
NOTE: Where the track from Windmill Hill

reaches the A4 there is a track directly opposite. This provides a shortcut to the prominent earthwork, but walkers should be aware that this short track is not a right of way.

3 Follow the track along the earthwork towards Oldbury Castle. At a T-junction just beyond the mound of a tumulus, turn left up a broad, rutted track. Reach a gate giving access to Cherhill Down and Oldbury Castle. Continue uphill to reach the summit of Oldbury. The route leads along the east side of the Oldbury embankment. Keep to the left of two hawthorn trees that stand in a hollow, and reach a wire fence. Go through a gate in the fence, then follow a path downhill amidst scattered hawthorn trees on Calstone Down. At a junction with the broad track of the Roman road that comes in from the left, turn right, signposted Wessex Ridgeway. Follow the track for about 1½ miles/2.4 kms to a junction with Wansdyke at a gate and information board on Morgan's Hill. (4 miles/6.4 kms)

4 Go left through the gate and follow the path along the dyke past Baltic Farm, to reach the A361 at Shepherd's Shore. Cross, with care, go over a stile on the right of a house, then continue along the line of Wansdyke for about 3 miles/ 4.8 kms, to reach a break in Wansdyke by a gate and bridleway sign at OS 081652 on Tan Hill. (4 miles/6.4 kms)

5 Turn left, then right along a track. At a bridleway sign, turn left and follow a track downhill, between wire fences. Merge with another track and keep straight ahead and downhill. Silbury Hill lies ahead. Reach a broad track and follow it for a short distance, until just above West Kennet Long Barrow. (*There is no right of way to the long barrow from here.*) Continue to the right along the track and follow it to a junction. Go diagonally across and continue up a lane. At a barn, turn left onto a grassy footpath. Follow the path downhill, cross a grassy track, then go over a stile into a field. Follow the path through fields, eventually bearing left to reach a junction with a track. Take the path immediately opposite. In a short distance reach the junction with the track leading uphill

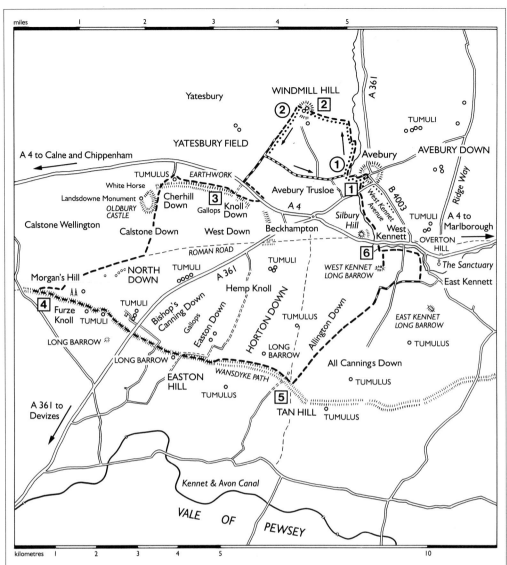

to West Kennet Long Barrow. On the main route keep ahead for a short distance, then go right down a track to reach the A4. (3¾ miles/6 kms)

6 Cross diagonally left, with care, then go over a stile signposted Avebury Village. Follow a path alongside a stream, crossing several stiles. Keep ahead past a bridge. *Silbury Hill can be reached by turning off left and crossing the bridge.* On the main route, reach the A4361 and the car park opposite. (¾ mile/1.2 kms)

CIRCULAR WALK
6 miles/9½ kms

A walk to Windmill Hill. There are few inclines and the ground is generally dry, but it may become muddy during prolonged wet weather.

Start Avebury car park, OS 099697

1 Follow direction **1** on the main walk to reach the summit of Windmill Hill.

2 Follow direction **2** on the main walk as far as OS 077704. Turn left here and follow the track to reach the public road at a corner. Keep straight ahead past some houses, then continue along a path to return to Avebury and the car park.

The Circle Road: Wiltshire
TOP The Cherhill White Horse, Oldbury Hill
BELOW The Cove, Avebury

The Saxon Shore: Kent
TOP Langdon Bay, Dover
BELOW Deal Beach
OPPOSITE Walmer Castle

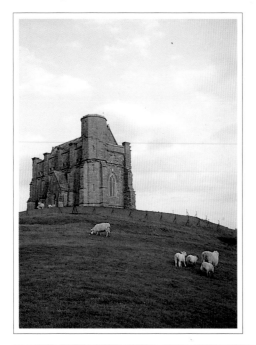

The Giant's Road: Dorset
TOP LEFT St. Catherine's Chapel, Abbotsbury
TOP RIGHT The Cerne Abbas Giant
BELOW Looking south from Maiden Castle

The Stone Road: Dartmoor
TOP Red Lake
BELOW Nun's Cross
OVERLEAF Stall Moor Stone Row near Dry Lake Ford

The Tinners' Way: Cornwall
TOP Wheal Edward and West Wheal Owles mine stacks
BELOW Mulfra Quoit
OVERLEAF Mine engine houses of the Crowns Mine, Botallack

The Saxon Shore
Kent

Deal to Dover 9 miles/14.4 kms

England's white cliffs have deep significance for the British people. Yet they are only a part of the remarkable Channel coast that runs from the mouth of the River Thames to Dungeness. This intriguing walk, from Deal to Dover, takes in shingle beach and chalk cliff and passes a number of historical sites on the famous Saxon Shore.

The white cliffs of Dover's 'chalk arena' seem more at risk from the waves of humanity that crowd to their edges than from the waves of the English Channel. They are marvellously abrupt, these great slices of crumbling chalk. They look as if they groan under the weight of Kent and may pitch head-first into the sea at any moment. Grassy slopes run to the very edge. Seen from a distance, worn paths veer perilously close to thin air. No half-measures here; England ends, white-faced with fright, it seems, though the chalk cliffs of the 'Saxon Shore' are the most cherished symbol of England's certainty and confidence; and of its insularity.

From the white cliffs on clear days, Europe seems touchingly close. The bearing of Cap Gris Nez on the French horizon makes you long for the beautiful South. This has always been a coast of arrivals and departures; now, we have even burrowed our way beneath it. Once, of course, it was locked to Europe by a low-lying stretch of land that alternated between frozen tundra and waterlogged plain, as successive ice sheets advanced and retreated.

The sea made its first great breach between Europe and Britain about 10,000 years ago, when the southern part of the English Channel was formed. It took another 1,000 years for the isthmus between England and Holland to be breached and for Britain to become an island. By then the Straits of Dover had widened. Great slabs of the white cliffs plunged, as if from calving icebergs, onto the salt pans of the shoreline, and the clay and mud of ancient river sediments drained away from the deep shingle beds further north.

During the Neolithic period, the Saxon Shore was settled by primitive farmers. These early settlers progressed more through integration and influence than through violent displacement by 'foreign' invaders. The Neolithic, Late Stone Age passed seamlessly into the 'Beaker' Bronze Age, because of cross-Channel connections and trading links with Ireland, and because of a shared trans-European culture. In turn, the Bronze Age evolved into the Iron Age by similar social and economic mechanisms.

During the final centuries BC, cross-Channel co-operation between Britain and Gaul continued, as long as there was an equitable balance in supply and demand of food and other materials. Territorialism and aggressiveness increased during the Late Iron Age, however, because of pressure from a growing population and its demands on overused farmland. But there was still a mutuality of interest between the tribespeople of south-east England and those of Gaul. They belonged to the same tribal confederation, the Belgae, and British chieftains supported local resistance to Rome's colonization of northern Gaul. Such help was enough to prompt the first real invasion of British shores.

Roman Might

On an August morning in 55 BC, Julius Caesar's galleys anchored off Dover. At that time the River Dour flooded between cliffs that extended several hundred yards further out to sea than they do now. A hundred Roman galleys stood at the 'front door of England'. But the white cliffs were a daunting barrier to the several thousand heavily armed troops of the Roman force, while the hostile Britons who lined the cliff top convinced Caesar that he needed a better landing place. The Romans waited for the flood tide, then rowed north to the low shingle shore near modern Deal.

The beach at Deal slides quickly into dark water. It was here that Caesar's deep-keeled galleys crunched, unexpectedly, into the shelving shoreline. They thought they had another hundred yards to go. The legionaries tumbled overboard and found themselves out of their depths. They thrashed their way to the beach, undaunted, and then routed the Britons in short order. A few days later, a violent storm wrecked half the Roman fleet. Undaunted, Caesar returned to Gaul where he built over 500 warships; this time the troop carriers were broad in the beam and had shallow draughts to make landing easier on the shingle beaches.

On his second expedition, Caesar fought his way beyond the Thames, then retreated, to subdue Gaulish rebellion and to make his bid for glory in Rome itself. It was enough that Rome had left its mark on island Britain. For 100 years after Caesar's invasions there was no official Roman presence in Britain. But Roman influence, and the momentous events of that seminal century in world history, were to shape Britain's future all the same.

There was a punitive element to Caesar's expeditions because of Britain's military support of Gaulish rebels, but at heart, the expeditions were imperialistic. After Caesar, Roman traders and adventurers developed links with Britain, and Roman ways were adopted in the Kent area especially, while British tribal leaders strengthened their associations with a Romanized Gaul. The Roman occupation that followed was inevitable, given that Rome had the will and the means. British tribes were not united against Rome and they had their own quarrels amongst each other. The Claudian 'invasion' of AD 43 was nominally a response to appeals to Rome by one British tribe, for military support against another. It was a useful excuse for Rome to attempt once again the conquest that it had always desired.

The Romans turned the Channel coast into a military beach-head from which they organized the occupation of Britain. Their main base was at Richborough, to the north of Sandwich, but Dover was also of military importance and by the second century it was the base of the Roman fleet, the *Classis Britannica*. For over 200 years Roman control of southern Britain was absolute. The *Pax Romana* was a reality, until the weakening of Roman influence in Gaul coincided with expansionist attacks on the Empire by aggressive Germanic tribes. Britain's Channel coast was attacked by Saxon and Jutish pirates, and it was during the third century AD that the term 'Saxon Shore' seems to have been introduced.

Germanic Influence

The Romans built forts on both sides of the Channel as part of their defensive system. Reculver, on the Thames Estuary, was one of these. The existing fort at Dover was strengthened, and forts were also established at Lympne, Richborough and Pevensey. In the fourth century, control of these was placed in the hands of a Roman officer known as the Count of the Saxon Shore. The name Saxon, so readily adopted, seems portentous. It covered the diverse yet related Germanic tribes of Angles, Saxons and Jutes who most influenced the Channel and North Sea coasts of Britain. It suggests that there was already a Germanic influence in the south-east by the fouth century AD, an infiltration similar to that of the Romans after Caesar's expeditions.

Germanic control of the Saxon Shore must have developed rapidly in the wake of Roman decline. Kent once more became a base from which a vigorous pagan race colonized Britain. Across the Saxon Shore came warriors, farmers, tradespeople, craftsmen, administrators and families seeking land. Kent became the richest of the Saxon kingdoms, absorbing the most fruitful aspects of Roman civilization and maintaining trade with Frankish Gaul.

It was from France also that the next of England's 'invaders' came, at the chaotic end of the Saxon era. When the turmoil of Norman conquest subsided, England was confirmed as a major participant in the great political and military struggles of medieval Europe. Now the Saxon Shore became, even more crucially, the first line of defence of a unified England, a nation that stood face-to-face with its European neighbours in mutual fear, distrust and, at times, violent conflict.

For the next 800 years England's defence of its Saxon Shore was of paramount importance. In Tudor times more castles were built to strengthen the chain of existing fortifications in response to fears of a Franco-Spanish invasion. They were linked to each other by earth embankments. In the nineteenth century the threat of invasion by Napoleon prompted the digging of a military canal between Hythe and Rye to ring-fence the Romney marshes, across which it was thought the

French would invade. A chain of martello towers was also built along this south-eastern shore. At the same time, Dover's defences were extended and strengthened and the town's Western Heights were hollowed out into caverns and brick chambers, the strategic last resort of the British Army. In the twentieth century the Saxon Shore was stitched with barbed wire, and sown with concrete pill boxes and anti-tank devices to guard against a threatened German invasion. The Saxon Shore has always symbolized Fortress Britain, writ large.

Deal

Today's Saxon Shore is more symbol than defence. The sea is the main protagonist now. Anything else is mere sentimentality about where England begins; never where it ends. At Deal there is not much on the shoreline to define a national identity that might be seen as being intrinsically Anglo-Saxon. Daniel Defoe got it about right when he summed up the sea-salted melting-pot of races out of which the 'English' climbed:

From this amphibious ill-born mob began
That vain, ill-natured thing, an Englishman.

The Englishman's 'Saxon Shore' at Deal unfurls along swaths of shingle. Beached fishing boats ride high on the banks, as if on a stony sea. These are small, sturdy vessels, with proprietorial names such as *Roseann Amy, Solo Sun, Aurora*. They are launched from the beach by means of portable metal rollers and, on their return, are drawn up on cables attached to winches. Deal boats catch cod, whiting and flatfish, and on the shallow waters of the Goodwin Sands their nets snag on the wreckage of 4,000 years of maritime history.

There is no evidence of a Roman past at Deal now. But the town is a remarkable example of a port that prospered, without the advantage of a conventional harbour. Offshore is the deep anchorage called The Downs that lies between Deal and the Goodwin Sands, and it is this anchorage that was the making of Deal. The Goodwins are fenced in by buoys and light vessels; they are breached only by the navigable channels of the Kellet Gut, the Gull Stream and the Ramsgate Channel. This is a sea place to make you shudder. The Goodwins were known always as the great 'ship swallower', and there is no telling how many thousands of vessels have broken their backs on these shifting sands and now lie in the belly of the beast. In one monstrous storm in 1703, several thousand seamen were drowned when over 150 ships tore free of their moorings. Many of the ships were wrecked. In the streaming daylight, over 200 survivors crouched on the temporarily exposed sandbanks. They screamed for help, and they howled at the rising tide. But the good people of Deal had to be bribed with silver before they suspended their looting of the wrecked vessels to mount a rescue. The balance to such callousness has been the outstanding voluntary service of local lifeboats in the years since.

In spite of occasional storms, The Downs anchorage turned Deal into a naval supply town. Boats carried supplies and materials to the ships by night and day. The Naval Yard covered 5 acres/2 hectares and was in service until 1864. Today, all that remains is the yard's famous Time Ball Tower, used as a semaphore and signal station until the nineteenth century.

Deal's older buildings have retained some richness of style, especially in the area of Middle Street, and in the alleyways that run between High Street, Middle Street and the shore road. The absence of a harbour robs the town of a focus, but the linear, tightly packed nature of Deal's seventeenth- and eighteenth-century buildings lends cohesion to the townscape. There is a European texture; Dutch gables and French-style cobbles reflect Deal's proximity to the great sea road that linked it to Europe, however turbulently.

Deal Castle was built in the late 1530s. It was part of the chain of maritime defences that a nervous Henry VIII built from Hull to Milford Haven in response to post-Reformation fears of a Franco-Spanish invasion. Other castles were built at Sandown to the north and at Walmer to the south. All three were linked by earth embankments, and they were known as the Three Castles of the Downs. Deal Castle is a massive structure, but it is low to the ground, sunk within an outer moat. It has a central tower, clasped within six small bastions, the whole lying within six outer bastions; a stone flower. The rooms of the inner core are designed as segments of a circle.

The Cinque Ports

From Deal it is a long, rhythmic stroll towards the white cliffs of Dover. The vast shingle beach sweeps away to the south, where once Tudor defences rose like a dyke, and where wreaths of barbed wire and anti-tank devices guarded against more recent threats of invasion. Beyond the outskirts of Deal, the way leads past lines of modest Victorian houses that have little turrets and cupolas, and red tiling above white wooden balconies. They give way eventually to modern mock-Georgian.

A paved walkway runs parallel to the public road and leads, in about 1 mile/1.6 kms, to Walmer Castle. Walmer has the typical Tudor design of central keep with four round bastions. The brute strength of its massive walls is still evident beneath mellow ivy. On the east bastion, hefty 32-pound/14.5 kg cannon point menacingly to seaward. But today, Walmer Castle is more of a luxury residence than an artillery fortress, being the home of the Lord Warden of the Cinque

Ports, a titular honour awarded for long service to the British Crown, but dating from the days of that other great defensive institution, the Confederation of Cinque Ports.

The original Cinque Ports – of Sandwich, Dover, Hythe, Romney and Hastings – were appointed in 1050 by Edward the Confessor as defenders of the Saxon Shore. The towns were responsible for providing ships and men, on a free and flexible basis, for fifteen days a year. In return the Cinque Ports, and their officials, the Portsmen, received privileges, many of which exempted them from various taxes, and which allowed them virtual self-government. By Norman times the Confederation was strengthened by the addition of Rye and Winchelsea as 'Antient Towns'. Other ports joined the Confederation as 'Limbs' of the Cinque Ports, and these included Deal as a Limb of Sandwich. The privileges of the Cinque Ports led to a degree of autonomy that eventually alarmed the Crown; and in the early thirteenth century a Lord Warden of the Cinque Ports was appointed to oversee the activities of the Portsmen.

The thirteenth century was the heyday of the Cinque Ports, when the Portsmen gave sterling service to the Crown while carrying on their own lucrative businesses of smuggling and privateering. The last full action by Cinque Port ships was in 1588, when they sailed as part of the English fleet that routed the Spanish Armada. But the random movement of sand and shingle in the Channel brought an ignominious end to many of the Cinque Ports, as harbours became silted and blocked. Today the old 'ports' of Romney and Winchelsea are 2 miles/3.2 kms from the sea, and Hythe, Hastings and Sandwich have lost their navigable harbours.

Walmer was made the official residence of the Lords Warden of the Cinque Ports in 1708. The present Lord Warden is the Queen Mother. Other Lords Warden have included William Pitt the Younger, who did much to create the beautiful gardens at Walmer; the Duke of Wellington; Winston Churchill; and, less grandly, the bookshop magnate, W. H. Smith, who set up a trust to preserve the historic furnishings of the castle. Walmer is decorated exquisitely. Even the serene blue-green paint applied to the corridor and stairwell in the late nineteenth century has been restored.

It is an easy stroll from Walmer Castle to Kingsdown Beach, where there is a seashore pub, the Zetland Arms. Latterly, the way is awash with shingle where the beach has shifted inland on high tides. Kingsdown was a notorious smuggling base during the eighteenth and nineteenth centuries and its free traders, together with those of Deal, accounted for vast quantities of smuggled silk, satin, scent, spices, fine teas, gin and brandy: enough to make your mouth water. Lifeboats were stationed at Kingsdown from 1866 to 1927, the same skilled seamanship of the old smugglers being directed to saving lives.

The Great White Cliffs

A broad expanse of shingle beach runs south from Kingsdown towards the first of the great white cliffs at Old Parker's Cap. The cliff here rises spectacularly from the flatness of the beach in a way that makes your head spin. Disappointingly, the top of the cliff cannot be reached directly from the beach. Instead, you have to wade along a shingle track to a junction with the coast road, then walk south along Undercliffe Road. The view of sea and cliffs is suddenly blocked by trees, but before the road ends, the view to seaward opens up once more, though now it is a bleak prospect of waste ground and sullen sea. Iron coffer dams have been erected along the shoreline as a storm defence, but they have been torn jaggedly by the pummelling of the waves, proof that storms on these Channel shores can be as savage as on the Atlantic coast, though they may not send in such massive swells. This stretch of beach is known, dismally, as The Swamp. In stormy weather, the sea is iodine-stained, murky and bleak; the shingle shifts and rattles gratingly against the twisted metal of the dams.

At the end of Undercliffe Road a flight of stone steps climbs amidst scrub and muddy clay to the cliff top. Ahead lies a narrow green corridor of rough ground pinned between thin air and the edge of a golf course. England and its suburban culture press close to the cliff edge yet again. A grassy path leads to the south and to the grim cenotaph of the Dover Patrol Memorial, which commemorates the men of the Royal Navy and the Merchant Navy who died while serving on vessels in the Dover Straits during the world wars. There are similar memorials at Cap Blanc Nez on the French coast and at New York Harbour.

Beyond the memorial, the coast path runs between dense thickets of hawthorn and sloes. The character of a cliff-top path is lost for a time, until, with splendid drama, the great bull-necked cliff of Ness Point bursts into view ahead, above St Margaret's Bay. The way drops quickly now; the narrow path is worn to an awkward angle, which makes it as glassy as ice in wet weather. Soon the path plunges into dark woods, then winds down broad steps beneath a shroud of gloomy trees, to emerge on the beach at St Margaret's Bay. The shingle here is held in place by a series of groynes that protrude from the seaward wall of the car park. This, too, was a notorious smugglers' beach at one time. Just inland is the Coastguard Inn, signalling by name perhaps the ultimate triumph of the Revenue over the runners. At the village of St Margaret's at Cliffe, on the high ground above the bay, is the splendid twelfth-century Church of St Margaret, a building that, though it was restored in the last century, retains a Norman integrity, not least in its decorative motifs and in its great scale.

The high edge of the great cliff is reached from St Margaret's Bay by a detour inland. A few yards up the steep road that climbs from the bay, a broad opening leads left to Beach Road and to the delightful Pines Garden, where there are 6 acres/2.4 hectares of trees, shrubs and flowers, and an ornamental lake. At the heart of the garden stands a statue of Winston Churchill, who led the last of the great defences of the Saxon Shore against the threat of military invasion. On the east side of Beach Road is the Bay Museum.

There is a crossing of rough tracks at the end of Beach Road, and from here a steep path leads uphill through scrubby ground. There is a fine view of Coney Burrow Point to the north, and of the Dover Patrol Memorial. Inland, the wooded slopes of Bay Hill are dotted with fine houses that look like Swiss châteaux. Ahead, the path leads south along the cliff edge until it reaches a wall of low trees and an ominous sign that warns of the sudden edge of the cliff to the left, where the deep grass ends in thin air. Above the swaying trees ahead, the top of an old windmill protrudes. A broad track leads past the inland side of the mill, and then between hawthorns and sycamores to the South Foreland lighthouse.

A narrow, paved pathway leads from the lighthouse to the sweeping expanse of the South Foreland cliffs. The South Foreland is a mere curve in the cliff profile, where the line of the coast turns to the south-west. But here the white cliffs are at their most awesome. On windy days there is an eerie sense of precariousness. The glossy grass slides magnetically towards the uncertain edge and into booming space. Paths make frequent sidesteps inland, to reassuring hollows where the grass is speckled with the bright yellow and orange of kidney vetch and bird's-foot trefoil, and the rose-pink of sainfoin. Visible in the distance are the arms of Dover Harbour, between which cross-Channel ferries glide in and out. The ferries are neither elegant nor romantic, but they still excite, with their irresistible promise of arrival and departure.

The cliff path leads round the steep funnel of Bantam Hole, then on to the deeper Langdon Hole. In places side-paths lead, alarmingly, to the very edge of the cliff, and there end. The ground is worn to a small, nervous circle, where people have stood as near as they dare, oblivious perhaps of the steady annual erosion of the cliff edge. It is this erosion that preserves the pristine whiteness of England's white cliffs; a curious irony, since the cliffs are such a metaphor for the nation's resistance to erosion of its sovereignty. But, for the determined Anglophile, Europe is at least being physically distanced from the white cliffs, bit by bit.

The cliff faces are patched with swaths of grass and sea beet, and are speckled with flint and chert. They have been scaled by some of the country's most accomplished rock climbers, but here using ice-climbing equipment: crampons, ice axes, and ice screws. A tradition of such eccentricity leads back to the infamous satanist Aleister Crowley, who climbed on the chalk cliffs in the 1930s. At Langdon Hole, the edge of the flanking cliff is like a slim, ghostly pillar rising elegantly from the beach. The climb that tackles its central prow is known, fittingly, as the Great White Fright.

Less outrageously, the cliff path curves securely round the rim of Langdon Hole. Another path drops down to the bottom of the hollow, where a glittering pile of flints lies amidst a copse of hawthorns and sloe trees. The climb back to the cliff top is breathlessly steep, but then the path leads on easily towards Dover. It passes below the slowly revolving radar scanner of the coastguard station at the edge of Fox Hill Down and ends at the National Trust car park and viewpoint, from where the great prow of Shakespeare Cliff can be seen to the west. Beyond the car park there is a swift descent into the whirling turmoil of Dover's seafront.

Dover Castle

Above it all, Dover Castle stands loftily on Castle Hill. The site contains a remarkable series of buildings and fortifications, which began with a probable Neolithic encampment that was later turned into an Iron Age fort. The great henge of this fort survives. The Romans built a *pharos*, or lighthouse, here, which, with another on Dover's Western Heights, acted as a navigation aid for the great fleet of *Classis Brittanica* that was based at Dover. During the fifteenth century the lighthouse's top section was rebuilt. The ruin of the *pharos*, its rough walls wonderfully eroded, stands cheek by jowl with the Saxon church of St Mary-in-Castro.

Dover Castle is monumental. The medieval castle – 'the key of England' said Matthew Paris in the thirteenth century – dates from at least 1066, though it may have been a pre-Conquest fortified Saxon *burh*. Dover is also recorded as having a Roman fort that defended the Saxon Shore. Whatever form of castle existed in 1066, it was adapted by William the Conqueror, and was added to and amended at various times from the reign of Henry II onwards. In the mid-eighteenth century a major re-styling of the castle began. It has left a less organic, less elegant complex than the medieval original, and our own age has added to that barrack-like element.

The town of Dover, caught between castle and container port, has probably always had difficulty in jostling for attention. Its position as the 'key of England' has made Dover a target as much as a town. It was badly damaged by shelling during the Second World War and there has been modern reconstruction of a kind that never quite re-creates the heart of an old community. Development continues at Dover's busy seafront and dock area, through which millions of travellers pass each year. But the magnificent white cliffs to either side of the town, and the powerful presence of the castle, give Dover a strong character. Its heritage is England's oldest, in spite of those fleeting elements of arrival and departure across the Saxon Shore.

The Saxon Shore
Information

Distance 9 miles/14.4 kms

Maps OS Landranger 179 (Canterbury & East Kent)

Nature of walk A generally undemanding coastal walk between Deal and Dover, along a shingle foreshore, then along the edge of high chalk cliffs. Easy going, but with some steep climbs along the latter part of the walk. *The cliff edge should not be approached too closely. Care is advised where the path runs close to the cliff edge.*

Accommodation Hotels, guest houses and B&Bs at Deal, Kingsdown and Dover. Camp sites north of Deal.

Transport Rail connections from London to Deal and Dover. Rail connection between Deal and Dover.

Further information Tourist Information Centre, Dover, tel. (01304) 205108.

Start Deal Pier

1 Walk south along Victoria Parade, passing lines of fishing boats drawn up on the shingle beach. Pass the Time Ball Tower and Deal Castle (reached by turning right down Deal Castle Road). On the main walk continue for about 1 mile/1.6 kms, then turn right, then left, and continue along the paved way of Wellington Parade until abreast of Walmer Castle. Continue along Wellington Parade, which becomes a gravel drive between the houses and beach, to reach the Zetland Arms at Kingsdown. (2¼ miles/3.6 kms)

2 From the car-parking area in front of the Zetland Arms, turn right and inland, along a shingle drive in front of a terrace of houses. At a junction (Rising Sun pub just to the right), turn left along Undercliffe Road. Beyond the junction, where Oldstairs Road turns sharply right and uphill, go right up some stone steps to reach the cliff top alongside a golf club. Continue along a grassy path close to the edge of the cliffs at Old Parker's Cap, and then past Hope Point to reach the Dover Patrol Memorial at OS 373453. (2¼ miles/3.6 kms)

3 Keep to seaward of the old coastguard lookout and follow a path alongside hawthorns and sloe trees. At a junction by a signpost, keep left, then follow a winding path downhill. *In wet conditions, the path can be slippery here.* Go through a tunnel of bushes and trees. At a junction, go left down a long flight of winding steps to reach the shingle beach at St Margaret's Bay. (½ mile/0.8 kms)

4 Walk through the car park, then follow the road uphill to where it bends to the right. Turn left along a rough track, then after a few yards bear left along Beach Road to pass the Pines Garden and the Bay Museum. Continue along a rough lane, with private houses on the left. At a crossing of tracks, bear up left by a signpost and follow a path that winds uphill. At the top of the slope, go straight across a broad track, then follow the grassy track opposite for a few yards to reach a T-junction with another grassy track. Go right along this track for ¼ mile/0.4 kms, to a point, just before a line of trees, where there is a sign warning of 'Dangerous Cliffs'. Turn right (*without question*), to reach a T-junction with a broad gravel track by a house. Turn left along the track, passing the windmill on the left. At a junction with a metalled road, turn left, then left again past the South Foreland lighthouse complex. Go through a gate onto a narrow paved path, signposted 'Langdon Cliff and Dover'. (1 mile/1.6 kms)

5 Turn right at the cliff path and follow it for about 1 mile/1.6 kms, passing Bantam Hole, to reach Langdon Hole. Follow the path round the rim of Langdon Hole, then continue towards the coastguard lookout ahead. Follow a good track past a signpost to reach a stile, then continue through hawthorns, to reach a flight of steps with a handrail. From the top of the steps, continue to a wooden kissing-gate below a big radar scanner. Continue to the National Trust parking area at Fox Hill Down, then follow the surfaced road to a junction with a minor road at a steep bend. Keep to the path along the verge for a few yards, then bear off left by three posts. Follow the path

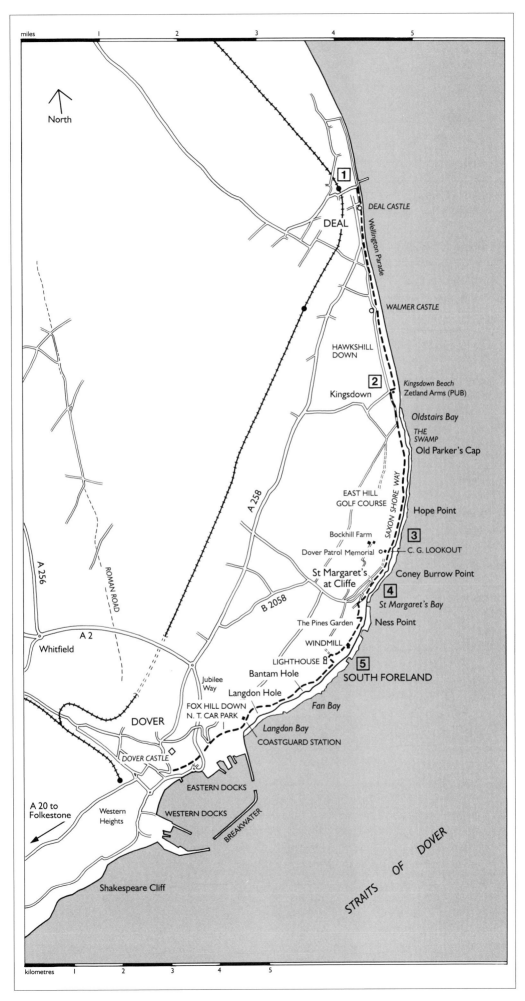

miles

North

DEAL

1

DEAL CASTLE

Wellington Parade

WALMER CASTLE

HAWKSHILL
DOWN

2

Kingsdown

Kingsdown Beach
Zetland Arms (PUB)

Oldstairs Bay

THE
SWAMP

Old Parker's Cap

EAST HILL
GOLF COURSE

SAXON SHORE WAY

Hope Point

A 258

Bockhill Farm

Dover Patrol Memorial

3

C. G. LOOKOUT

St Margaret's
at Cliffe

Coney Burrow Point

A 256

ROMAN ROAD

B 2058

4

St Margaret's Bay

The Pines Garden

Ness Point

A 2

Whitfield

WINDMILL

LIGHTHOUSE

5

Jubilee
Way

Bantam Hole

SOUTH FORELAND

Langdon Hole

FOX HILL DOWN
N. T. CAR PARK

Fan Bay

DOVER

Langdon Bay

COASTGUARD STATION

DOVER CASTLE

A 20 to
Folkestone

Western
Heights

EASTERN DOCKS

WESTERN DOCKS

BREAKWATER

Shakespeare Cliff

STRAITS OF DOVER

kilometres

downhill, then down some steps and below the underpass of Jubilee Way. Join Atholl Terrace and continue to East Cliff. Follow the signs to the seafront. (3 miles/4.8 kms)

CIRCULAR WALK
3½ miles/5.6 kms

Start St Margaret's Bay car park

1 Follow direction **4** on the main walk as far as the South Foreland lighthouse.

2 Go inland from the lighthouse along a track. After about 300 yards/274 metres reach a junction. The left-hand branch leads to Wanstone Farm. Turn right and keep straight ahead to reach Lighthouse Road. At a junction with the main road to St Margaret's Bay, cross diagonally right, then after a short distance turn left along Granville Road for about ¾ mile/1.2 kms to reach the Dover Patrol Memorial at OS 373453.

3 Follow direction **3** on the main walk to return to St Margaret's Bay.

The Giant's Road

Dorset

Cerne Abbas to Abbotsbury 16 miles/25.7 kms

'In this landscape, with the chalk staring through the grass in a way red earth could never do, something like a man or a beast seems to be lurking in every field and on every hillside ready to jump out.'

Patricia Beer, *Wessex*

Several ancient sites are visited on this long walk from Cerne Abbas to the sea at Abbotsbury. They include the famous Cerne Abbas Giant and the Iron Age hill fort of Maiden Castle. The route follows riverside paths and field tracks through peaceful countryside.

The Cerne Abbas Giant is a ludicrous rather than lewd figure. He neither leaps, nor does he lurk. The giant is a caricature, rigid with discomfort, and a little forlorn in his rampant nakedness. Faced with such absurd masculinity, Shelley's poem *Ozymandias* springs usefully to mind: 'Look on my works, ye mighty, and despair. . .' We do, indeed.

Dorset has numerous archaeological features of greater antiquity and power than the Cerne Abbas Giant, though few command such prurient interest. It is the startling details that make the giant so outstandingly noticeable. He lies, in outline, on the west-facing slope of Giant Hill above Cerne Abbas village. The outline is formed by a continuous chalk-filled trench of about 2 feet/0.6 metres in width. The figure is 180 feet/55 metres high; it brandishes a club 120 feet/37 metres long. Depicted also are nipples, ribs, the monumental phallus of 22 feet/7 metres, and facial features of eyebrows, eyes and vestigial mouth. At one time the giant had a nose, and nose and eyes were said to represent the outline of the phallus downcast. From the air, the ghostly outline of a short cloak has been spotted hanging from the giant's outflung arm. Only the raucous would suggest that he has just whipped it aside with a flourish.

Today, the Cerne Abbas Giant is in the care of the National Trust. Grooming of the figure is now done commercially, but local people once gave the giant an occasional short-back-and-sides. Every seven years or so they trimmed back the outline on the taut skin of the hill, and grubbed out weeds from the trenches. They carried chalk dust up those plump slopes and sprinkled it on the scoured earth. They tended the great phallus with a matter-of-fact briskness. Down-to-earth indeed; but there must surely have been a giggle here and there, an earthy epithet to suit the earthiness of the occasion. Gilding, rather than gelding, the giant during times of moral rectitude must have been deliciously reassuring to those who clung to country ways and had a healthy, though hidden, contempt for piety and prudishness.

There is a viewing enclosure alongside the busy main road below Giant's Hill: the only example of publicly facilitated voyeurism in Britain. But the angle of view disappoints. Car-bound visitors peer through their windscreens at the blurred and distorted outline. The giant is best seen from the hills to the west; a slight tilting of the landscape lends some fluidity to the awkward posture and makes him look much more in control of himself.

Pagan Gods

There are no written references to the Cerne Abbas Giant before the eighteenth century, but some authorities believe that he derives from images of pagan gods of the ancient Britons, or from the 'priapic' cult of the Roman god Hercules. Records show that St Augustine founded Cerne Abbey after 'breaking in pieces Heil, the idol of the heathen English Saxons'. Augustine, reformed roué that he was, may then have gone on to eradicate all representations of a priapic god, especially if one existed in such brazen form as that of a bare-faced giant carved on a hillside. Later generations of inhabitants, clinging to folk-memory, may then have reinstated the Cerne Abbas giant in the form that we see today.

It is all speculative, of course. Sceptics say that the Cerne Abbas Giant originated in the eighteenth century, at a time when there was an antiquarian fashion for marking out chalk horses and giant human figures across the malleable downlands of southern England. The first written record of Cerne Abbas's Giant dates from 1754, when Dr Richard Pococke recorded in his *Travels Through England* that he had seen at Cerne Abbas 'a figure cut in lines'. Pococke speculated that the figure was ancient, and added: 'It seems to be Hercules, or Strength and Fidelity, but it is with such indecent circumstances as to make one conclude it was also a Priapus.' It is from Pococke that we learn that the outline of the giant was scoured and re-cut by local people every few years. The job was not always precisely done. The giant is said to have sported a navel at one time, but the navel seems to have been absorbed by extension of the phallus. In 1764 the antiquarian, William Stukeley, recorded details of the giant, and records prove that his 'Mightiness', as the giant was known locally, was manicured until well into the twentieth century.

As a fertility symbol the Cerne Abbas Giant is strikingly obvious, though local larkiness may have exaggerated the most fertile proportions. The giant is associated with the maypole dancing that once took place inside the small earthwork known as The Trendle that stands on the brow of the slope above the giant's head. Consummation of barren marriages on the tip of the phallus was certain to produce children, according to local lore. Enthusiasm for fertility rites amongst the young people of the area must have been fervid. The giant roused prurience and prudishness in equal measure. An eighteenth-century illustration of the Abbot's Hall at Cerne shows the giant 'lurking' in the background, crestfallen and ridiculous, his loins draped with a makeshift nappy. At times the outline of the phallus was left untrimmed. Ironically, the entire figure was covered with cut bracken and grass during the Second World War so that German aircraft could not use it as a landmark.

Fastidiousness

In Cerne Abbas there seems to be a healthy reluctance to make too much of the giant. This may reflect a mix of diffidence and fastidiousness. Refreshingly, there are no 'themed' outlets, and no overt exploitation of his 'Mightiness'. The village makes clear that the giant is the appendage, and not vice versa, although tourism generated by the giant has helped Cerne's economic survival.

The village developed during the tenth century, on the skirts of its Benedictine abbey. It thrived until the Dissolution of 1539, after which neglect by absentee landlords caused economic decline. There was a recovery during the nineteenth century, when rural industries flourished and when Cerne was a main coaching stop.

Good buildings add to Cerne's appeal. They include a handsome row of timber-fronted Tudor town houses in Abbey Street; the best is The Pitchmarket, once the home of the aunt and uncle of the American president, George Washington. Adjoining this is The Old House, which has an eccentric and charming shell porch, an eighteenth-century indulgence. Opposite The Pitchmarket row, and cramping its Tudor style a little, is the Church of St Mary. A big, three-staged tower and an embattled south porch add to the severity. The church is the ecclesiastical focus of Cerne today; there is not much left of the ninth-century abbey, remnants of which stand at the top of Abbey Street. One outstanding survival is the porch to the Abbot's Hall, made doubly attractive by its well-preserved medieval oriel window, complete with leaded lights and decorative shields.

The rest of old Cerne is mainly vernacular buildings in russety stone and brick, and dark flint. There are some fine old pubs in the village, including the sixteenth-century Royal Oak on the corner of Abbey Street and Long Street; as good a starting point as any for a long walk to the sea.

The Cerne Valley

The Cerne Valley runs due south from Cerne Abbas. It is a mere fold in the Dorset hills, down which the River Cerne glides unfussily between green banks. Smooth pastures rise to a skyline, which on cool, misty days seems to merge with the blurred landscape. From Cerne Abbas, a good path leads down the east bank of the river. It is hedged in at first by blackthorns and by old coppiced beeches, then breaks free into open fields. After rain, the Dorset clay sucks at your feet; on the approach to farms, cattle have churned the clay into a satisfying potter's mix, which looks ready for the wheel.

Walking is undemanding here, in spite of the occasional muddiness. In spring the cheerful yellows of primrose and celandine light up the edges of the path; in the fields, the young grass is like green velvet. This is deepest Dorset, utterly pastoral and restrained; it should not excite devotees of rough country, yet the gentleness of it all is persuasive. You could walk for ever through such passive countryside.

The way leads through Pound Farm and then past reed-fringed ponds, whose banks are out of bounds to walkers. The right of way leads across the centre of a tree-studded field, and then into tangled woodland, where thickets of hart's-tongue fern line the track. Beyond is the little hamlet of Nether Cerne and the Church of All Saints, a mix of thirteenth- and fifteenth-century features, although its roofs and some of its stonework are Victorian restorations. Nether Cerne was a Benedictine chapelry of Cerne Abbey, until the Dissolution.

All Saints has been in the care of the Redundant Churches Fund since 1973, when a decline in its congregation led to its merging with the parish of Cerne Abbas. The church stands close to the River Cerne, where plump trout hover amidst the Ophelian water weed. A broad lawn of close-cropped grass lies between the church and the river, and gives the tower especially a strong emphasis. Alongside All Saints is the small manor house of Nether Cerne, a late seventeenth-century building of local stone and flint. It is privately owned, and visitors to the church are asked to respect this privacy.

To Bradford Peverell

Beyond Nether Cerne field tracks lead south for just under 1 mile/1.6 kms to a place where the little village of Godmanstone can be reached across the bubbling race of an old millstream. There is an endearing little pub here called the Smith's Arms; it has a thatched roof and is low-ceilinged, in keeping with the cramped style of the Cerne Valley and its steeply pitched fields. At Godmanstone the path climbs away from the river bank across the open field slope, then leads downhill to the attractive buildings of Forston Farm.

At Forston the main road is crossed, and a steep path is followed uphill, before it turns south to follow field walls and fences along the rambling crest of Charminster Down. From the high ground, a roller-coaster track spills down to the valley of the River Frome, where the quiet village of Bradford Peverell lies beyond river, railway and the busy main road. A Roman road once ran alongside the Frome. It linked Durnovaria, the Roman Dorchester, with Lindinis, modern Ilchester. The Romans built an aqueduct along the southern slopes of the valley; it can still be detected as a slight terrace here and there. The aqueduct carried millions of gallons of water from a point on the river above Bradford Peverell to Dorchester, where it supplied public baths, villas, drinking fountains and sewers.

Beyond Bradford Peverell's Church of St Mary, a Victorian building with a fine broached spire, a track leads past houses and then past a graveyard of old vehicles and machinery. Beyond this it climbs steeply over Penn Hill, then descends through fields that are golden with corn stubble in late summer. Ahead, beyond a patchwork of fields and lanes, lies the great Iron Age hill fort of Maiden Castle. The long, elegant lines of the fort's northern ramparts emerge slowly from the summer haze; there is a blurred ghostly impression of some vast desert fortress.

Maiden Castle

Maiden Castle was southern England's most ambitious Iron Age hill fort. The multivallate defences enclose a 'plateau' of 47 acres/19 hectares. The site lies on a northern rampart of the Dorset Downs and commands the broad river valley of the Frome. A Neolithic causewayed camp occupied the eastern end of the hill from about 3000 BC. Traces of a Neolithic axe industry have been found close by. Late in the Neolithic period a huge barrow mound was erected; it was over ⅓ mile/0.5 kms long. Its eastern end was excavated in the 1930s and the crouched skeletons of two young children and the skeleton of an adult male were found. The latter seemed to have been dismembered and trepanned, but whether or not this was done for sacrificial purposes is speculative.

Maiden Castle was unoccupied after 1500 BC. This coincided with the emergence of a Bronze Age culture that had less need of centralized communities. By 300 BC, however, the hill top was again occupied by more territorial and more defensive Iron Age people, who extended and strengthened the ramparts. There may have been scores of buildings within the defences, although the remnants of only a dozen round houses have been found. During the last century BC the defences were extended again, possibly in response to the increasing use of the sling as a war weapon. Bank and ditch reduced the range of attackers' slingshot fire and increased that of defenders. The people of Maiden Castle stockpiled thousands of rounded pebbles gathered from the great shingle bank of Chesil Beach. Yet, in AD 44, slingshot did not save Maiden Castle from the relentless war machine of the Roman Second Legion Augusta, under Vespasian.

The Romans battered at the defences of Maiden Castle with ballista, the powerful arrow-bolts that had overcome the defendants of the mighty hill fort at Badbury to the north-east. Then the soldiers edged forward through the eastern maze of embankments, sheltering from a rain of slingshot beneath overlapping shields. They set fire to wooden outbuildings and tinder. The pungent smoke rolled across the final rampart and, through cloud and flame, Rome poured into the heart of the hill top. Men, women and children were slaughtered mercilessly.

Today, upon the vast, green plateau of Maiden Castle, it is easy to imagine the panicked rout; the people suddenly overcome, their great fortification now a trap. Some may have spilled over the flanking rim of the hill and found a way out through the bank and ditches to the south and west, though the western entrance was probably blocked by Vespasian's hard-faced soldiers. Excavation of the ditches has uncovered mass burials of men, women and children. Grave offerings of food vessels and domestic artefacts were hurriedly buried with them, probably by traumatized survivors. Lodged in the backbone of one skeleton was an iron arrowhead; a Roman farewell.

The soldiers burned and razed the round houses of Maiden Castle; they demolished the wooden revetments that had strengthened the ramparts; then they marched on to the west. People continued to live upon the great hill, but soon after the conquest the Romans built a new Romano-British town at Durnovaria on the banks of the nearby Frome, and within sight of Maiden Castle. Here they showed the demoralized Britons the advantages of even the trappings of civic life. The great hill fort was abandoned for ever. Yet, on the summit of Maiden Castle, lie the meagre remains of a late Romano-British temple of the fourth century AD, indicating perhaps that the site continued to hold a spiritual significance for many. It was a lingering significance. A Saxon burial ground of the seventh century has been found on the great empty hill top, where today visitors wander freely, and always with room to spare.

Tamed Landscape

To the south of Maiden Castle, farm tracks thread a way through a rather bland landscape, then on to the ridgeway of Bronkham Hill, which is visible from north and south. Long before the Romans, one of the great linear cemeteries of the Bronze Age dominated this high place. The Bronze Age culture was based on settled farming and territorialism, and a chain of skyline burial mounds proclaimed to newcomers that the surrounding countryside was the land of 'ancestors', an inherited land.

Today, the ground to either side of the ridgeway has been rendered featureless by centuries of ploughing. But the ancient tumuli survive, and on the western end of the ridgeway, wafer-thin slabs of stone protrude from hedge banks, possible remnants of more durable artefacts. The skyline of Bronkham Hill is now criss-crossed with power lines strung between huge pylons, the brutal artefacts of our twentieth-century inheritance. Beyond the sizzling wires, a line of tumuli signpost's the way to Black Down and the stony brutalism of the Hardy Monument.

The Dorset Hardy who is immortalized by the great stone monolith on Black Down is not the famous writer, but Nelson's flag-captain at Trafalgar. This was the Thomas Masterman Hardy immortalized uneasily by the famous 'Kiss me, Hardy' of Nelson's dying breath.

Fastidious commentators still claim that Nelson murmured 'Kismet', and that rough old Masterman Hardy was unlikely to kiss anyone, least of all in the heat of battle. Lord Hardy was born at Portesham, the village that lies just south of Black Down.

From the Hardy Monument, the way leads down through alien pine trees, then climbs over the shoulder of Portesham Hill and past the remains of the Hell Stone, a chamber tomb of the Neolithic period. Its rocky ribs were rearranged by Victorian enthusiasts, but the cluster of stones is still impressive. Other local antiquities have struggled to survive. West of the Hell Stone, on Hampton Down, the path leads past the forlorn remnants of a stone circle. It is a cramped little feature that may be part of a demolished tumulus, rather than a circle. Rank grass and scrub have overpowered the scant remains.

Ahead lies a deep combe, its slopes ribbed with cattle tracks. The land to the south falls away steeply now. From the western edge of the combe, the way leads onto White Hill and across a vast field that, in its openness, has an almost moorland quality about it. From the field's southern edge, the ground swoops down across the area known as Abbotsbury Plains, once in the ownership of Abbotsbury Abbey and still a splendid open space today. The descent is helter-skelter, exhilarating and random, until you are brought up short at the foot of the Plains, from where a narrow lane leads down into Abbotsbury itself.

The village has been rather overpowered by traffic. A main road wriggles between the houses of Red Lane, and through sharp bends that were meant for the stately progress of horse and wagon. Abbotsbury's Benedictine abbey was wrecked at the Dissolution of the monasteries. Most of the abbey's buildings were pillaged for stone, but the walls of the cavernous tithe barn survived. Now the huge building contains a museum of rural life. The Church of St Nicholas also survived the Dissolution. Most churches did so – they were an insurance for the godly landowners who annexed monastic property, with dutiful relish.

On the shoreline below Abbotsbury is the medieval Swannery, once a food store for the monastery. Today, nearly 1,000 mute swans spend the winter here. Half this number stay to breed during the summer. And on St Catherine's Hill above Abbotsbury stands the fourteenth-century St Catherine's Chapel, another survivor of Henry VIII's wreckers. It is a curious building, tall and narrow, with a solid stone roof and walls corseted by sturdy buttresses. The interior roof is tunnel-vaulted. The building is like a small castle rather than a chapel. From its hill top, St Catherine's commands one of the finest views on England's south coast. It is a striking landmark that draws the eye from every quarter, though it may not draw as many sidelong glances as the Cerne Abbas Giant.

The Giant's Road
Information

Distance 16 miles/25.7kms

Maps OS Landranger 194 (Dorchester, Weymouth & Surrounding Area)

Nature of walk There are some long uphill climbs, but there are long descents to compensate. Sections of the route, especially in farming country, can become very muddy during wet weather. The upland sections are exposed and may be very cold and windy in late autumn and winter. Weatherproof clothing and strong footwear are essential.

Accommodation Hotel, guest house and B&Bs in Cerne Abbas and Abbotsbury. B&Bs at Martinstown. Camp sites to the west of Weymouth.

Transport Train connections from main centres to Dorchester. Bus services between Dorchester and Cerne Abbas, and between Abbotsbury and Dorchester, via Weymouth. Further information from Dorchester TIC.

Further information Tourist Information Centre, Dorchester, tel. (01305) 267992.

Start Car park and picnic site at Kettle Bridge on the northern outskirts of Cerne Abbas, just below Giant Hill, OS 664015

1 Turn left out of the car park and then, at the bridge, go right alongside the river. After 200 yards/183 metres, at a junction, go left to reach Abbey Street. Turn right to reach Long Street by the Royal Oak. Turn left along Long Street for about 100 yards/91 metres, then cross over and go down an alleyway to reach Back Street. Turn right and then, in another 100 yards/91 metres, turn left to reach a track by Cheshurst Lane. Go through a gate, then continue down the left edge of a field to reach a line of trees. Turn right and follow the edge of the trees, then turn left over a stile. (½ mile/0.8 kms)

2 Follow a tree-shaded path along the base of Black Hill and reach a junction after ¼ mile/ 0.4 kms. Go down to the right beneath hawthorns, then go over a stile and continue across open fields to reach Pound Farm. Keep ahead, through the farm, often muddy underfoot, then keep straight ahead across a field past some ash trees. *Keep well away from the ponds on the right. The banks of the ponds are on private property.* Reach the corner of a wood, then follow the right edge of the wood to reach a gate. Go through the gateway and follow a track to another gate into a farm lane at Nether Cerne. Follow the lane opposite to reach All Saints Church. Continue south from the church along the lower edge of sloping fields. (At OS 667974 a stile on the right leads to Godmanstone, where there is a pub. (2 miles/3.2 kms)

3 On the main walk, keep straight ahead alongside the field edge to cross a stile into another field. Bear diagonally left and uphill on the side of Cowdon Hill, passing below a clump of trees. Reach a line of hawthorns, just west of Forston Barn, then follow these down right to the far corner of the field. Bear down right past two sycamores to reach a field gate. Continue to Forston Farm. Follow the drive in front of the house to reach the A352. (1 mile/1.6 kms)

4 Cross the A352, with care, then go through the gate opposite. Continue uphill through fields. Where the hedge in the third field turns sharply to the left, go left and head towards a tall tree, then continue alongside the field edge. Pass above Brooklands Farm, then go through a gate. Bear right across the next field to a gate, then continue over a rise and past old field barns. Continue downhill on a wide track to reach the busy A37 at Ash Hill. (1¾ miles/2.8 kms)

5 Cross the A37, with great care, then turn left along a footpath/cycle track. After a short distance, turn right down the road to reach Bradford Peverell. Go right at a T-junction, then immediately left. Pass the church and keep straight ahead past houses and onto a track, signposted New Barn Field Centre. Pass a scrapyard, keep left at a fork, then follow the curving track uphill. In a few yards turn right up a permissive path. Go steeply uphill, to where the track levels off. Soon cross another track, then

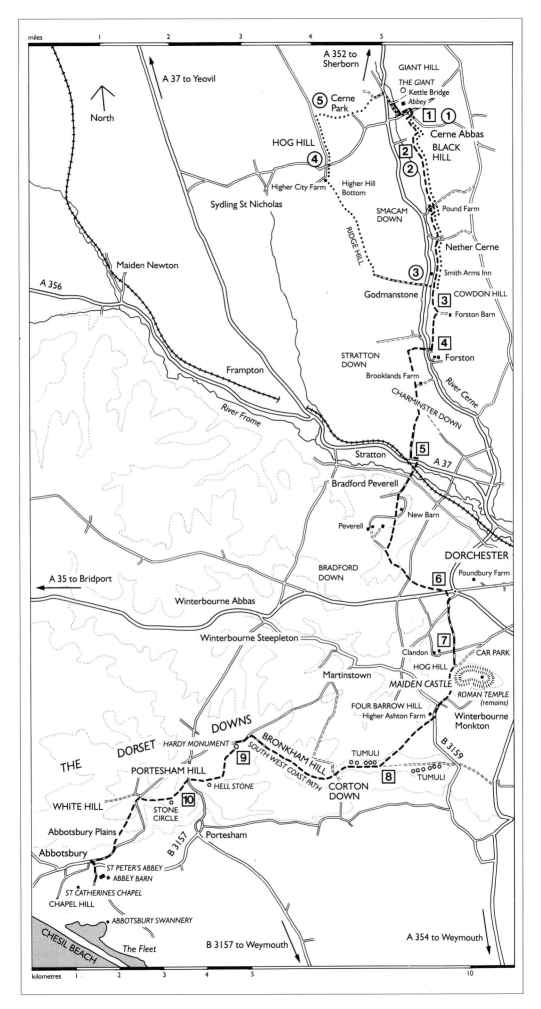

keep straight ahead and downhill, first with trees on the right, then alongside a wire fence. Reach a gap in a narrow belt of trees. Pass through the gap, then turn left down a broad track. After about 50 yards/46 metres, where the track bends to the right, go left through a gateway, then diagonally right across a field. Pass through a tree belt, then continue across an undulating field to reach a minor road. Cross over, then over a stile into a field. Cross the field to a stile into the next field. Head slightly rightwards across the next field to another stile. Follow the next field edge to reach the A35. (2½ miles/4 kms)

6 Cross the A35, with care, then follow a short stretch of abandoned road opposite, to reach another road. Go right for a short distance, then cross over at a corner, to take a track leading left, signposted Maiden Castle. Follow the track to Maiden Castle. At a junction of tracks on the west side of Maiden Castle, turn right through a gate. *The castle can be reached easily from this point, or it can be reached over a stile a little further ahead.* (1 mile/1.6 kms)

7 On the main walk, continue downhill, between Maiden Castle and Hog Hill, to reach a metal gate into a lane. Keep ahead down the lane, go straight across at a crossroads to reach the B3159 (Martinstown is about 1 mile/1.6 kms to the right). Turn left down the B3159, signposted Weymouth, then after a short distance bear off right at Higher Ashton Farm, signposted Bridleway to Friar Waddon. Go straight through the farmyard, then go up to the right along a concrete farm road to reach a junction of three tracks. Keep straight ahead into a field and follow its right edge to a gate in the field corner. Go left and alongside the field edge to reach another gate. Go through this gate, then continue for 80 yards/73 metres to reach a gate on the right. Go through this gate and cross a field, keeping left of a clump of trees. Pass to the left of a row of tumuli (burial mounds) and continue to a gate in the corner of the field, where there is a signpost. Continue diagonally across the middle of the next field, signposted Bridleway to Friar Waddon. Reach a gate and a stone wall, with two burial mounds on its other side. (2 miles/3.2 kms)

8 Turn right, signposted Inland Route, then continue directly on a track along Corton Down, and then along Bronkham Hill. Pass beneath pylons near a junction with a path to Martinstown. After about 1½ miles/2.4 kms you reach the road just down from Hardy's Monument. Turn up left to reach the monument. (2¼ miles/3.6 kms)

9 From the monument, walk to the far south-western corner of the car-parking area, passing a clump of trees on the way. Go down a narrow stony path at a concrete marker, signposted Inland Route West Bexington. Go left at a T-junction and continue to an open area at a junction with cross-tracks. Keep straight ahead and follow a path, signposted Inland Route West Bexington, downhill through trees. Where the track leaves the trees, go between two rough wooden posts, then turn right along a field track. Go through a gateway into a field, then bear left to reach a stile. Go over the stile and then along the field edge. Continue along the next field edge to reach a group of stiles at junction of a hedge and fence on Portesham Hill. *The Hell Stone burial chamber can be reached by crossing the field on the left.* On the main walk, cross the field ahead, keeping right of the wire fence, to reach a road. Turn left for a few yards, then go right along a track by a sign for Evershot Farms Hampton Dairy, signposted Abbotsbury 2 miles.(1 mile/1.6 kms)

10 Go down the track for a short distance, then, where the track curves to the right, keep straight ahead, through a gap. Follow a muddy track, past a rookery and a silage pit, then continue along a grassy track, passing the remains of a circle of stones. Reach a gate and a stile above the head of a deep combe. Cross the stile and follow a fence on the right past a hollow, and then round the slope to reach a road. Go left down the road, then, after a few yards, cross over at a bend and go through a gate on the right, signposted West Bexington. Go up a field track on White Hill. After 100 yards/91 metres, keep straight ahead where the fence veers off left at a signpost, for Bridleway Abbotsbury. Keep slightly left across the open field, to reach a hidden hollow leading down to a gate. Beyond the gate, continue downhill, keeping left of some hawthorn trees. Go through a gap at a fence, then continue downhill to reach a gate onto a road just to the right of a group of trees. Turn right and follow the road into Abbotsbury. (2 miles/3.2 kms)

CIRCULAR WALK
7 miles/11 kms

The route leads from Cerne Abbas alongside the River Cerne to Godmanstone, crosses the Cerne Valley, then leads back north to its starting point, along field tracks and paths.

Start Car park and picnic site at Kettle Bridge on the northern outskirts of Cerne Abbas, just below Giant Hill, OS 664015

1 Follow directions **1** and **2** on the main walk to reach point OS 667974, then go right over the stile to reach Godmanstone and the main road.

2 At the main road, cross with care, then go left, then right by Manor Farm. Follow a bridleway uphill for about ¾ mile/1.2 kms, then go through a gateway into a field. Turn right and keep to the edge of the field. Go through a small wooden gate. Keep the next field edge on your right. At the field corner, go left for a short distance, then sharp right through a gate. Continue over Ridge Hill, with the hedge on your left, to reach a small wooden gate. Continue with the hedge on your right to reach a big metal gate. Follow the track through several fields to reach Higher City Farm, then continue to a junction with a public road.

3 Cross the road and follow the lane opposite for about 1 mile/1.6 kms until you are abreast of a radio mast. Turn right and walk past the radio mast to reach a hedge corner. Turn right and follow the hedge for a short distance to an opening into woodland. Go left and follow a track through hazel woods, descending steeply to reach a stile where the trees thin out.

4 Bear slightly right and downhill across the large field of Cerne Park, which is dotted with oak trees. The Cerne Abbas Giant is visible in the distance. Cross a stile, then continue to another stile by a field gate. Continue along a muddy track that curves round the base of a hill. Where the track rises slightly and curves left, bear off right to cross a stile into woodland. Follow the path to join a track on a bend. Keep ahead along the track to reach the A352 between large buildings. Cross, with care, then go right. Pass the giant's viewpoint and keep left down a side road. Take the first turning left to reach the car park.

The Stone Road
Dartmoor

Princetown to Ivybridge 14 miles/22.5 kms

Dartmoor is a rich repository of ancient remains that have sunk back into the wilderness. This moorland walk leads from Princetown, at the heart of the Dartmoor National Park, to Ivybridge on the park's southern edge. The route crosses wild and lonely country and passes prehistoric burial sites and stone rows, ancient tin-works and medieval cattle pounds.

You need good sea-legs, rather than a head for heights, to ramble across the heaving deck of Dartmoor. The rise and fall of the great moor have no breathtaking peaks or ridges to lead you ever upward; there are no vertiginous slopes to draw you down, helter-skelter. Few landmarks therefore; and only distant uncertainties, which demand a sailor's skills in navigation. If you travel across this quaking wilderness without map and compass, you may find yourself adrift.

High Dartmoor is composed of a bedrock of granite surrounded by an aureole of quartzites and shales. The moorland hills of today are the eroded roots of ancient mountains, which were formed by cataclysmic earth movements millions of years ago. Dartmoor was not glaciated, but the permafrost conditions and the inter-glacial sequences of freeze and thaw, which were generated by the proximity of northern ice sheets, played a major part in shaping the moor's landscape. After millions of years of erosion, Dartmoor emerged as an undulating plateau of smooth hills, the highest of which reach heights of just over 2,000 feet/610 metres. Many of the tops are crowned with rocky tors, the surviving stubs of iron-hard granite bosses that resisted total erosion.

Within a few thousand years of the final retreat of the ice, Dartmoor became well wooded, with birch and oak trees growing up to the contour line of 1,500 feet/457 metres. By 10,000 BC Middle Stone Age/Mesolithic hunters were felling, or burning, areas of woodland and clearing the ground during seasonal forays. Later New Stone Age/Neolithic people settled on the moorland fringe and began an irreversible process of deforestation, a process that transformed most of Dartmoor into the treeless wilderness that we have inherited with such enthusiasm. Bronze Age people completed the process of deforestation and, soon after 2000 BC, early farmers began to divide sections of open land into primitive fields and territories. They marked these off with low walls, known as reaves, miles of which still survive on Dartmoor today.

Stone Rows

The cairns and burial cists, stone circles and standing stones of Dartmoor belong to this Late Neolithic/Bronze Age culture. The most intriguing artefacts are the long rows of stones that run like stitch-marks across many parts of the moor, often terminating at stone circles or burial sites. Cairns, tumuli and chamber barrows have defined their purpose by the human remains and grave goods discovered within them. But stone rows remain enigmatic. There have been various suggestions as to their purpose – that they are simple boundary lines or guide posts; that they are battle memorials; that they are Druidic 'temples', astronomical calculators, or memorials to the dead. Popular superstition has added much colourful nonsense, which casts the stone rows as works of the Devil, petrified maidens or giants' skittles. But the most intriguing aspect of the stones is their enduring mysteriousness; they taunt our modern 'need to know' with a mute dignity.

All of Dartmoor is peppered with ancient stone artefacts. But there is a particularly striking group of ruins located on Erme Plains at the remote heart of the South Moor. They include stone rows, burial cairns, walled cattle pounds and Iron Age hut foundations. They lie within a landscape that also displays the chaotic remains of medieval tin-works: the digging pits, crushing mills, blowing houses and shelters of ancient industry. The route to this remarkable outdoor museum begins at Princetown at the high, lonely heart of Dartmoor.

Princetown

Princetown's eponymous prison cannot disguise its sinister atmosphere. It is a grim contradiction of the sense of freedom that attracts so many of the law-abiding to Dartmoor. The prison was built in 1808 to house French captives of the Napoleonic Wars, and in later years American prisoners of a trade war that had flared up between British and American ships were held here. Few escaped, but many died; at the rate of four a week during the period 1809–14. Even in such deathly times, prisoners helped build Princetown's St Michael's and All Angels' Church, in whose graveyard – bleached of colour – are rows of gnomic headstones that mark the graves of unknown prisoners. Princetown became a civil gaol in 1850 and is still so, though it is no longer classified as a maximum-security prison. Today it holds approximately 600 inmates.

The inescapable grimness of the prison, its Victorian severity, rubs off on the little settlement of Princetown, a village by any other name. For long months, winter imprisons everything here. Yet the 'town' is a generous, unassuming place with good shops and pubs. In summer Princetown enjoys its deserved advantage of lying at the heart of Dartmoor. Open moorland is reached within a few hundred yards. Freedom beckons from all quarters.

A straight track leads south from Princetown across South Hessary Tor, with its squared-off crown of granite, to Nun's Cross on the watershed between the brimming marshes of Foxtor Mires and Newleycombe Lake. Nun's Cross stands over 7 feet/2 metres in height.

It was first recorded in 1240 as a bond-mark of the Royal Forest. The name *Syward* is inscribed on its eastern face and refers to a Northumbrian earl who was granted Dartmoor manors by William the Conqueror. On the cross's western face is inscribed *Boc Lond*, said to be the ancient form of Buckland; this suggests that the cross may have also been a boundary mark of the monastic lands of Buckland Abbey. The 'Nun' part of the cross's present name is thought to be a corruption of the old British word *nans*, meaning 'valley', perhaps referring to the Newleycombe valley to the west.

Abbot's Way

At Nun's Cross, the route to Erme Head breaks off from the broad, stony track that leads due south towards Sheepstor and Ditsworthy Warren. The way now followed is said to trace the line of an ancient monastic track that linked Tavistock and Buckland Abbeys on the western side of the moor with Buckfast Abbey on its eastern side. The route was dubbed the 'Abbot's Way' in the nineteenth century, though there are earlier records of its being named simply the 'Jobbers' Way', a suitable name for an ancient pack-horse route, whatever its provenance. The way leads past Nun's Cross Farm, whose present building is a replacement for an original turf-roofed dwelling of the 1870s, which was built to go with the land that was 'taken in' from the moor. Before then, there may well have been other dwellings on the site. The building stands at a true moorland crossroads that throngs with the ghosts of travellers. On windswept days, light and shade flicker across the landscape, where the colour and texture of dark walls and scrub contrast sharply with the emerald carpet of close-cropped bent and fescue grasses in the low-walled intakes. These are days of breathtaking skies, crammed with billowing cumulus and with occasional streaks of blue beneath the steel grey of rain clouds.

There is no clear path over the high ground of Crane Hill. The vestigial line of the Abbot's/Jobbers' Way simply flounders along random paths through rough waste. Some of these paths are the remnants of old ways that are long redundant; many are aimless trods that have been broken out by ponies, cattle and sheep. On the brow of the hill, a smooth whaleback of silvery granite breaks surface from the tiding moor grass. A tiny metal cross protrudes like a dart from its stony spine. From here, stranded paths lead south through ground that is never dry; this is classic blanket bog, a soggy morass of sphagnum moss, purple moor grass and white-headed cotton grass. It is desolate country, where the Dartmoor weather can be splendidly hostile. In thick mist, you peer ahead, anticipating monsters in the murk. During storms, icy rain slices across the weeping moor and the air smells of wet moss and mud. You wade rather than walk. In the dead of winter, conditions can be vicious; the wind cuts like a knife.

On the south side of Crane Hill a clear path leads down, through the corrugated ground of some old tin-works to Plym Ford, where the infant river sends threads of glittering water fussing amidst the stones. From the ford, a well-defined track rises steadily across the south-eastern flank of a hill known as Great Gnat's Head. The track runs across close-cropped turf that sprays water from beneath your feet in drenching rain. It rises steadily amidst the smooth, concave hills that sweep away to all sides. To the south-west, the land slowly subsides towards Plymouth and the sea. Soon the track leads to Broad Rock, a slabby boulder of granite that heaves its grey shoulder out of the moor. There was a guidepost here at one time, and the stone has the words 'Broad Rock' and the letters BB carved deep into its surface. The BB stands for Blachford Boundary, indicating that Broad Rock defines the boundary between the old Blachford Manor, now within the parish of Cornwood, and the bounds of the Royal 'Forest' of Dartmoor, the emphatically treeless hunting demesne of Norman kings.

Erme Head

From Broad Rock, the moorland sweeps away to the east. Below lies the broad apron of Erme Head. The horizon is a barely interrupted line of smooth hills, which runs from Naker's Hill in the north, through Green Hill and Brown Heath, to Quickbeam Hill above Erme Plains. Midway, the line is broken by the upstart cone of clay waste at the abandoned Red Lake China Clay Works. On dull days this is a gloomy place, but when light and shade flicker across the landscape beneath slate-blue skies, the moorland colours are transformed. At dusk, in late autumn on Dartmoor, the low-pitched sun sends a cascade of fiery light across the bronze and saffron hills; the colours change every few minutes as the sun glides between layered clouds.

The descent to Erme Head from Broad Rock is through a broad apron of marshy ground, where any semblance of path or track is satisfyingly lost. At one time the River Erme was known as the Arme. It emerges meekly from waterlogged ground, then winds between the tumbled chaos of Erme, or Arme, Pits, the scene of medieval tin-streaming. Here the tinners delved into the ground, and sifted the earth and rubble in water chutes to extract fine deposits of tin ore, which they smelted in primitive 'blowing-house' mills. The wrecked and scarred ground, now mellowed beneath a pelt of moss and moor grass, reflects the extent of primitive tin-streaming that went on here from pre-Roman times until the intensive workings of the seventeenth century. The Erme Head area was said to produce a fine tin deposit, known as 'zill', which was of high mineral content.

From Erme Pits, the way leads more easily alongside the north side of the stream and through more tin-works, to where the Blacklane

Brook comes down from the north across the low, marshy ground of Wollake. Old tin-works run high into the moor alongside Blacklane and towards the famous Ducks' Pool and the site of a plaque commemorating William Crossing, the great chronicler of Dartmoor, who died in 1928. Beyond Wollake, the path leads on to Dry Lake Ford and another stream crossing.

Stall Moor Row

Just beyond Dry Lake, the line of the remarkable Stall Moor Row is reached. The stones are gnomic; a line of stunted boulders only, yet dramatically significant within this remote moorland. The row is 2¼ miles/3.6 kms in length. From this point, it leads south for over half its length to a terminal circle on Stall Moor. From the same point, it leads north on an uncertain line; the stones become sporadic, and the row ends 200 yards/183 metres short of the tattered remains of a stone burial cist and barrow on top of Green Hill.

Over sixty stone rows have been recorded on Dartmoor. A mile/ 1.6 kms to the south is the much shorter, but more majestic line of Staldon Row and near Piles Hill, towards the end of the walk, there are several fragmented rows. At Merrivale, to the west of Princetown, are dramatic double rows, which are similar to the stone avenues of Avebury, though not as grand. The Stall Moor Row may have been constructed over many years by several generations of people; it may have evolved from two separate lines that were later joined across the marshy ground, known as The Meadow, that lies just upstream from Erme Pound. It is the longest example of its kind in Britain, and though its stones are modest, the row is longer even than the great megalithic settings of Kerzerho, Kerlescan and Menec in Brittany, those heartstopping massed ranks of giant pillars near Carnac in the French *département* of Morbihan. The suggestion that the rows may have been the ceremonial sites, the sacred precincts, of their time, constructed to celebrate the memory of its builders' ancestors, seems to be the most reasoned of all.

The stone row is followed south across the red-pebbled bed of Red Lake stream and on past the great stone corral of Erme Pound. The pound is a large, irregularly shaped enclosure of drystone walling, with a circumference of about 345 yards/315 metres. The pounds, or pinfolds, of Dartmoor were used from the Norman period onwards for holding cattle, sheep or horses that had either strayed onto the moor from adjoining common ground or were pastured there illegally. The rounding up of such strays was known as a 'drift' and was carried out by drift masters appointed by the manorial authorities. Drift pounds were probably in use from Norman times, but there is evidence that most surviving pounds are of a medieval date and are built on existing structures, or on the framework of Iron Age settlement enclosures.

Erme Pound

Erme Pound contains the vestigial remains of a number of Iron Age hut circles, and there are low-lying remains of medieval stone shelters outside the pound. Above the pound are the rambling walls of a much bigger enclosure and just south of this lies another, its walls composed of very large stones. South of this again lies a fourth enclosure, containing the low remains of several hut circles. Between these last two enclosures lies a short stone row. At the junction of Stony Brook and the Erme are the remains of an old blowing-house where tin was smelted. Across the river to the south-west lie other remains of hut circles and burial cairns that flank the distinctive line of the Stall Moor Row. The river flows down its stony bed, where dippers and grey wagtails flit from rock to rock. In the marshy ground, yellow-flowered bog asphodel and the pinky-white bogbean grow.

From Erme Pound, the way leads south-east across the meagre ditch of Stony Bottom, and then climbs steadily uphill until it reaches the rough track of the old Red Lake Tramway. The tramway served the clay pits at Red Lake from 1909 to 1932 and it is still known locally as the 'Puffing Billy' track. It is a long, open corridor into the heart of Dartmoor and is part of the long-distance trail, The Two Moors Way, which runs between Ivybridge and Lynmouth on the Exmoor coast. The track now winds its level way south and the Erme Valley deepens below it. The occasional spoil heaps of old clay workings, the tramway, the slime pits and troughs have not merged gracefully with the moorland in the way that Erme Pound and the scattering of ancient artefacts on Erme Plains have done. There is something too industrial, too intrusive about the clay remains. Feet thud jarringly against the flinty bed of the track, and the clay pits look desolate and colourless. The undulating route along the swelling hills of Ugborough Moor, just east of the track, is a more strenuous but more entertaining alternative.

Yet the tramway track is a fast way off the moor, and the views across the shoulder of Sharp Tor are exhilarating. The way is lined with the fragmented remnants of stone rows, burial barrows, boundary stones and cists, which seem to have been tossed aside by the 'Puffing Billy'. Above Harford, the track begins to descend towards Ivybridge. It passes Hangershell Rock and skirts Butterdon Hill and Western Beacon, where there are more scatterings of ancient stone artefacts, though they lack the impressiveness of the lonely ruins of the high moor. Soon the downhill track veers away from the tramway and descends between field walls. Below lies Ivybridge, pinned between main road and railway, a world that is wholly disengaged from the high, lonely waste of Erme Plains.

The Stone Road
Information

Distance 14 miles/22.5 kms

Maps OS Outdoor Leisure 28 (Dartmoor)

Nature of walk A challenging walk through high moorland, mainly on good tracks and paths, but with sections where the paths are indistinct, or even non-existent. The walk can be accomplished in a day by experienced walkers. Weatherproof clothing should be carried at all times of the year. A winter crossing should be considered only by those with winter hill-walking experience and with full winter clothing and emergency bivouac equipment. Visibility is often poor. Competency in the use of map and compass is essential.

Accommodation Guest houses and B&Bs at Princetown and Ivybridge. Plume of Feathers camp site at Princetown. Some accommodation may be seasonal. Further information from Ivybridge TIC.

Transport Summer bus services from Plymouth and Exeter to Princetown. Limited winter service. Bus service between Ivybridge and Plymouth. For further information contact Devon Bus, tel. (01752/01392) 382800; Western National, tel. (01752) 222666. Regional railway connections to Ivybridge from Exeter and Plymouth. Ivybridge Station is about 1 mile/1.6 kms east of the town centre.

Further information Princetown High Moorland Visitor Centre, tel. (01822) 890414; Tourist Information Centre, Ivybridge, tel. (01752) 897035

Start Princetown High Moorland Visitor Centre

1 Walk to the junction with the B3212. Cross, with care, then go along the track between the Prince of Wales Inn and the Devil's Elbow (The Railway Inn). Follow the track over South Hessary Tor to reach Nun's Cross. (2½ miles/4 kms)

2 Bear left from Nun's Cross and head south-east across open ground to the left of Nun's Cross Farm, and to the left of a solitary tree. Just beyond the tree, reach a track leading right. Follow the track for about 100 yards/91 metres to reach the Devonport Leat. Cross the leat by a slab bridge, then, within a few yards/metres, cross Nun's Cross Ford. Follow the rough track uphill, then descend to cross a rough ditch. *There is no clear path for the next mile/1.6 kms to Plym Ford. In misty weather good compass navigation is essential.* From the rough ditch, continue along an indistinct path in a south-easterly direction for about ¼ mile/0.4 kms to where a faint green track crosses the line of the route at OS 613695 (about 200 yards/182 metres to the left, there is a stone cross). Straight ahead lies the slope of Crane Hill. Cross the faint track and go uphill on a bearing of 122 degrees. There is no discernible path. Reach a large, smooth rock at the top of the slope. A small metal cross is embedded in the top of the boulder. (¾ mile/1.2 kms)

3 Go due south from the boulder and, within a few yards/metres, reach a very narrow path. Follow this path for just under ¼ mile/0.4 kms to reach some low-lying heathery hummocks at OS 614687. Pass to the left of these (there is usually a small pool here) and continue to a boulder-strewn, reedy area. Bear south-west here and soon reach a grassy track. Follow a gently descending track to Plym Ford. (½ mile/0.8 kms)

4 Cross Plym Ford and follow the obvious track that bears left and uphill. Continue in a south-easterly direction across the western flank of Great Gnat's Head for about 1 mile/1.6 kms to reach Broad Rock at OS 618673 (rock inscribed 'BB Broad Rock'). *Below and south-east lies Erme Head, the head of the River Erme valley. The path down to Erme Head is indistinct and fades out in places.* Head south-east and downhill from Broad Rock, keeping to the right of the marshy ground and aiming for the spoil heaps in the valley bottom. Reach the infant River Erme, which is a mere stream at this point. Cross the stream at Erme Head Ford, then continue through the chaos of old tin-pits and spoil heaps, bearing slightly left to re-cross the stream at Erme Pits Ford. Soon a path develops along the north bank of the stream. Follow the path to the place where

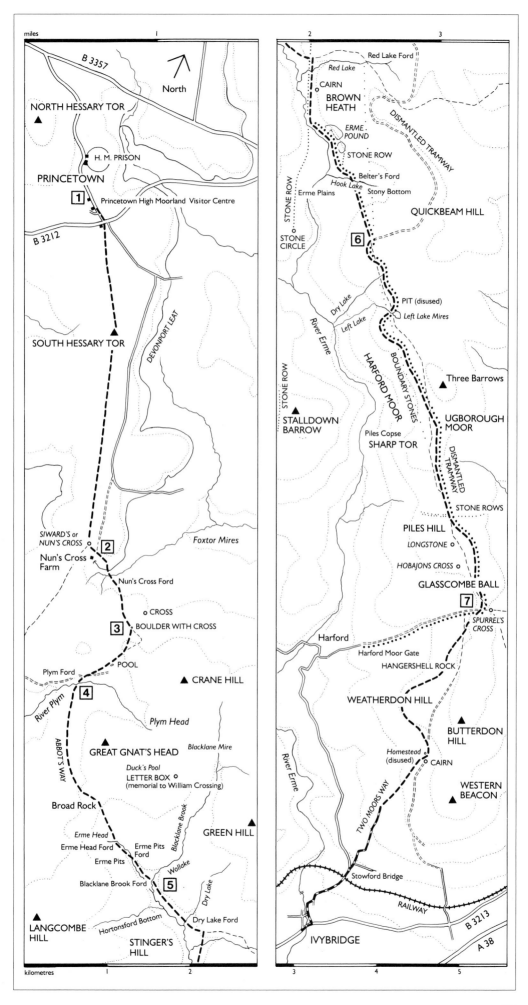

miles

1

B 3357

North

NORTH HESSARY TOR

H. M. PRISON

PRINCETOWN

1 Princetown High Moorland Visitor Centre

B 3212

DEVONPORT LEAT

SOUTH HESSARY TOR

Foxtor Mires

SIWARD'S or
NUN'S CROSS **2**

Nun's Cross
Farm

Nun's Cross Ford

○ CROSS

3 BOULDER WITH CROSS

Plym Ford

POOL

ABBOT'S WAY

River Plym

4

▲ CRANE HILL

Plym Head

▲ GREAT GNAT'S HEAD

Blacklane Mire

Duck's Pool
LETTER BOX ○
(memorial to William Crossing)

Broad Rock

Erme Head

Erme Head Ford

Erme Pits
Ford

Erme Pits

Blacklane Brook

Wollake

Blacklane Brook Ford **5**

Dry Lake

▲ GREEN HILL

▲ LANGCOMBE
HILL

Hortonsford Bottom

Dry Lake Ford

STINGER'S
HILL

kilometres

1

2

2

3

Red Lake Ford

Red Lake

CAIRN

BROWN
HEATH

ERME
POUND

DISMANTLED TRAMWAY

STONE ROW

Belter's Ford

STONE ROW

Hook Lake

Stony Bottom

Erme Plains

QUICKBEAM HILL

Erme Plains

6

STONE
CIRCLE

Dry Lake

PIT (disused)

River Erme

Left Lake

Left Lake Mires

STONE ROW

HARFORD MOOR

BOUNDARY STONES

▲ Three Barrows

▲ STALLDOWN
BARROW

Piles Copse

UGBOROUGH
MOOR

SHARP TOR

DISMANTLED
TRAMWAY

STONE ROWS

PILES HILL

LONGSTONE ○

HOBAJONS CROSS ○

GLASSCOMBE BALL

7

SPURREL'S
CROSS

Harford

Harford Moor Gate

HANGERSHELL ROCK

WEATHERDON HILL

River Erme

Homestead
(disused)

CAIRN

▲ BUTTERDON
HILL

▲ WESTERN
BEACON

TWO MOORS WAY

Stowford Bridge

RAILWAY

B 3213

IVYBRIDGE

A 38

kilometres

3

4

5

the Blacklane Brook joins the Erme at the marshy ground of Wollake at OS 628667. (1¾ miles/2.8 kms)

5 Cross Blacklane Brook Ford, then continue on a good path for ½ mile/0.8 kms, crossing Dry Lake Ford to reach a line of low standing stones running north–south above the spot where the Erme Valley turns south. Turn south yourself and follow the stone row downhill. Cross a stream and continue alongside the stones for about ¼ mile/0.4 kms to reach the stone-walled enclosure of Erme Pound. Continue downstream from Erme Pound, passing below another stone-walled enclosure. Just before a solitary tree, and by a big rock, bear left and uphill, at a slight angle, to another stone-walled enclosure. Walk through the enclosure, heading for its far top-left corner. From the edge of the enclosure, bear left and uphill for about 200 yards/182 metres, then bear right and cross Belter's Ford at Stony Bottom. Continue uphill on a bearing of 164 degrees for ½ mile/0.8 kms to reach the broad, stony track of the old Red Lake Tramway at OS 644644. (2 miles/3.2 kms)

6 Turn right (south) and follow the old tramway track. In just over ½ mile/0.8 kms, pass a flooded clay pit at Leftlake Mires. Continue along the track. Pass east of the summit of Sharp Tor and of the low mound of Piles Hill, to where the track is crossed by a grassy track at OS 658599 (about 200 yards/182 metres to the east is a stone cross called Spurrell's Cross). (3½ miles/5.6 kms)

7 Continue down the track, passing Hangershell Rock, then follow a long, curving section round Weatherdon Hill. At OS 652583, where the track swings to the right by the low ruins of a stone enclosure and ancient hut circles, leave the track, bearing off right on 220 degrees, to reach a gate. Beyond the gate, follow a green lane downhill. At a junction with another lane, turn right for a few yards/metres to reach the public road to Harford. Turn left down the road, cross the railway at Stowford Bridge, then, at a junction, cross over and go down the lane opposite. Pass the entrance to a paper mill, then continue alongside the River Erme to the centre of Ivybridge. (3 miles/4.8 kms)

CIRCULAR WALK

There are no satisfactory opportunities for short circular walks along the line of this route, because of the remote nature of the most interesting sites.

Erme Pound and the Stall Moor Row can be reached along the course of the Red Lake Tramway from a small car park at Harford Moor Gate, OS 644595, above Ivybridge. The track of the Red Lake Tramway is reached by walking east from the car park for 1 mile/1.6 kms. Follow the tramway track north for 3½ miles/5.6 kms to OS 644644, where the tramway curves to the right. This represents direction **6** on the main walk, in reverse. Follow direction **5** in reverse to reach Erme Pound. Then retrace your steps to Harford Moor Gate car park. (11 miles/17.7 kms)

The Tinners' Way

Cornwall

Cape Cornwall to St Ives 16 miles/25.7 kms

The Land's End peninsula lies within the district of Penwith, the 'furthest end' of Cornwall, and is famed for the beauty of its landscape. The area was a major source of tin during the Bronze and Iron Ages and again during the eighteenth and nineteenth centuries. This long walk passes through the coastal and moorland landscape of the peninsula where prehistoric and industrial artefacts reflect centuries of human occupation and mineral mining.

The Land's End peninsula thrusts its rocky claw into the Atlantic and the ocean responds with its storms. The bare bones of the peninsula are made of gold and silver granite and jet-black greenstone and slate. The granite cliffs soar like temple walls; fantastic pinnacles and columns, ribs and buttresses of golden rock rise from a restless sea. The slate cliffs are no less impressive, though they are more Gothic in their dark irregularities, more angular. They slice into the land and form gloomy, sea-washed chasms, known in Cornwall as 'zawns', where seabirds nest on lime-streaked ledges. The tidal rocks are draped with kelp and bladderwrack and with purple carragheen. Deep in the narrow zawns, massive boulders lie jammed together. During Atlantic storms, when torrents of water pour in and out of the zawn beds with enough energy to light up London, you can hear the boulders grinding against each other.

Above all this, the cliffs rise to rounded summits or to sharp, dizzying edges. Their upper faces are gilded with saffron- and lime-coloured lichen, the slopes above and between swathed in pink thrift, stonecrop and white sea campion. In many places along the 50 miles/80 kms of the peninsula's rocky coastline, the cliffs are breached by crescent-shaped bays with beaches of bone-white sand, and by rocky coves where wooded valleys end at a sea of Mediterranean blue. Inland lies an endearing countryside of small, irregularly shaped fields interspersed with farm settlements and villages with handsome granite churches. All are linked by a network of narrow lanes and vegetated stone walls, the famous Cornish 'hedges', which blaze with the brilliant colour of wild flowers in spring. Along the north coast the ground rises to a broad, inland ridge of rock-fretted moorland, which lends some shelter to the sloping southern half of the peninsula where it sweeps down to Penzance and the shining crescent of Mount's Bay.

This is one of Britain's most cherished landscapes, minuscule in its forms, yet complex and varied; it is loved for its clarity of light, for its island-like character and for the seductiveness of its often brilliant summers. But, behind the great cliffs, below the grass, and below the seabed even, lies another landscape, the labyrinthine world of coastal tin-mines, the unseen country that has defined the soul of Penwith and the character of its people. On the north coast of the peninsula, and along the ridge of tumbling moorland, mining was the arbiter of life for hundreds of years. It dictated the lie of the land – above ground as well as below. The result, especially in the coastal area of St Just and Cape Cornwall, is a still-visible desolation and a wrenching of the landscape, which is made bearable only by the exhilarating presence of the Atlantic.

Diaspora

In Cornwall tin-ore is always spoken of as being 'won', rather than mined. There is a proud, but awkward doggedness in the way that the word is used to lend dignity to a moribund industry. Today, only the South Crofty mine at Camborne in mid-Cornwall survives, out of hundreds of ventures that once made the county the world's greatest producer of tin and a crucible of the Industrial Revolution. Cornwall too had its diaspora, just as much as did Ireland and Scotland; and it was desolate. Cornish miners and their families left their homeland in droves during the slumps of the Victorian mining era. They took with them, to South America and to Australia, their proud spirits and a matchless experience of the raw, rough world of hard-rock mining, to which the convoluted geology of their homeland had bent them.

Four hundred million years ago, within the primeval landscape of which the Cornwall of today was an unformed part, great domes of molten granite burst like nuclear bombs into the sedimentary roots of ancient alps. The sediments metamorphosed into shales and hardened clays in the white heat of the eruptions. As the mingled igneous and metamorphic rocks cooled and contracted, mineralizing liquids and gases bubbled along a network of fracture lines that ran through the mass. They crystallized into veins, or 'lodes', of copper, tin, silver, wolfram, zinc and uranium, Cornwall's cornucopia of mineral wealth. There followed millions of years of further upheaval and erosion, from which emerged a primitive landscape, the surface of which was scattered with mineral-rich debris. Below ground, great vertical sheets of tin and copper plunged deeply into the ancient 'country' rock.

Tin is cassiterite, a mineral that is more easily smelted than copper. In its refined form it has a coating of oxide, which protects it from corrosion. But tin, like copper, is a soft metal and was of little functional use in prehistoric times, until it was found that by mixing copper with tin a hard metal called bronze was produced. Tin was the alchemist's key to the Bronze Age and may have brought European bronzesmiths and technicians to the Late Neolithic Cornwall of 2000 BC.

There are enduring claims that the fabulous St Michael's Mount, the tidal island in Mount's Bay, was the 'island in front of Britain called *Ictis*, a peninsula at low tide', described by the Greek historian Diodorus Siculus as being the main British tin-trading base of prehistory. But strong cases have also been made for other locations being *Ictis,* including the Isle of Wight, Mount Batten Point in Plymouth Sound and Ile d'Ouessant off Finistère. Nor is there any substance to claims that tin-trading Phoenicians ever grounded their Mediterranean galleys on the shores of Mount's Bay. What does seem certain is that, by the final centuries BC, there were coastal clearing-houses from which Irish and British metals were shipped to Gaul and then carried along pack-horse trails to eastern Europe and the Mediterranean; there may also have been a strong tin trade between Cornwall and Ireland. It is probable therefore that smoke-blackened *astragali*, rough ingots of tin, were carried from Penwith's north coast across the high ground of the Land's End peninsula to the shores of St Ives Bay and to Mount's Bay, from where they were shipped to Ireland and to Gaul.

The Old St Ives Road

The line of a ridgeway track is still traceable along the high ground of the peninsula. There is anecdotal evidence that it was once known as the 'Old St Ives Road'. Today parts of this ridgeway track have been incorporated into an imaginative walking route that leads from Cape Cornwall, below St Just, to St Ives. The route has been dubbed 'The Tinners' Way', although the 'tinner' connection is still wishful thinking. In Cornish it is known as *Forth an Stenoryon*. In anyone's language it is a splendid outing through coastal and moorland landscape, within which the evocative monuments of ancient people survive alongside the artefacts of Victorian industry.

There is no historical precedent for starting the Tinners' Way at Cape Cornwall. But the idea sits well with the area's mining traditions, of which the sturdy granite town of St Just is the focus. Today Cape Cornwall is the pivotal property of a 3-mile/4.8-km stretch of old mining coast, which is now in the care of the National Trust. It is a spectacular coastline, once industrialized and now of immeasurable archaeological value, and historically of world significance. This is not an easy landscape to manage; but the Trust seems to be taking a thoughtful approach, which seeks to reconcile the demands of 'heritage' tourism with the sensitivities of a local community that lost so much when the last of the coastal mines at nearby Geevor closed in 1990.

The Tinners' Way begins as a broad track leading eastwards from Cape Cornwall. The track leads on for ½ mile/0.8 kms to a point where it drops steeply into the Kenidjack Valley and a remarkable post-industrial landscape. The earliest form of mineral extraction was by 'streaming' of surface deposits and alluvial gravels, using methods similar to those of the early lead industry in the Yorkshire Dales.

Industrialization

Over time the basics of metal production did not change. But the methods did, as steam power facilitated deep-shaft extraction and led to the industrialization of Cornish mining during the eighteenth and nineteenth centuries. In the nineteenth century the scene in the Kenidjack Valley was one of spectacular industry. Rumbling water wheels were fed with water from channels known as 'leats', which led from ponds higher up the valley, whose dried-up courses can still be seen as level lines along the valley slopes. Everywhere there were granite engine houses with tall stacks; wooden trestles and gantries supported coupled flat-rods, which transmitted power from the water wheels to mine-shaft pulleys and stamping mills. The air was filled with the staccato thud of ore-crushing stamps and the hissing of steam engines. The whole valley was wreathed in the smoke and fumes that poured from the engine houses, where huge beams rocked and bobbed above gaping mine shafts. The river supplied much of this motive force and was essential to the sluicing and separation of tin from waste material.

Crushed granite reeks of sulphur. The steam engines were driven by blazing coals that fumed with tarry smoke. In mine galleries there is a dense, sweet smell of mud and de-oxygenated air. The mix would have been stifling and potent; the smell clung to clothing and impregnated the skin. Several hundred men, women and children worked in the Victorian mines of the Cape Cornwall area. The surface workers were mainly women, older men and children. The women were called Bal Maidens – the Cornish word *bal* means 'a place of digging' (as opposed to the word *huel* or *wheal*, which is translated more specifically as 'mine' and is used to prefix the named mines of the area). The Bal Maidens wielded long-handled Cornish shovels and used small hammers for breaking or 'cobbing' the ore. They wore long black skirts and white aprons and bonnets. Below ground their menfolk fretted at the hard rock, which could crush them at random or collapse about their heads under the pressure of masses of drowning water.

The way across the valley passes close to the ruins of an arsenic labyrinth – its tall, cowled chimney still intact, its broken arches and smoke-blackened tunnels like the ruined cells of some medieval prison. It was here that tin ore was baked in a calciner to rid it of unwanted arsenic and other impurities before smelting. The toxic fumes were drawn through the labyrinth, where the arsenic crystallized on the walls and was then scraped off by women and children. It was exported to the cotton fields of America, where it vanquished the boll-weevil. It also vanquished many of the Cornish workers. They absorbed the poison through their bare, sweating skin in the heat of the labyrinth's tunnels. There is not much romance in this Cornish heritage. And there was little mercy from market forces, either. A major collapse of Cornish tin prices in the 1870s closed down most of the ventures in the Cape Cornwall area. Twenty years later, in November 1893, a torrential flood swept through Kenidjack and destroyed many of the buildings and equipment. Thereafter the history of coastal tin-mining was of sporadic resurgence and of twentieth-century decline.

Imposing Ruins

The path out of the Kenidjack Valley climbs steeply to the airy promontory of Kenidjack Castle, a fortified Iron Age site that may have had connections with the early tin trade. The coast running north from here is dominated by the remains of Victorian mining. Below ground is a vast uncharted network of tunnels and galleries, which extend in places for up to a mile/1.6 kms beneath the seabed. Above ground, as if to spurn the subterranean darkness, the summer slopes are bright with creamy-white bladder campion, pink thrift and the yellow western gorse.

The track along the cliff top is flanked by the imposing ruins of the old mines of Wheal Edward and West Wheal Owles. Visible ahead is the Botallack area, with its famous cliffside mine-stacks of The Crowns and its numerous mining remains. Just north of Botallack is the National Trust's Levant engine house, which is open to the public and where there is a magnificent beam-engine worked by steam. Close to Levant is the Geevor Tin Mine Heritage Centre with its absorbing interpretations of Cornish mining. But at Wheal Edward, the route of the Tinners' Way turns inland by the scant remains of the pumping house of West Wheal Owles. Field paths and tracks lead to the hamlet of Truthwall on the main road between St Just and St Ives, a road that still manages to enchant, with its tortuous course and its unforgiving, reef-like walls.

From Truthwall, narrow lanes climb to the breezy moorland of Tregeseal Common and to the site of a Neolithic stone circle. On the crown of the hill stands Carn Kenidjack, a cluster of rock tors where fluted grooves and gaps orchestrate the wind into an eerie moaning. This is the famous 'Hooting Carn', where benighted travellers are said to have become demented by the sight of grotesque giants wrestling in the icy moonlight, and from where dishevelled girls and scared youths came home after midnight with dazed talk of having met Old Nick; as nice an excuse as any.

Chun Castle

From Carn Kenidjack, the Tinners' Way runs in a determined line to the north-east, along the 'Old St Ives Road'. Muddy tracks cross Woon Gumpus Common, then rise to the stone 'mushroom' of Chun Quoit, once partly covered with earth and turf and still the best preserved of Penwith's Neolithic/Bronze Age chamber tombs of a type known as a portal dolmen. Just east of the quoit and post-dating it by 3,000 years is Chun Castle, an Iron Age fortified site of impressive proportions. The castle's walls were once twice their present height of 5 feet/1.5 metres, but were robbed of stone during the eighteenth and nineteenth centuries.

From this high ground, monolithic drystone walls slice across the green fields that run down to the edge of the great cliffs of the Atlantic's edge. You can see the weather coming a mile away on this coast, and the way east is just as wide-eyed. The track leads past the site of an Iron Age settlement at Bosullow Trehyllys, further evidence that the area was of great strategic importance in its day. Paths lead on across the summit of Morvah Carn, where enormous slabs of rock lie embedded in the green turf, as if abandoned there in the midst of some megalithic enterprise. Ahead lies a great widening swell of moorland across the rising ground of Watch Croft and Bosullow Common. To the south-east, the sentinel mine-stack of the Ding Dong mine at Greenburrow dominates the horizon.

Men-an-Tol

Towards Greenburrow the way leads past the celebrated Men-an-Tol, the 'stone of the hole', an artefact that has become hugely popular with visitors, partly because of its aura of healing mysticism and the alleged symbolism of its alignments. There is more artifice than artefact about the Men-an-Tol, however. The holed stone and its flanking pillars may once have been part of a large burial chamber or stone circle, but there is evidence that they were disturbed and realigned in recent centuries. The magic is what you make of it. A short distance further on, in a field to the left, is the more persuasive Men Scryfa, the 'stone of writing', a solitary standing stone inscribed in dog-Latin with the words *Rialobrani Cvnovali Fili*. The script translates as 'Rialobran [the Raven], son of Cunoval [Famous Hound]' and probably refers to Romano-British tribal chieftains who had a penchant for hunting.

Beyond the Men Scryfa, open ground is reached at the Four Parishes Stone, where a flat boulder, marked with a cross, once bore a metal pole that indicated the meeting of the bounds of the old ecclesiastical parishes of Morvah, Madron, Zennor and Gulval. To the north is the rocky hill of Carn Galver. To the south lies the Greenburrow mine stack; the ground between is riddled with ancient tin-diggings. But the Tinners' Way keeps its eastern course across sweeping moorland. It passes close to the stone circle of the 'Nine Maidens' at Boskednan, and a mile/1.6 kms further on reaches the Bodrifty Iron Age settlement with its scattering of low-walled ruins of courtyard houses. The site has been cleared and made accessible through the goodwill of the landowner and through an arrangement with the Ministry of Agriculture's Environmentally Sensitive Area scheme, which has operated successful conservation agreements on these marginal lands of Penwith for over ten years. On a nearby hill top, above slopes of bleached and windswept moor grass, is Mulfra Quoit, a stone chamber of the same period as Chun Quoit and with the same compelling beauty.

From here, the way leads in a straight line along roads and tracks, and then by narrow paths across the lonely moorland of Amalveor Downs. When the wind is from the sea and brisk beneath cloud-torn skies, there is a sweet freshness about this empty landscape. To the north are the rock-studded summits of Zennor Hill, Sperris and Trendrine. West of Zennor Hill the Foage Valley opens a blue window to the sea and to a distant mosaic of Iron Age fields around the village of Zennor. Ahead lies the thickening waist of the peninsula, where the land is more determinedly bent to farming. Soon a hollowed lane leads down from the moors to Embla, the way to Amalveor and the charming medieval church of Towednack, a Christian acknowledgement on this emphatically pre-Christian trail of antiquities.

Towards St Ives

A long, straight road leads from Towednack towards the coast. Several small fields are crossed, then a lane like a deep trench wriggles through the ancient farm settlement of Trevessa to the point where a field track turns north towards the sea. This was the access track to a group of mines known collectively as Trevega Bal, of which one prominent ruin survives. At Trevega, in 1700, it is claimed that blasting powder was used to break out a lode – the first record of its use in Penwith mines. For the next 2 miles/3.2 kms the way follows paths through the flat shelf of land at Trevalgan and Trowan, where the mosaic of stone-hedged fields reflects a working landscape that was first set out in the Iron Age. To the south lie the rolling hills of Rosewall and Trendrine, where the Cornish also adventured for minerals.

Soon the way turns north along a hedged lane. It leads to the coast path at Hellesveor, from where it is a straightforward walk to St Ives along the rim of coal-black cliffs. Old St Ives was dependent on pilchards and tin. Here, miners and fishermen lived cheek-by-jowl: the fishermen in Downlong, by the sea; the miners in Uplong, the tin and copper country. They rarely mixed or matched. Now St Ives is emphatically a tourist town; its mining hinterland has succumbed to suburbia; its beautiful harbourside enclaves are given over to art, craft and Cornish cream, although the best values of old St Ives and its people have survived. The coast path emerges at the surf-lined Porthmeor Beach, above which stands the dazzling white building of the St Ives Tate Gallery. It exhibits work by such distinguished painters as Peter Lanyon, Patrick Heron and Terry Frost, all powerful interpreters of the ancient and deeply rooted landscape of Cornwall's 'furthest end', through which the Tinners' Way makes its wandering course.

The Tinners' Way
Information

Distance 16 miles/25.7 kms

Maps OS Explorer 7 (Land's End, Penzance and St Ives)

Nature of walk A moorland and coastal route that is quite strenuous but can be covered in a day by experienced walkers. *The Tinners' Way is not an official route or regional trail. It is an informal route, sections of which follow rights of way and permissive paths. Permissive paths are used by arrangement with the landholder and at the landholder's discretion. Their use does not signify that their use are rights of way. A number of mining sites are passed on the way. Mine adits (tunnels) can be extremely dangerous and should never be entered. Never approach the edge of mine shaft openings. Keep dogs under control in mining areas, both coastal and moorland. The walls of ruined buildings should not be tampered with, for safety reasons, and because of their important archaeological status.*

Accommodation Hotels, guest houses and B&Bs in and around St Just. Youth hostel at Cot Valley, St Just. Camp sites at Trevaylor, near Botallack, and at Kelynack, St Just. Numerous hotels, guest houses and B&Bs at St Ives. Camp sites at St Ives and at Trevalgan Farm.

Transport Mainline rail connections to Penzance. Bus connections between Penzance, St Just and St Ives. Seasonal bus connection between St Ives and St Just. Rail connections from St Ives to Penzance.

Further information Tourist Information Centre, Penzance, tel. (01736) 62207; Tourist Information Centre, St Ives, tel. (01736) 796297.

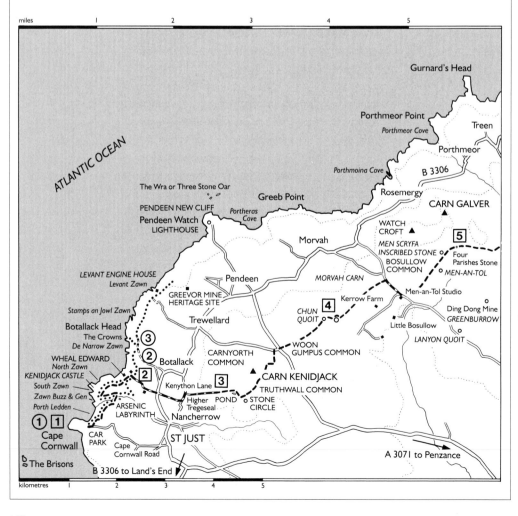

Start Cape Cornwall car park, near St Just, OS 354317

1 From the car-park entrance, go up the road for about 50 yards/46 metres. Turn left along a stony track. At a fork, keep left. At the next fork, take the left branch into the valley, which is crossed via a small bridge. Reach a stone 'Coast Path' sign at a junction with a track below a house. Turn left and in 50 yards/46 metres turn right at some waymarks. Follow a path steeply uphill to reach a track high above the valley. Go left down the track for 100 yards/91 metres, then turn up right by a waymark. Climb steeply along the rim of a quarry, then follow a level grassy track to a stone stile by a gate. Go along the grassy track for about 50 yards/46 metres to reach a waymark at a junction with the bend of a stony track. Keep straight ahead along the track to the point where

it branches, just above the preserved Wheal Edward building at OS 361328. (1¼ miles/2 kms).

2 Take the right branch of the track. Pass the sketchy ruin of the West Wheal Owles Winding House, then in 50 yards/46 metres turn right along a walled lane to reach a stile by a gate. Continue through fields and gaps to a stile and gate by the remains of the Wheal Owles pumping engine house at OS 366325. Follow a muddy track round left and past a house, to reach the B3306 at Truthwall. Cross to the right, with care, then go left past the Trevaylor Caravan and Camping Park. Follow Truthwall Lane, then at a T-junction turn left and, after 100 yards/91 metres, turn right by a row of cottages. Follow the stony Kenython Lane uphill. Pass the entrance track to Kenython and keep straight ahead through a gapway, by a wooden stile, at OS 382325. (1¼ miles/2 kms)

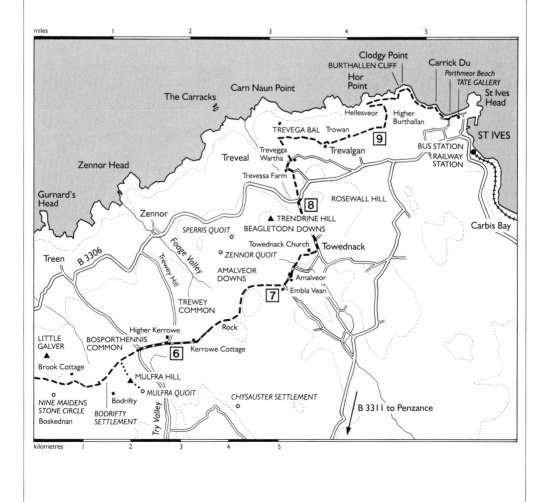

3 Follow the track downhill, passing to the right of a pond. Keep ahead where the tracks cross, then in 50 yards/46 metres, at a fork, take the right branch. *A few yards/metres ahead a narrow path leads to Tregeseal stone circle.* On the main walk, keep straight ahead, keeping left where the path forks. Follow the trenched path uphill, across Botallack Common, passing Carn Kenidjack on your left, to the moorland corner, where a path comes in from the left. Turn right, and pass a row of three telegraph poles. Continue to where the path joins a farm track. Go down the track and follow it round left to reach a road. Turn right to reach the B3318. Cross the road, with care, to an open area, then take the right-hand track across Woon Gumpus Common. Keep straight ahead when the track merges with another track. Keep left at a fork, then reach a gap and stile into a field. Cross the field on a permissive path to another stile onto the open moorland of Chun Downs. Continue uphill to Chun Quoit. (2 miles/3.2 kms)

4 From the quoit, follow a broad track to the right to reach Chun Castle. The castle is entered through a double gapway. Go left and follow the wall of the castle to its far side at a point directly opposite the entranceway. *The next section as far as a public road is along permissive paths.* Look carefully for a narrow path leading off left (north-east) and downhill through thick gorse (bare legs not advised). At the bottom of the slope, continue down a walled track, past Trehyllys Iron Age settlement (access by arrangement only), then cross a stile and keep straight ahead through fields to another stile into rough ground. Follow a path through the gorse, passing to the right of the slabby rocks of Morvah Carn to reach a stile onto a walled path that leads to a road. Turn right and follow the road downhill to reach the Men-an-Tol Studio. Turn left opposite the studio, signposted Men-an-Tol, and follow the track for about 1 mile/1.6 kms, passing Coronation Farm and an access-stile to the Men-an-Tol about halfway along. Reach open ground and a gate onto open moorland at the Four Parishes Stone, a low boulder with a small cross cut into it, at OS 430354. (2½ miles/4 kms)

5 *The next section, as far as the road at OS 452360, is along permissive paths.* Follow the path that leads uphill from the boulder for about 30 yards/27 metres, then turn left and off the main path via a very narrow path. Continue uphill on stranded paths, then, where the ground levels out at a crossing of paths, take the leftmost branch, which converges with a field wall on the left. Keep on this path over the moor and down to a huge rock at a junction with a track leading down from Brook Cottage. Turn right along the track to a junction with another track. Turn left, along the track, go through a gateway, then in 50 yards/46 metres turn off right to reach a granite stile onto open moorland. Just beyond the stile and just past a big leaning rock, the path forks. *The right branch leads in 100 yards/ 91 metres to the remains of Bodrifty Iron Age settlement (explanatory noticeboard at site).* On the main walk from the stile, follow the left-hand path across the moor, crossing two more granite stiles. Keep ahead across the moor, to reach a road junction at OS 452360. Keep straight ahead along the road signposted Zennor and St Ives for ½ mile/0.8 kms. (2 miles/3.2 kms)

6 At a left-hand bend, at Higher Kerrowe, leave the road and keep straight ahead along a broad, stony track for about ¾ mile/1.2 kms, passing several houses. Where the stony track ends by a house, continue along a grassy track, keeping left where the track branches just before a gate. Follow a path between walls to reach open moorland by a huge fallen rock. Follow the path round to the right and then continue across Amalveor Downs. Keep straight ahead at a crossing of paths. Soon the walls to either side close in, and alternative paths run parallel to each other. Follow the descending path to reach a surfaced road by Embla Vean. (2 miles/3.2 kms)

7 Go left along the road and uphill. Pass a group of houses at Amalveor, and continue downhill to where the road swings right. Leave the road at the corner, cross a triangle of grass by the entrance track to Beagletodn, then follow a path through wet ground and to the left of a telegraph pole. Cross a stream by a slab bridge and go up to a stile. Follow some white-painted blocks between fish-ponds, then follow a rubble track round to the right and alongside a pond. At a large boulder, go left through a wooden gate and into a field. Follow the right edge of the field, then go right and through a wide gateway. Cross the next field diagonally left, to reach a stile into Towednack Church parking area. Go down the church lane to a public road. Turn left and follow the road to a T-junction with the B3306. (1¼ miles /2 kms). *About 200 yards /183 metres along this road, a lane leads off to the right. This is Towednack Road which leads directly to the outskirts of St Ives and the B3306 into the town. Distance 2½ miles/4 kms.*

8 Cross the road, with care, then go right and uphill for 100 yards/91 metres. Turn left at a waymark and go over a granite stile, then continue in a direct line, over stiles and through small fields to a stile into a narrow lane. Turn left and follow the lane, past Trevessa and Trevega, for ¼ mile/0.4 kms. Turn left down a field track by a signpost just before Trevega Wartha. *This track may be overgrown with nettles in summer.* In ¼ mile/0.4 kms reach a stone stile on the right, by a signpost. Cross the stile, then follow a path through several fields, and over stiles, to Trevalgan Farm. Detour round the back of the farm and continue on field paths, guided by black and white posts. At Trowan Farm follow the signs through the farmyard to a stile and a signpost to St Ives. Continue through more fields to reach a stile into a walled lane at OS 502405. (2¼ miles/3.6 kms)

9 Turn left down the lane for ¼ mile/0.4 kms to reach the coast. Turn down right at Hellesveor Cliff by a 'Coast Path' sign. Pass a National Trust sign, then continue along the coast path to Burthallan Cliff, and then to Clodgy Point. Continue along the coast path past Carrick Du to reach Porthmeor Beach car park, by St Ives Tate Gallery. (1½ miles/2.4 kms.)

CIRCULAR WALK
2½ miles/4 kms

A pleasant walk that takes in most of the mining sites of the Kenidjack and Botallack areas.
Start Cape Cornwall car park, near St Just, OS 354317

1 Follow direction **1** on the main walk.

2 Where the track branches at Wheal Edward mine-stack, follow the left branch to reach the cliffside area of Botallack mine-remains, and a track down to The Crowns mine-stacks.

3 Retrace your steps to the fork by Wheal Edward mine-stack. Follow it back towards Kenidjack, keeping to the track as it swings left. Follow it inland, keeping straight ahead at a junction with a track from the right. Continue downhill to another junction. Turn sharp right and walk down to the start of direction **2**, by a stone 'Coast Path' sign below a house. Turn left and follow direction **1** on the main walk in reverse to reach Cape Cornwall car park.

Bibliography

Allan, R. and Candlish, I. (joint editors), *The Scottish Borderland – The Place and the People*, Border Country Life Association, 1988

Brown R. Allen, *Dover Castle*, English Heritage, London, 1995

Bryant, Arthur, *The Medieval Foundation*, Collins, London, 1966

Chapman, Malcolm, *The Celts. The Construction of a Myth*, Macmillan, London, 1992

Coad, J. G. and Hughes, G.E., *Walmer Castle and Gardens*, English Heritage, London, 1995

Crawford, Thomas, *Walter Scott*, Scottish Writers Series, Scottish Academic Press, Edinburgh, 1982

Crossing, William, *The Ancient Stone Crosses of Dartmoor and Its Borderland*, J. G. Commin, Exeter (first published 1902)

Crossing, William, *Crossing's Guide to Dartmoor*, Peninsula Press, Newton Abbot, 1990 (first published 1912)

Cunliffe, Barry, *Iron Age Communities in Britain*, Routledge & Kegan Paul, London, 1974

Daiches, David, *Scotch Whisky, Its Past and Present*, André Deutsch, London, 1969

Hamilton Jenkin, A. K., *Mines and Miners of Cornwall*, Truro Bookshop, 1962

Hawkes, Jacquetta, *A Guide to the Prehistoric and Roman Monuments in England and Wales*, Chatto & Windus, London, 1951

Hoskins, W. G., *The Making of the English Landscape*, Hodder & Stoughton, London, 1955

Jeffries, Richard, *Wild Life in a Southern County*, 1879

Jennings, Bernard (editor), *Pennine Valley, A History of Upper Calderdale*, (Hebden Bridge WEA, Local History Group), Smith Settle, Otley, 1992

Knight, Jeremy K., *The Three Castles (Grosmont Castle, Skenfrith Castle, White Castle)*, CADW: Welsh Historic Monuments, Cardiff

Macdonald Fraser, George, *The Steel Bonnets. The Story of the Anglo-Scottish Border Reivers*, Barrie & Jenkins, London, 1971 (revised edition, HarperCollins, London, 1995)

Maclean, Calum L., *The Highlands*, Club Leabhar, Inverness, 1975 (first published by Batsford, London, 1959)

Malone, Caroline, *The Prehistoric Monuments of Avebury*, English Heritage, London, 1990

Margary, I. D., *Roman Roads in Britain*, Vols I and II, Phoenix House, London, 1956

Moir, D. G., *Scottish Hill Tracks. Old Highways & Drove Roads*, revised edition, Scottish Rights of Way Society, Edinburgh, 1995 (first published by Bartholomew, Edinburgh, 1947)

Pochin Mould, D. D.C., *The Roads from the Isles. A Study of the North West Highland Tracks*, Oliver & Boyd, Edinburgh, 1950

Raistrick, Arthur, *Lead Industry of Wensleydale and Swaledale, Vol. 1 The Mines*, Moorland Publishing Company, 1975

Rees, Sian, *Dyfed: A Guide to Ancient and Historic Wales*, CADW: Welsh Historic Monuments, HMSO, London, 1992

Rosenthal, Michael, *Constable*, Thames and Hudson, London, 1987

Rowley, Trevor, *The Norman Heritage 1066–1200*, The Making of Britain Series, Routledge & Kegan Paul, London, 1983

Smiles, Samuel, *Lives of the Engineers*, Vol. II, 1862

Speed, Peter, *Dorset, A County History*, Countryside Books, Newbury, 1994

Spencer, Colin, *The History of Hebden Bridge*, Hebden Bridge Literary and Scientific Society, 1991

Stanford, S. C., *The Archaeology of the Welsh Marches*, (second edition) Collins, London, 1980

Waltham, Tony, *Yorkshire Dales National Park*, Webb & Bower/Michael Joseph, Exeter/ London, 1987

Watson, Godfrey, *The Border Reivers*, Sandhill Press, Warkworth, 1974

DOCUMENTS AND RECORDS

The Archaeology of Rural Dorset, Past, Present and Future, L. M. Groube and M. C. B. Bowden, Dorset Natural History and Archaeological Society, Monograph 4, 1982

Dartmoor Fact Sheet Series, Dartmoor National Park Authority, 1996

Excavations at Chun Castle in Penwith, Cornwall, E. Thurlow, Leeds, 1926

Glenlivet Estate Management, information documents, Glenlivet Estate Ranger Service, 1996

Kintail Estate (Kintail, The Falls of Glomach and West Affric), management plan, 1995–2000, National Trust for Scotland, 1995

Lead Mining and Smelting in Swaledale and Reesdale, Cleveland Industrial Archaeology Society Research Report No. 2, 1979

Lead Mining in Swaledale, from manuscript of Edward R. Fawcett, Faust Publications, 1985

St Just: An Archaeological Survey of the Mining District, Vols I and II, Adam Sharpe, Cornwall County Council, 1992

Statistical Account of Scotland, Vol. XVII – Inverness-shire, Ross and Cromarty 1791–99, EP Publishing Ltd, London, 1981

The Third Statistical Account of Scotland, Vol. XVl, Scottish Academic Press, Edinburgh, 1985

Index